HISTORY
CIVILIZATION AND CULTURE

HISTORY
CIVILIZATION AND
CULTURE

An Introduction to the
Historical and Social Philosophy of
PITIRIM A. SOROKIN

by
F. R. COWELL

WITH TWELVE PLATES AND
THIRTY DIAGRAMS AND TABLES

Boston · THE BEACON PRESS · *1952*

MADE IN GREAT BRITAIN
PRINTED BY ROBERT MACLEHOSE AND CO., LTD.
THE UNIVERSITY PRESS, GLASGOW

Preface

So deeply ingrained is the scepticism aroused by the many efforts which have been made to find rhyme or reason in the infinite complexity of history that any new attempt will need to have much to recommend it if it is to get a sympathetic hearing.

In the belief that the continuing debate on this great theme can thereby be illuminated and helped forward, this book is devoted to a summary of new and striking theories about historical change and the development and decay of human societies which have been worked out by Pitirim A. Sorokin, a Russian-born Professor of Sociology in the University of Harvard.

As his work seems relatively little known or noticed in the English-speaking world outside the United States, it is necessary to say at the outset in what respects his views have more to recommend them than have those of others who have written on the subject.

In three ways he has sought to enlarge knowledge about the rise and fall of civilization and cultures.

In the first place he analyzes and describes in a more thoroughgoing manner than any of his predecessors the nature of those systems of culture whose varying fates provide the very subject matter for the history of man and of civilization.

He next examines, on the basis of an exhaustive survey of the history of Western civilization as a whole, the manner in which changes have actually occurred in cultural life. More persistently than any other writer, he has attempted, with the aid of teams of helpers, to measure and to weigh the evidence which historians have amassed. Finally, he asks and seeks to answer the questions inevitably provoked by the long and fascinating record he unrolls; why the changes occurred and how they took place.

Sorokin's great and solid achievement provides more than a new approach to the explanation and understanding of past ages and of vanished civilizations markedly different from our own. His work also offers a new basis for the study of sociology, the study of man in society which a few people in the last hundred years have hoped to develop into a new science.

It would be a most serious disservice to Sorokin as well as to the cause of scholarship, learning and of knowledge which he labours to serve, if in making these great claims on his behalf, any impression were given that he considered himself finally to have answered all the questions and to have resolved all the difficulties which so vast a subject inevitably raises. He has presented his work for critical review in the hope that the suggestions which he has offered and the theories which he has proposed will provoke thought to improve or to supplant them.

The present book can have no other motive. It is likely to have greater imperfections than Sorokin's original work which it attempts to reflect, to condense, and to a lesser extent to illustrate. It aims in fact to summarise and to restate, as far as possible in less technical language, the main outline of his vaster work particularly as it is to be found embodied in his four large volumes *Social and Cultural Dynamics* to which it is hoped it may serve as an introduction. The fact that it is a condensed summary version made independently, with of course Professor Sorokin's consent although without his oversight, must be an added reason for referring readers to his own much larger work, in which he has explained and defended his opinions at greater length than is possible here. His own volumes provide not merely a fuller, better balanced and more accurate statement of his views but will also be found to yield a deeper, richer satisfaction of the many-sided interests in new lines of thought and conjecture which it is the ambition of the present book also to stimulate.

London, 1952   F. R. COWELL

Acknowledgments

IT would not have been possible to produce the present work had not consent to use copyright material been generously given by Professor Sorokin and the publishers of his treatise in four volumes, *Social and Cultural Dynamics*. Gratitude is accordingly here expressed to The American Book Company, New York, and to Messrs. George Allen and Unwin Ltd., who published the first three volumes of it in London. Acknowledgment is also made to Messrs. Harper and Brothers, publishers of Professor Sorokin's *Society, Culture and Personality*, 1947, in which many of his earlier views are restated and amplified.

The author's thanks are due to the Editor of *The Times Literary Supplement* for permission to use parts of an article on Professor Sorokin's philosophy which appeared in that journal, and to the Librarian of the American Library in London for help in obtaining reference material.

Acknowledgment is made of the courtesy of the respective copyright-owners in giving permission to reproduce the illustrations in this book. The name of each appears after the title of the appropriate plate on page xi.

Other Books by Professor Sorokin

IN addition to the volumes mentioned above, Professor Sorokin has published many others, of which some are referred to in the pages of this book. For convenience of reference a brief selection is listed here:

The Sociology of Revolution, 1925. Philadelphia: J. B. Lippincott & Co.

Contemporary Sociological Theories, 1928. New York: Harper and Brothers.

The Crisis of Our Age, 1941, New York: E. P. Dutton & Co.

Sociocultural Causality, Space, Time, 1943. Durham, N. Carolina: Duke University Press.

Russia and the United States, 1944. New York: E. P. Dutton & Co.

The Reconstruction of Humanity, 1948. Boston: The Beacon Press.

Social Philosophies of an Age of Crisis, 1950. Boston: The Beacon Press. 1952. London: A. & C. Black, Ltd.

This is not a complete list and it omits all mention of Professor Sorokin's many contributions to learned journals.

Contents

Illustrations

PLATES

xi

FIGURES

TABLES

HISTORY
CIVILIZATION AND CULTURE

CHAPTER ONE

The Search for
Explanations of Historical Change

U ntil very recent times the great majority of people have not looked to history for more than stirring stories of the deeds of men and women of bygone days. In the form of epic poems or of chronicles, such stories have fascinated generations of listeners and readers.

The story is always the important thing. It may be a story with a moral, and most stories can provide some sort of moral, but thousands value a story compared with the few who value its moral.

History evidently arises and depends for its progress on those few who wish to be enlightened by stories of the past as well as to be entertained by their recital. Not content merely to hear endless stories, they want to know how the stories hang together; what wider significance they may have for others than the actors in the scenes and events they describe; what light they may throw on various aspects of the past, upon human nature in general or upon the people and happenings in the everyday world in which they are themselves actually living.

The hope that obscure events of past times may illuminate the present has greatly strengthened interest in history, for it gives the study of history a very practical value. If 'History repeats itself,' as the popular saying alleges, then he who knows what has happened in the past may hope for the distinction and prestige which humanity would be very willing to confer upon anyone able to foretell the future. Such a power would moreover yield intellectual satisfaction to its possessor even although it did not happen to be rewarded by any social advantages.

Aristotle may illustrate the argument, when, after examining the long history of Greek cities and over a hundred and twenty of their constitutions, he pointed out how aristocracy had again and again been replaced, after popular revolt, by democracy which had been turned by the demagogues it bred into a tyranny; or, as we should now say, into a totalitarian state at the mercy of a dictator. We have our own reasons to be interested in such a lesson of history, and it is not difficult, in the light of an example of this kind, to see how history came to be regarded as 'philosophy teaching by examples'.

During very many centuries the wisdom of old men had no other basis than the knowledge they had acquired through long experience. What could be more natural than to suppose that mankind would gain a very valuable guide if such experience could be preserved and accumulated by historians?

Such a notion was not slow in developing among intelligent peoples in the past. Thucydides in the fifth century B.C. expressed it when he wrote that 'the accurate knowledge of what has happened will be useful because according to human probability similar things will happen again'. In the second century B.C., Polybius said much the same. 'The knowledge gained from the study of true history,' he wrote, 'is the best of all educations for practical life. For it is history and history alone which, without involving us in actual danger, will mature our judgment and prepare us to take right views, whatever may be the crisis or posture of affairs.' So strongly did he emphasise this practical, pragmatic view of history that he took the extreme view that, 'if you take from history its element of practical instruction, what is left of it has nothing to attract and nothing to teach'.

When history is endowed with oracular powers to guide and influence conduct in this way, historians have a tremendous responsibility. The temptation to tamper with the record becomes obviously great. It is but a short step from an attempt to extract moral rules and political principles from history to the much more dangerous attempt to rewrite history and to fake it in some way so that it seems to teach the doctrine that the fakers wish to popularize. The danger is all the greater in proportion to the trust put in history, as philosophy teaching by examples, because it then becomes one of the most powerful influences on public opinion. This is why one of the first things a propagandist does is to try to exhibit the doctrine he has to popularize as one with its roots in history. Then Clio, the fabled Muse of History, ceases to inspire mankind and becomes instead a kind of ventriloquist's dummy.

Volumes could be written to illustrate the dangers arising from deliberate efforts to pervert history in this way. Volumes have been written in the honest search for real clues through the tangled record of the past. The need for them is clearly great. Confronted by the tremendous tale of human achievement from the dawn of time, with its records of the rise and fall of empires, principalities and powers; by the epic stories of heroes, king, princes, warriors and statesmen and by the struggles of whole peoples to survive natural catastrophes or wars and civil strife; it seems essential to try to find some clue, some guiding principles, to explain what would otherwise be a vast welter of meaningless events.

Powerful as the motives have been to search for some philosophy of history, they cannot yet be said to have achieved any very deep satisfaction. They take the historian beyond history, and the plain man still farther out of his depth into the vast sea of philosophical speculation from which most people shrink as from the unknown.

It is rare to find an historian willing to take the plunge into philosophy which a fully professed theory about the inner nature of historical change would require. This does not mean that historians have always succeeded in writing history without any philosophical assumptions. What actually happens is that they are content to tell their story and to rely upon currently accepted general notions about the causes of change to provide any deeper explanations which may seem to be necessary. In the age of faith it was sufficient to refer to the will of God in order to explain the mysterious course of human events. An eleventh-century writer, Gilbert de Nogent (1053-1124), called his story of the Crusades 'God's deeds through the French' (*Gesta Dei per Francos*), a title which was borrowed again in the early seventeenth century by Jacques Bongars. By no means discarded in our own time, this dogma is now far less used than are more secular, mundane notions.

In the eighteenth century, men's eyes turned earthwards. Climate for instance was one of the elements which Montesquieu emphasised as the ground or cause of national character and all that flows from it. The Rationalists, who said that they saw no need for the hypothesis that God exists, nevertheless pinned their faith upon predominantly mechanistic notions, invoking various 'forces' to explain the movements they thought they discerned in history. These forces were little less mysterious than the operations of that 'Providence' they attempted to replace, and they really explained nothing.

Thus began the fashion of endeavouring to account for human development and change in purely material terms. The idea of a materialist interpretation of history is for ever associated with the name of Karl Marx. Certainly no one else has employed the materialist interpretation of history with more effect or has gained greater influence through it than he did. Expressed in cruder and more limited forms by smaller men who followed his lead, it was widely applied in the effort to find an economic explanation for everything of any importance that has happened in history. The result has naturally been that the Marxists have been betrayed into endless imbecilities as are all those who hope to solve the riddle of the universe by one simple idea. The story is the same in all sciences. The doctors and surgeons of the eighteenth century, whose first act for the relief of human maladies was to drain their patients of considerable quantities of blood, operated on a theory which contributed as little to human health as the Marxian materialist doctrine of the necessary class war, a type of economic blood-letting, can add vigour and harmony to human society. In medical science the men of one idea no longer find so many gullible disciples, but social science has been slower to escape from the ethussiasm of the well-meaning amateur or from the attempt at domination by the charlatan and the quack.

One safeguard against deception may well be the great variety of competing theories about the true nature of history, for there certainly has been no lack of ingenious speculation in recent times.

The idea that history might be found to fit some pattern or follow an ascertainable form of development is relatively new in Western European thought. The destiny of man which history unfolds was, in an age of faith, confidently supposed to be determined by the will of God. Not that there was a complete lack of interest in the past, especially in the lives and fortunes of famous men. Chronicles and anecdotal histories seem to have been all that was needed in the Middle Ages to satisfy such interest.

The Reformation and the dynastic and religious strife at the close of the Middle Ages introduced new passions into history which began to be written on behalf of Protestants or Catholics or, as Professor Butterfield has shown in *The Englishman and his History*, for or against Tudor or Stuart claims.

In the seventeenth century a new interest in objective truth arose. A fascinating account of the two generations of English scholars who, after 1660, laboured to retrieve the early history of their country has been given by Professor Douglas. Towards the close of the eighteenth century it might still be said, as Dr. Johnson is recorded as having remarked at breakfast on the 17th September, 1773, during his tour of Scotland, 'that it was but of late that historians bestowed pains and attention in consulting records to attain to accuracy'.

The general search for a philosophy of history did not occur until the nineteenth century. One or two powerful minds at the beginning of the eighteenth century were moving in that direction, but their work was little known or indeed entirely unpublished. The contribution that Vico (1668-1744) or Leibniz (1646-1716) might have made to the study of historical development has only begun to be realised in our own time.

They were the forerunners of a movement which was to gather momentum at the hands of German philosophers such as Herder (1744-1803), Fichte (1762-1814) and Schelling (1775-1854). Powerfully stimulated by Hegel (1770-1831), the search for underlying explanations of historical events attracted many minds. Frenchmen took up the study with enthusiasm. The contributions of Cousin (1792-1862) and Saint-Simon (1760-1825) were dwarfed by the work of Auguste Comte (1798-1857), whose theories attracted considerable interest in England. Not that Comtism had a very wide or lasting influence. Indeed, despite a considerable interest in the philosophy of history in England during the last half of the nineteenth century, it was not a study which won much support or approval from either philosophers or historians. It seemed as though the English, who have ever liked to believe that the spirit bloweth where it listeth, refused to give a very attentive ear to the notion that the study of man in society can become an exact science. Some early enthusiasms for that view in the nineteenth century seemed to show promise of exciting discoveries when statistics and history, or history and geography, or history and biology, combined to produce some strange new offspring. But, in spite of their apparently robust physique, the brood was sterile, and Herbert Spencer and Henry Thomas Buckle founded no school, although their immediate influence can be underrated.

If more recent schemes of continental origin, and particularly of German inspiration, such as the momentarily fashionable notions of Oswald Spengler, have not been altogether ignored in the United States of America or in the British Isles, they have provoked little more than mild surprise at their popularity in the lands that gave them birth.

Yet in England and America also in recent years many have been led to ponder upon the setting in which civilizations rise and fall, thanks to the monumental *Study of History* by Professor A. J. Toynbee. There is always a ready interest in such wide-ranging historical surveys during periods of great crisis. So to-day, the very evident peril of our civilization is compelling people everywhere as never before, to diagnose its causes and to seek for remedies. To do so seems the condition of survival.

It is from this point of view, as well as from a purely philosophic or scientific standpoint, that the work of Professor Pitirim A. Sorokin commands attention. He brings an unusual experience as well as vast erudition to the subject of sociology that he has made his own. He was, he says, born and reared within the lowest classes in Russia, an 'ethnic mongrel' in Nazi eyes, subsequently passing through various strata of the Russian social pyramid from the status of poor peasant and itinerant worker to the position of Professor of Law and Sociology in the University of St. Petersburg. During his career in Russia he was thrice imprisoned for his opposition to the Tsarist regime and twice by the Communists, by whom he was condemned to death. In the interval between those events he had been Kerensky's private secretary, editor-in-chief of a metropolitan newspaper, a founder and member of the All-Russian Peasant Soviet, member of the Council of the Russian Republic and Constitutional Assembly, all before his thirty-fourth year.

Banished in 1922 he went to Berlin and Prague, and later to the United States, where he became Professor of Sociology in the University of Minnesota (1924). He there continued his sociological work, publishing a number of volumes including *Sociology of Revolution* (1925), *Social Mobility* (1927), *Contemporary Sociological Theories* (1928), and *The Principles of Rural Urban Sociology* (1929), the last in collaboration with Carl C. Zimmerman.

These works were a prelude to his main enterprise, the analysis and restatement of the course of history and of human progress as it is to be seen in the development and change of cultural life. This work was published after he had been appointed Professor at Harvard University in 1930, where he founded the Department of Sociology.

It is the aim of this book to give a summary outline of the main principles by which Professor Sorokin's work has been inspired. He has stated his views on the nature of history and has explained their basis in the four large volumes, *Social and Cultural Dynamics*, of over 2,800 pages, and they have been followed by a number of other works. Of these, special mention must be made of *Society Culture and Personality, their Structure and Dynamics* (Harper and Brothers, 1947), which contains Sorokin's general system of sociology; and more especially of *Social Philosophies of an Age of Crisis*, in which he critically reviews recent interpretations of historical change by eight well-known writers whose views he discusses in relation to his own theories summarised in the present volume. These eight philosophers are Danilevsky, Spengler, Toynbee, Schubart, Berdyaev, Northrop, Kroeber and Schweitzer. This work, which forms a most stimulating commentary upon his contemporaries, is also an indispensable addition to his other books setting out his own views.

CHAPTER TWO

Discovering Patterns
of Historical Development

What has been wrong in all the attempts during the last three hundred years to explain the nature of social development and historical change has been, in Sorokin's opinion, that their authors have remained prisoners of their own limited set of values, so they have been blind to other systems of values including those by which countless generations of mankind were once willing to order their lives and their actions.

What is needed, therefore, is a revolution in our way of looking at history. We have as much to gain by trying to understand the peculiar values of cultural systems foreign to our own as the astronomers gained when they gave up the old Ptolemaic standpoint which took the earth to be the centre of the universe and replaced it by the Copernican standpoint, which views the earth as one planet among many thousands of independent constellations. The Copernican revolution for which Sorokin, as Spengler before him, pleads, entails giving up the idea that all human history has conspired to produce the modern age as its finest flower, and taking instead the standpoint of relativity which has already revolutionised ways of regarding physical science. Then the record of former times will suddenly shine forth in a new and truly enlightening form.

The Middle Ages, for instance, will cease to be a dull, dark and mysterious period in which men and women were trying without much success to develop into people like ourselves or were miserable and frustrated because they failed to do so. Sorokin believes that the civilization of the Middle Ages provided a satisfying system of thought and ideas to the vast majority of the human beings who lived through it. The same can be said, he thinks, about Ancient Greece or Byzantium whose ways of life and ideas of values were very different from our own.

Many other people have, of course, said very much the same thing

7

about the essentially unique nature of the cultural life of past periods. What distinguishes Sorokin's views is the thorough-going way in which he works out the implications of the theory of historical relativity to create what is in effect a new theory of social development also. It is upon his historical investigations and his philosophical study of the methods of the social sciences that he bases his trenchant criticism of many previous writers. They have, he thinks, mostly been misled by insufficient attention to this problem of method. Hence there has been confusion of thought over the meaning and significance of the words 'culture' and 'civilization' used in a historical and in a sociological sense.

Some writers have not bothered to sort out their ideas on these matters, so they lump together all sorts of factors, which in reality are essentially unrelated, merely because they happened to occur in one place and proceed to regard them as making up the cultural life or civilization of that place. They then personify the civilization and speak of it as though it were endowed with something in the nature of life and even of personality, without pausing to analyse the serious and far-reaching consequences which ought to follow from such a claim.

Culture, from Sorokin's point of view, is a word which must, in the first place, relate to purely human phenomena because it has essentially to do with the life of the mind. He does not use it in the sense in which it is applied to plant and animal life.

Sorokin lists meanings, values and norms as particularly the subjects of culture. Translated into more simple everyday terms, it may be said that culture is concerned with anything that men consider to be useful, beautiful or right, in short, with everything which for humanity has Value.

Because many if not all these cultural values can arise only when men are gathered together in communities or societies, cultural matters are also social matters, and Sorokin constantly uses the rather ugly word 'socio-cultural' as a short way of expressing this fact in dealing with the main subject of his enquiry.

To talk about any single system of culture, such as the culture of Egypt, India, Greece or of Medieval Europe is to imply that the men and women whose activities made up that culture did in fact recognise special and distinctive values which gave their age its peculiar character. They had their own notions about art, architecture, literature, economic welfare, social conditions, ethics, philosophy, law, justice and religion.

To the extent that their culture was a true culture, all these cultural manifestations should, Sorokin holds, show an inner harmony and cohesion; a unity and style of their own. Unless all these miscellaneous cultural manifestations can be so related, it is not possible to speak about a true cultural system at all. He believes not merely that the course of history does reveal these truly unified, distinctive cultural systems, but that history is vital and real to the extent that it is able to recognise them and to follow their development and their changing fortunes. For no true cultural system is eternal. Change is the law of life, and it applies to cultural systems as it does to all living things.

One very important consequence of taking this view about the nature of cultural systems is that it gives a much deeper meaning to the idea of civilization, as that word has commonly been used. For the study of successive cultural patterns shows up clearly the danger of speaking and writing about civilizations—Egyptian civilization, Græco-Roman civilization and so on—as though they were some easily identifiable, single, individual thing. The facts are, and Sorokin's work has the great merit of emphasising them clearly, that civilizations, such as those of Ancient Greece or of Western Europe, have shown a succession of cultural systems which cannot be described by the same label throughout their history as 'Greek civilization' or 'Western European civilization' without grave risk of misunderstanding and error.

These preliminary considerations underlie Sorokin's own theories and contrast them sharply with those of many other well-known writers. He is not content, as a number of geographers and anthropologists, for example, have been content, to leave the analysis of a culture as soon as they discover some external similarities or links between the various aspects of the area or peoples they study. Sorokin remarks that heavy timber houses, vodka, skis, felt boots, and winter evening entertainments, all of which are found together in North Russia, offer no explanation of the true nature of Russian culture. They merely happen to have a common link in the external, geographic factor of the great cold of North Europe.

Unless some deeper explanation is forthcoming, all such things should be regarded as odd mixtures or chance products. Sorokin christens them 'spatial and purely mechanical congeries of various cultural objects and values'. He thinks that the 'culture areas' of many anthropologists often consist of nothing more than of such chance occurrences and that they should not be spoken of as true cultures. He applies the same criticism to the 'civilizations' of Spengler and Toynbee, all of which are vast and complex conglomerations of multitudes of true cultural systems, in Sorokin's own sense, and of congeries. They are cultural and social dumps, not true cultural systems. For Sorokin, a culture must possess an inner unity; its various parts and aspects must hang together as a whole. It must change as a unified system, that is to say in togetherness. Unless this is true, it is meaningless to talk about the death of a civilization. What has not been a unity cannot grow as a unity and cannot be disintegrated, since it never was integrated. All the sweeping conclusions made by so many writers about the fate of civilizations are quite untenable because they start from a false premise, the assumption of some unity, some vital organic nature, in their 'civilizations' which they neither fully describe nor demonstrate.

Often when some unifying principle is sought, as it instinctively seems to be in order to endow the story of the growth of civilizations with more plausibility, the search is wrongly directed. Many theories seek the unifying principle in some one common factor *external* to the life of the society they describe. The great progress made in the study of geography in recent years which have seen the development of human geography with all its fascinating contributions to the study of social life and of history, has very notably strengthened the tendency to rest content with external factors as a sufficient source of explanation. It is a tendency fortified by faith in other external factors, such as the biological factor seen in theories about evolution, heredity and race-selection.

All such views are partial, incomplete and inadequate.

It was therefore an advance from reliance upon theories based upon common external factors when writers and thinkers sought to discover powerful *internal* factors within societies and cultural systems capable of explaining their nature and the way they work. Such writers were led by a sound instinct, but where they have gone wrong is in their effort to find a *single* principle able to account for the whole rich and varied cultural life of a developed community. Whether economics, religion, family organisation or technology are proposed as the key to the explanation of all history, each fails because none can claim tangibly to condition all cultural phenomena in all fields. For Sorokin as for Hegel, a true culture must possess a unity of its own from which the meaning of all its various parts or components is derived and to which they all contribute. Far from economics being able to explain the whole of culture therefore, it is the form and nature of the dominant culture that determines the economic pattern of life within the culture. Greek culture in the fifth century B.C., for example, cannot be understood by reference to the climate and geography of the Eastern Mediterranean or by discovering how the Greeks ate, slept, worked, loved, fought and earned their livings. Eculid's geometry, Plato's metaphysics, the sculptures of Phidias demand a wider framework because they are fragmentary parts of a true culture, and true culture must be seen as a whole with a specific style, physiognomy and personality of its own. A central meaning or idea or mental bias should and can be discerned permeating all life and activity of those who sustain and bear a true culture, which may therefore be said to have its own meaning and logic. By 'meaning,' Sorokin understands anything which, for some mind, stands as a sign of something else. By 'logical', Sorokin means not so much indulging in the rigorous use of chains of reasoning as exhibiting a consistent inner pattern in which the parts hang together to form a coherent whole.

This logico-meaningful integration, as Sorokin calls it, is therefore to be sought in the individual, the smallest culture area, as well as in the group or society of such individuals. This does not, of course, mean that all individuals and all groups everywhere show such integrated personalities but merely that a culture is a strong, well-knit whole to the extent that it approaches such a condition.

Advocating such a view of cultural life, Sorokin necessarily confines himself to civilizations of which a tolerably adequate record is preserved. His *Social and Cultural Dynamics* is based upon a detailed study of the Greek, Græco-Roman and general Western cultures from about 600 B.C. to 1920 A.D., although he also gives more cursory references to Egyptian, Hindu and Chinese cultures. Almost the whole recorded history is therefore within his scope.

Looking back over this great stretch of time, he thinks it possible to detect the rise and fall of three main types of human culture with which are mixed some secondary forms of lesser importance. These three main types of 'socio-cultural super-systems', as he rather forbiddingly christens them, are distinct and are each capable of surviving for several centuries. Before long, however, he thinks one great culture dies away to be replaced by a second and before long the second by the third, after which the second, or possibly the first, may again recur to capture the loyalty, devotion and enthusiasm of mankind. He has not merely a theory about the form of cultures, but also about their change or, as he calls it, their 'Dynamics'. He calls each of these three 'super systems' by a special descriptive name of his own. The first is the 'ideational' system, the second is the 'idealistic' and the third the 'sensate'.

Sorokin's main concern is to achieve greater precision in thought and deeper insight, so he does not hesitate to use words in special senses if he thinks he can thereby better drive home his argument. Despite his lavish use of apparently difficult, technical words, his central ideas are simple and easy to grasp.

'Ideational' and 'sensate' are words demanding explanation. So also is 'idealistic', for it is used by Sorokin with a definite meaning, distinct from that of its ordinary everyday use. He uses 'idealistic' to describe a special form of culture which is a blend between the 'ideational' and the 'sensate' systems. An 'idealistic' culture is therefore a mixed one; it endeavours to achieve a synthesis of the other two. The special meanings to be attached to these three systems will become much clearer in the light of their actual application to the facts of historical development, in the succeeding chapters, but some preliminary description of their scope and content may be given at once.

At the risk of oversimplifying matters, an ideational culture may be described as that of an age of faith, and a sensate culture as that of an age of science and of the common man. The old theological distinction between the Word or Spirit and the Flesh also corresponds fairly closely to the two classes.

An idealist culture gives more emphasis to the creative activity of the human mind in reasoning and philosophy, but the word idealist also carries with it, in addition to ideas of philosophical reflection, the notions of tremendous vitality and creativity in art, literature and thought, all of which are characteristic of an idealist cultural system.

The oversimplification of which this summary statement is guilty will best be remedied in the sequel.

Each main cultural system, ideational, sensate, and idealist is intended to describe a well-marked, distinctive system or pattern of human culture. They each differ in what Sorokin describes as the sharply contrasting 'major premises of their mentality', that is to say in the different views which the human beings who support them take about the nature of reality; about what for them constitute beauty and truth; about the kinds of means and the sorts of ends they try to attain. It is a contrast equally evident in the different ways in which they go about the task of achieving the results at which they aim.

To men who create and maintain an ideational cultural system, reality appears as non-sensate, non-material everlasting Being; their needs and ends are mainly spiritual, to be satisfied as fully as possible on the highest level and by minimizing or eliminating most physical needs. They reject the notion that the world revealed by the senses has any self-sufficient meaning or value. In its extreme form, the ideational system may amount to the special type of 'ascetic ideational-ism' in which the world and self are viewed as unreal and illusory. A less extreme form would be the 'active ideationalism' of the early Christian Apostles and Popes, such as Gregory the Great and Leo the Great, who sought to reform the sensate world and to transform society and culture along lines of spiritual reality. Wordsworth has some lines in 'The Prelude' which well characterize the mentality of such a period:

> *Princes then*
> *At matins froze and couched at curfew time*
> *Trained up, through piety and zeal to prize*
> *Spare diet, patient labour and plain weeds.*

The mentality of the sensate culture stands in striking contrast. It believes in no supersensory reality, or at most displays an agnostic attitude towards the world beyond the senses. Reality is regarded as a becoming, process, change, flux, evolution, progress, transformation. Aims and needs are mainly physical, their fullest satisfaction is sought not by trying to modify the characters of human beings but by modi-fying and exploiting the external world. There are three main ways in which members of a sensate culture go about the task of reshaping the only reality in which they are truly interested. The 'active sensate mentality', wrestling with its environment, is seen incarnate in the great technologists, medical men, business organizers and empire-builders. They may appear as altruistic and as devoted to a high ideal as an ideational character, but the difference between the two is that the kingdom of the ideational culture is not of this world. The 'passive sensate mentality', on the other hand, consists of passive not active Epicureans. Their ideal is a parasitic exploitation and utilization of external reality as a source of sensual pleasures. 'Eat, drink and be merry,' 'Wine, women and song' are their mottoes. Somewhat more cunning is a third sensate type of 'cynical Epicureans,' who borrow respectable ideational masks if thereby their sensate aims can the better be achieved. With a shrewd judgment of the side on which their bread is buttered, they become communist, Nazi, monarchist or liberal as the situation seems to demand. All, however, are forms of the sensate outlook on life and are easily referable to it and identified with it. The world is never too much with them, for in getting and spending they seem to find full exercise for their powers.

Unlike so many of his predecessors who have written about the history of culture and civilization, Sorokin does not pretend to have worked out a neat and perfect pattern into which all the multitudinous facts of history can be fitted, like the pieces of a gigantic jigsaw puzzle. He is not so naïve as to suppose that either the ideational or sensate culture has ever existed in an absolutely pure form. He does not suppose, for example, that ideational man lost or never found the use of his five senses. The point of his argument is that great varieties of cultures can be explained and undertsood by relating them to the two poles of his system, the ideational type and the sensate type, and that no better method has yet been devised whereby such understanding can be achieved. Unless, with one exception, the cultural life of a people can be brought under one of these two principle rubrics, 'ideational' and 'sensate', they are 'eclectic, self-contradictory and poorly integrated'—in other words, not genuine cultures at all.

The one exception is the 'idealistic culture mentality' in which the meaning and value of life are found in a consistent, balanced harmony of spiritual and material activity, guided, directed and sustained by a predominantly spiritual inspiration. Idealistic culture does not therefore regard the world as an illusion, or at best as a merely negative value, but endeavours to use the sensate world for the greater glory of the human spirit. Clearly it requires active, creative people to build an idealistic culture, and they have ever been in a minority.

This broad threefold division of men and women in history according to their basic mental outlook or their active spiritual character does not exhaust the matter, for Sorokin recognizes that there have always been large groups of culturally negative people. Such, for example, are those whom he includes as a 'pseudo-ideational' cultural type characterized by a passive, spineless attitude in which spiritual and carnal needs are alike suppressed by external influences and compulsions. Slaves, prisoners and great masses struggling with the direst poverty are often broken to this condition from which they may seek to emerge. If successful, they often relapse into some easy Epicureanism. Such folk do not make history; it is made for them by the more energetic or more fortunate people able to mould events. The latter alone create, sustain and amend cultural systems, and it is with their work that Sorokin is concerned. They are the true bearers of culture, for they give each cultural system and period its distinctive tone and style. They may, as in antiquity and the Middle Ages, be but a small proportion of the people as a whole.

It should therefore be clear at the outset that the various cultural systems did not necessarily all penetrate to the same depth the societies they characterized. How far each cultural system did in fact penetrate is a question with which Sorokin does not directly deal. To ask it, indeed, raises a problem impossible to solve, simply because not enough is known about the ways of thought of vast masses of mankind, particularly those who lived in ages of faith and in remote antiquity. Inevitably it is necessary to concentrate upon what is known about such epochs, and we often know little, all too little, about the leaders or bearers of cultural systems in the past, and nothing more. Sorokin estimates that out of the billions of human beings who have lived on this planet, not more than a bare 200,000 at the very most are names of any significance in the annals of history. It is not until the record advances to the age of the common man, the sensate culture, that it is possible to survey cultural life at a far greater depth than in previous ages, if only because we are more familiar with it as the cultural pattern dominant in our own time.

For Sorokin's purpose it is sufficient if he can demonstrate that over the centuries, recognisably integrated cultural systems have emerged, flourished and changed, carrying along with them not merely the leaders of men, who as the true bearers of culture both maintain and reshape it, but also the culturally inert, but probably imitative, masses. Some further clarification of these points will be provided in Chapters Nine and Ten.

The bulk of the first three volumes of Sorokin's principal work, his *Social and Cultural Dynamics* contains the results of a series of historical inquiries from which the three main cultural patterns might seem to emerge in their own right. The theory of the whole work purports to be based on history. It contrasts, therefore, with the work of many writers on cultural problems who bring history into their books to the extent that it seems to support and illustrate views they have formed about human destiny on other than historical grounds. So vast is the record that it is seldom difficult to find material which can be twisted or adapted to serve such a purpose. Sorokin, on the contrary, seeks to weave his theory from the fabric of history itself.

With immense industry he set himself to survey the entire history of Western European culture from its earliest times. With the help of collaborators, he has listed and dated almost every known contribution of any significance to this cultural stream in the fields of painting, music, literature, science, technology and invention, philosophy and law, deriving therefrom statistics out of which he has constructed a series of graphs. With these he claims to show what fluctuations have occurred in the creative achievements of Western man from the dawn of history in the realms of religious, secular and sensate art; in scientific invention and discovery; and in various philosophical, ethical and legal theories. These findings are brought together in charts, such as those showing the rise and fall through the centuries of materialism, the ethics of happiness, relativism, determinism, nominalism, temporalism and singularism. In his third volume he seeks to discover how far, if at all, the movement of these creative cultural activities is paralleled in all its significant (that is, ideational-idealistic-sensate) trends by broadly similar movements in social relationships, particularly as these are revealed in economic fluctuations, in the relative magnitude of wars, and in the occurrence of internal disturbances in the countries of the Western world.

Although he finds that the relationship of conduct and culture is less marked than the relationship of the basic cultural mentality with the various forms in which it finds expression, Sorokin concludes that the relationship is none the less real and that it is not merely in ideas, opinions and beliefs but also in personality and behaviour that ideational man has differed from sensate man. This contradicts the popular supposition that common underlying biological or economic drives always and everywhere produce the same type of behaviour, and that whatever differences they seem to show are nothing more than clever disguises, the 'rationalizations', 'derivations' or other manifestations of the subconscious which have recently been so fashionable in popular psychology. Sorokin dismisses the biological egos, the id, libido, and similar hypotheses of the psychoanalytic schools of Freud and Jung and others, as bugaboo paintings and degrading fairy-tales. He considers that human personality has at least four selves of which the personalities and selves in the individual reflecting the various social groups of which he is a member, what he calls the set of conscious socio-cultural egos, alone are significant for the cultural history of mankind and for the study of sociology. He recognizes but subordinates to them the set of conscious biological egos which in turn arise from unconscious biological drives, reflexes and instincts. He also recognizes, but does not discuss, because its analysis belongs to religion and metaphysics, a super-conscious, egoless self.

With this effort to prove that there has been an intimate connexion between the character of the dominant culture on the one hand and the conduct of the people who sustain it on the other, Sorokin concludes the factual, statistical, historical part of his work. He then attacks the more difficult problem of the way in which these major cultural systems change and the reasons by which such changes may be explained. The direction, character, rhythm and periodicity of all such movements are shown as far as it is possible to do so. As a result he is able to demonstrate conclusively the crudity of earlier single-track theories of steady evolutionary progress in one direction. He also exposes the inadequacy of previous cyclical theories of history, such as that propounded by Oswald Spengler in *The Decline of the West*, which took Germany and some of the rest of the world by storm in the early twenties of the present century.

Holding firmly to the doctrine that cultural changes arise from within the cultural system itself, that they are self-generated or immanent changes, Sorokin also seeks to show that all such change has limits and he tries to indicate how these limits arise.

Such in broad outline are the main characteristics of Sorokin's approach to the perennial problem of the nature and the processes of historical reality. The relative novelty, plausibility and undoubted interest of this new view of the history and progress of humanity and of the rise and fall of cultures warrant a strong claim for further study and reflection.

A specially attractive feature of Sorokin's theories is the way in which they take the reader through all branches of human cultural achievement: architecture, painting, sculpture, music, literature, philosophy, science, law and social theory and, in addition, bring in the broad lines of political and social development; the rise and fall of states and empires and the varying fortunes of war and peace.

This preliminary review of the nature of the problem with which Sorokin deals and these general indications of the main lines upon which he seeks to solve it will be taken further in Chapter Eleven, but, before these matters are again discussed, his main historical studies claim detailed attention.

We may therefore look first, as Sorokin himself does in *Social and Cultural Dynamics*, at the cultural history of art through the ages, for it is in the painting, sculpture and architecture of any epoch that the distinctive character of the age is most clearly seen, revealed as it inevitably is, by its marked individual style.

B

CHAPTER THREE

Painting
Sculpture Architecture

The written word is a poor vehicle by which to attempt to convey ideas about the arts, particularly to describe and contrast their developments through the ages. It would be much easier to examine, explain, illustrate, question or defend Sorokin's principles by a conducted tour through some of the principal museums and galleries and to one or two of the cities of ancient culture than to attempt to give an intelligible, convincing summary of them in one short chapter.

Nevertheless the main contrasts which Sorokin seeks to establish can be grasped by the aid of one or two illustrations and by reference to works of art which many readers will have seen either in their original form or in reproductions. It must be stated emphatically at the outset that Sorokin's views cannot yet be said to have won general assent, principally because they are not generally known, but also because any efforts to frame a general theory of history applicable to all branches of human endeavour, as Sorokin's tries to be, must necessarily be advanced as a guess, or hypothesis, for study, reflection and further refinement and amendment.

The first question to raise is whether his notions about the two main kinds of culture, the ideational and sensate, are applicable to the works of artists, past and present, and what the words mean in relation to styles of painting, sculpture, music, architecture, literature and the drama. Sorokin claims that in their light we shall be better able to understand the true inward nature of the art of any particular epoch and be helped therefore to understand more thoroughly those epochs themselves. His views provide a clue to the way in which now one form or style of art, and now another, rises, becomes dominant and then declines. They offer an explanation of the relationship between the changes in one form of art; in painting, for instance, and in other forms, such as architecture, music and literature. To provide a satisfactory account of the rise and fall of different schools of art is however but the beginning. In order to understand a culture thoroughly in the 'logico-meaningful' sense described in the previous chapter, page 11, it is necessary to discover the wider relation of its art to its science, philosophy, law, economics, politics and religion. The findings of this chapter should therefore be capable of relation to those of succeeding chapters on other aspects of cultural life, particularly if they succeed in suggesting uniformities in cultural sequences and changes.

Never before have so many questions about the true nature of culture and of cultural change been raised and answered as by Sorokin. There have of course been a vast number of earlier theories; many of them have been stimulating and suggestive, as Sorokin is very ready to acknowledge. Yet efforts such as those of Auguste Comte, Herbert Spencer and Oswald Spengler to discover stages of development, laws of progress or of evolution in all fields of culture, including art, have not yielded much more than facile and oversimplified analogies between cultural development and the development of individuals from childhood, adolescence and maturity to old age and death. Spengler's much vaunted work has no deeper basis than this. 'Cultures are organisms,' he says, 'and world history is their collective biography.' 'Every culture passes through the age-phases of the individual man. . . . Each has its childhood, youth, manhood and old age' (*Decline of the West*, Vol. I, pp. 104-108).

Without quarrelling with the self-evident idea that cultures appear, blossom and decay, Sorokin points out that merely to say this adds nothing to our knowledge, while the claim that the forms of art in all cultures show the same or similar patterns of development of childhood, maturity and senility is equally meaningless as long as concrete evidence of the essential characteristics of art childhood, art maturity and art senility is lacking. Unfortunately this is just what such author fail to provide in any satisfactory form. We are never able to point to unmistakable evidence of such qualities at specified epochs of all the various cultures, so the pretended explanation is never more than an empty analogy or a figurative expression. It is not an operative concept; not a real tool or means whereby new knowledge or new insight can be gained.

More serious efforts have been made to show that art develops in a sequence of archaic, classical and decadent forms. Such notably have been in sculpture and painting the views of W. Deonna (*L'Archaeologie, sa valeur, ses méthodes*, 1912) and Frank Chambers (*Cycles of Taste*, 1928; *The History of Taste*, 1932); in literature and music, E. Bovet (*Lyrisme*,

Épopée, Drame, 1911), Charles Lalo (*Esquisse d'une esthétique musicale scientifique,* 1908). The themes of these writers, being based upon a deeper insight into the nature of the arts, are more impressive, but Sorokin shows that they do not fit all the facts, notably the facts about the development of Egyptian, Chinese and Hindu art.

Sorokin sums up his criticism of the various views hitherto advanced as explanations of the nature of cultural change by saying that they impose a complete uniformity where it either does not exist at all, or exists in a much more limited form than is claimed. Human culture is much more variable and creative than such limited views allow. Yet it cannot be denied that sequences, recurrence, and repetition of various types, modes, or forms of art do in fact occur, although their nature is not fully explained by such descriptions as archaic, classical and decadent.

Sorokin's view is that their true explanation is to be found in the repetition and fluctuation in space and time of the ideational, the sensate (visual), the idealistic and of other mixed styles in all their varieties and with all their minor secondary characteristics. By following such a classification, many essential traits of a given art in a given period become comprehensible which otherwise would appear as meaningless unconnected fragments. More important still, the mentality behind the art, the true inner nature of the culture from which it springs, can be grasped by the aid of Sorokin's principles, which then become real aids towards a fuller understanding of the rise and fall of cultures. He seeks to combine in one study a comprehensive account of the changes through time in the ideas men have formed about the source and nature of the beautiful, the true and the good.

What, then, in art, are the characteristics of these new terms or categories by which the rise and fall of human cultures can be described and understood?

The ideational style in its finest form, Sorokin says, is purely symbolic, having no resemblance to the visual or sensory appearance of the object depicted. Examples of such an art are to be found in the Christian pictures in the Catacombs—an anchor, a dove, an olive branch, etc.—which signify ideational phenomena quite different from these objects.

The sensate style in its finest form, on the other hand, gets as near to real objects as possible in the actual form in which they are offered to our sense perceptions. It is, Sorokin says, purely empirical and material, and the rendering is purely impressionistic, that is to say it tries to be illusionistic. A good camera snapshot and the most com-

PLATE I

IDEATIONAL ART
SIVA NATARAJA. SIVA AS LORD OF THE DANCE
Bronze. Madras Presidency. *Circa* 11th century A.D.

See page 27

PLATE 2

IDEALISTIC SCULPTURE

HEAD OF A KORE

Acropolis, Athens. 530-500 B.C.

*See page 29 and
compare also Plate 6*

pletely impressionistic pictures are the best samples of the purely visual style.

For artists of this school, such as Manet, Monet, Pissaro, Sisley, Courbet, Cézanne, Renoir, Degas and others, the only reality is the visual appearance of the objects. Behind it and beyond it there is nothing. The choice of subjects is vast, because it does not matter at all what is depicted. What matters is the extent to which the illusionistic effect is caught. There is, therefore, small scope for thought or mind, what above all is necessary is a good eye and a good co-ordination between the eye and the painting muscles. Hence he holds that impressionism was not only anti-intellectual but was radically sensate. No thought, no brain, no ideationality is present or required for it. It just 'snaps' or 'shoots' the visual surface of the empirical objects.

One outstanding quality of this sensate art is its dynamism, due to restless striving to catch just a passing moment in the ever-fugitive appearance of the visual surface of the empirical world, the impression of change, of becoming. Another of its qualities is described by the untranslatable German word *malerisch*, used to denote the rich paint-like quality of a work of art in which patches of different colours, light and shade merge imperceptibly into one another. Rembrandt and Rubens are outstandingly *malerisch*, and Rubens shows outstandingly also the dynamism of the sensate school.

The purely ideational and the purely sensate or visual forms of art contrasted in the above paragraphs are extreme forms at each end of a wide scale. Between these opposite and completely incompatible poles are a wide variety of subclasses and mixed forms. Sorokin admits that there may be such a mixture of the elements of both styles that one cannot recognize in it either the ideational or the visual and is obliged to put it into an intermediary mixed or ideational visual style.

The ideational style admits of fewer subclasses, but Sorokin recognizes as an impure ideational style that used by artists trying to embody some visual resemblance of spiritual or super-empirical reality, such as allegorical figures of Virtue, Vice, Patience, Temperance, or the Muses, and pictures of Paradise, Inferno or the Last Judgment. There is also a less familiar form found, for example, in the geometric designs of primitive peoples, such as the Red Indians, symbolizing buffalo, snakes, hunting and fishing and other objects and activities of theirs giving meaning to their lives.

Two mixed or 'impure' varieties of the sensate or visual style call for special mention. The first occurs when some general idea or non-visual element is introduced into a visual or sensate work of art, as for example in the production of a 'character' portrait or picture in which emphasis is given to what is thought to be the essential, dominant nature of the subject at the expense of its purely momentary appearance.

Again, the subject may not be the ordinary everyday matter-of-fact things of this everyday world, which form the staple topic of sensate visual art. Despite the fact that a purely realistic empirical treatment may not be possible, the subject is nevertheless treated in a matter-of-fact way. Most of the religious pictures by the Italian masters of the Renaissance are in this class, for, although their subject-matter was often not of this world, they rendered it in a most worldy way giving personages, such as the Virgin or St. Anne, the likenesses of their friends, wives or mistresses.

It may sometimes be difficult or impossible to decide whether a mixed or impure style of art is preponderantly ideational or sensate. However, one such mixed category is sufficiently oustanding to be easily recognizable as a separate class. This is the idealistic style mentioned in the previous chapter, page 14. Simultaneously ideational and visual, it was a remarkable blend of each. The idealistic form of culture is most strikingly exemplified by the Greek art of the fifth century B.C. and the religious art of Western Europe in the thirteenth century. It merits the name idealistic because it modifies, typifies, transforms and idealizes visual reality in conformity with its ideas and ideals. The subjects of the idealistic style of art are, moreover, always carefully selected and are never debasing, vulgar, coarse, immoral or eccentric. Decay, senility, death, imperfection, or any excess of emotion or passion, are excluded. Seeking no mere photographic reproduction of reality, it presents instead a beautified, re-created, idealistic manifestation. Sorokin describes in detail how he discriminates between idealistic and sensate or visual styles in art.

The idealist style, like the sensate but unlike the ideational style, is, he points out, always a self-sufficient æsthetic value created for its own sake, but it is always more than this. Here it differs from the sensate, because it expresses, teaches and propagates an ideal. Ideal values lie outside art. To the extent that it serves religion, moral or civic virtue, or other ethical ends of a non-æsthetic character, as idealistic art usually does, it is always more closely correlated with the ideational than with purely sensate visual forms.

The sensate, visual style, on the other hand, is much more likely to be art for art's sake. It serves no values other than artistic values. It is therefore, says Sorokin, often associated with æstheticism in a particular sense, with that period in art history when art for art's sake appears, with its crowds of aesthetes, connoisseurs, collectors, professional critics, theorizers of beauty, and professional artists who want to be artistic and nothing more. Links with religion, public safety, decency and morality are spurned by the extremist sensate school. Here Sorokin interjects a moral note by pointing out that such supposedly realistic and free art is in reality the victim of its own illusions. In fact it becomes also a servant, but a servant of other masters than those served by the idealistic or ideational art. Sensate art is dedicated to the Golden Calf; to the empirical visual reality, to sensate needs (eudæmonistic, hedonistic and utilitarian, on which see Chapter Seven); to the sensual fancies of the Epicureans, the rich, the powerful.

Idealistic art is like ideational art in that it also serves purposes beyond itself, but these are the ideals or values of a genuine collectivity. The artist's own personality, needs and ambitions are of no account in his creations. Indeed idealistic artists are usually anonymous and unknown, as are those of the creators of many medieval Gothic and Romanesque or Byzantine cathedrals.

Sensate art, on the other hand, is jealously prized as a means of personal distinction, so it is individualistic to a high degree. A further clear distinction between the two styles is found in the choice of subject-matter which artists of sensate cultures always take from their own everyday world, made up of familiar individual objects, persons, events, historical scenes and landscapes. It is rare for idealistic art to illustrate such themes, just as it never chooses scenes of common or low life; the drunkard, criminal, street urchin, pretty faces or erotic figures which are the staple subjects of sensate, visual art.

While sensate art strives after a dynamic effect, is charged with emotions and agitated by passion; idealistic art is quiet, calm, serene, immobile and at peace. Its products partake of the same quality. They endure as ever-present sources of spiritual and æsthetic satisfaction, whereas the products of sensate art are incessantly changing in form and style in a desperate search for novelty and effect. Sensate art deals in 'best sellers', in 'hits and sensations'. The effort to create a sensation need not of course always be made upon established sensate lines and a number of other mixed forms may arise, which do not merit the name of idealistic art but which are nevertheless not wholly sensate.

Cubist and futuristic art present one such special type which, Sorokin points out, has no ideational character except to the extent that it seeks, by reaction against sensate, impressionistic art, to restore the peace of mind and thought which sensate art rejects. For the most part, however, such modernistic art does not seek to represent the super-empirical, non-materialistic reality but tries to find new ways of presenting the solidity, weight, spaciousness, movement and other properties of the material world.

An apparent mere juxtaposition or mechanical union of sensate and ideational styles occurs in Egyptian sculpture, even from the Old Kingdom which yields examples of a mixed style in which clear and beautifully rendered portrait heads of a pronounced visual sensate type are combined with what from the sensate standpoint is a quite unnatural rendering of the rest of the body, particularly its anatomy and posture.

These few examples by no means exhaust the wide variety of mixed styles observable in the long course of the history of human art. Their value lies merely in illustrating the chief principles and major concepts by means of which Sorokin seeks to interpret, not merely the forms of artistic creation so far achieved by mankind, but to explain also their inner nature and to show the manner in which they have been developed and transformed. If he is able to succeed in this task, the result will be not merely a useful clue to the history of art but a most suggestive guide to the history and progress of humanity as a whole in all its spheres.

That his theories are able to achieve this tremendous ambition is very clearly Sorokin's belief. He makes bold claims on behalf of his classification of styles in art into the three main groups—ideational, sensate and mixed. It is, he thinks, one of the most 'natural'; that it goes to the core of the predominant mentality shown in each style; that it uncovers the essentials of the *Weltanschauung*, i.e., the general philosophy of life of the artist and of his society; that it stands in the closest relationship with the characteristics of other aspects of a given culture; its science and philosophy, religion and morals, forms of social and political organization, the nature of the social relationships—in brief with all the essential traits of the given culture and its mentality.

To substantiate such theories is the large task that remains. Plausible and interesting as the new classification undoubtedly is, Sorokin has still to show that the concepts it enshrines can be operative as agencies of historical interpretation and explanation. Completely to vindicate the claims of this theory would involve rewriting the entire history of painting, sculpture, architecture, music, literature, the drama and all other human arts and sciences. It is obviously a colossal task beyond the unaided powers of any single individual to achieve in its entirety. Sorokin enlisted specialist helpers and with their aid he has succeeded in presenting a very thorough survey, if not of the entire history of human artistic achievement, at least of its most notable forms, whose nature and influence any theory of art must attempt to explain. Sorokin begins at the beginning with prehistoric art, whose manifestations particularly in paintings of mammoths, buffaloes, bison, deer and other game animals in rock and cave dwellings of palæolithic and neolithic man have been brought to light in recent times to astonish the world. Surprise at the remarkably realistic life-like achievements of these primitive artists has no doubt provoked this reaction, since other primitive peoples do not seem to have given evidence of any comparable skill. On the contrary their work often seems crude and clumsy, lacking the maturity of the artist of the early stone age. The explanation of the apparent mystery, Sorokin holds, is that these palæolithic peoples were predominantly sensate types whose art was naturally visual. The art of the later stone age peoples in the neolithic period was, on the contrary, much less visual and much more ideational. The idea that it is strange to find what seems to be a 'mature' art in the earliest period results from our mistaken belief that our own art, which is also visual and sensate, is a fine flower of human endeavour which all time has conspired to realize and that therefore anything resembling it must be 'modern'.

Sorokin is not merely taking a revolutionary view of the evolution of art in upsetting unreflective current assumptions, but he also establishes the important principle that there is not, as popular expectations would seem to indicate, any straight line of progress in art *from* ideational *to* visual sensate forms. Indeed to the extent that his description of sensate art as lacking any profound intellectual content or reflective power is true, it seems plausible to believe with Sorokin that it is not strange to find that visual art precedes ideational art in these earliest centuries of human existence. To have established at the outset the possibility of a 'modern' visual form of realistic pictorial art developing among primitive people helps also with the study of Egyptian art.

It is not possible here to do more than give a summary indication of his own outline sketch of the main broad developments of art since these prehistoric times.

Sorokin considers that a marked fluctuation, in the nature of a relative increase or decrease of ideational or sensate elements, is observable during the long course of Egyptian culture. Its four main epochs were:

Old Kingdom, to about 2700 B.C.—Non-sentimental depicting of a sound material world in a mildly ideational style, containing elements of naturalism and visuality, increasing from the fourth dynasty and manifest in portrait sculpture representing private and ordinary persons.

Middle Kingdom, from about 2400 B.C. to about 1600 B.C.—The art, mainly sculptural at the beginning, is much less visual, but in the thirteenth dynasty a visual style becomes much more pronounced, manifest particularly in art depicting the everyday life of the common people, houses, gardens, musical parties, baking, brewing, fishing and so on.

New Kingdom, from about 1600 B.C.—A notable turn to ideationalism and idealism occurred in the time of Akhenaton (1380-1362 B.C.). A sharp turn towards intimacy, picturesqueness, dynamism, to the visual and baroque occurred in the period of Tutankhamen (around 1360 B.C.), after which there was a gradual shift once again toward ideationalism. The fourth epoch of the history of Egyptian art is obscured by alien invasions in the early seventh century B.C. and by Assyrian and Persian domination. It was not until Egypt came under Greek kings and Greek inspiration (from 330 B.C.) that there was some revival. Sorokin believes it possible to trace similarly alternating cultural patterns under the Ptolemies and in the Roman period.

Chinese culture flowed in two main streams, the ideational represented by Taoism (and later by Buddhism) and the mixed, represented mainly by Confucianism. A purely sensate mentality was also always present, Sorokin holds, but it was a minor current.

These two streams are characterised by their products. The subjects of Buddhist art are essentially super-sensate and super-empirical in which the invisible inner world and its values are depicted by visible symbols. The great artists of the Han period attempted in this way to reveal the inner character, the spirit or soul of things, and the same is true during the growth of Buddhism in the Transition period and in the early T'ang period beginning in 618 A.D., especially during the Sui dynasty which preceded it (about 590-618 A.D.). The same is true of the later period of the five dynasties down to the Sung period (907-960 A.D.).

The topics for the most part are supersensory, such as the figure Kuan-yin, of Bodhidharma the first Buddhist missionary, the tiger and the dragons and other symbolic designs.

Divergencies towards visualism accompanied periods marked by a decline or persecution of the Taoist-Buddhist believers. Orthodox Confucianism or Passive Epicureanism in the Middle T'ang period characterized the second part of the reign of Ming Huang, which witnessed the rise of an Epicurean humanism. The beauty of the everyday world then furnished the subject matter of art. The court-painters, such as Wu-Tao-Tzï, with their mastery of perspective and fidelity to natural appearances, produced pictures possessing an extraordinary power of illusion. Ideational art concentrating upon religious subjects was not given up, but it appears to be the style of a minority, as it was again in the period of the Northern Sung (960-1126 A.D.), particularly at the end of it with the reign of the Emperor Hwei Tsung (1101-1126 A.D.), himself no mean painter.

Few styles of art have been more consistently ideational for a longer period than has the Hindu. Sorokin has no difficulty in quoting eminent authorities who stress this other-worldly aspect of Hindu art, pointing out that it has no counterpart in 'modern' (i.e., visual sensate) European art. Sanskrit lacks a word for art, in the sense it is used in modern European languages. Art for Hindu peoples is life as it is interpreted by religion and philosophy. Art for art's sake is consequently unknown. Instead a symbolism was created to express the various qualities of the Supreme Soul in imaginary superhuman figures. In this way arose the designs of many-headed gods and goddesses with many arms. Incomprehensible to the average uninstructed spectator trained to recognize and to like modern Western European art, they may not become more comprehensible by being labelled 'ideational'. However, the first advantage of such a label is that it points to the fact that in Hindu art such a spectator is in touch with the products of a civilization which is radically different in kind from his own, based upon different presuppositions about the nature of reality and of the values to be put upon the things of this world. See, for example, Plate 1.

From this first awakening, the spectator can be led to enquire in what other qualities also Hindu civilization is distinctive and from that, if Sorokin is correct, to an understanding of a way of life which in its innermost essence is entirely foreign to our own.

With the earliest manifestations of human art in the Mediterranean world, a very different civilization comes in question. Between the twelfth to the ninth century B.C. a form of art flourished in the isle of Crete which was markedly visual in character; at times extremely impressionistic, with excellent renderings of animals and human figures based upon a mature knowledge of their anatomy. Slender pretty voluptuous feminine figures, visual landscapes, picturesques, drama, dynamism and sensuality are marked features of this Creto-Mycenæan art which may indeed have begun in the sixteenth century B.C.

The Archaic period of Greek art (about 900-500 B.C.) which appeared after the so-far unexplained disappearance of Creto-Mycenæan art, is fundamentally different. Simple geometric patterns, characteristic, as often said, of an uncultivated race, but actually entirely different in meaning and purpose, were used by the early Greeks in striking contrast with the vigorous and life-like representations of the Cretans. Vase painting at this time in Greece was purely linear, at first using merely one tint or colour, resembling drawing rather than painting. Beginning in the sixth century B.C. a change becomes observable. Efforts were then made to render subjects somewhat more visually. Visual or sensate art began to rise in favour; ideational art to decline. Then came the miracle of the Greek achievement of the fifth century B.C., when, in Sorokin's words, the descending curve of ideationalism and the ascending curve of visualism cross each other and produce a marvellous blending in the form of sublime idealistic art. The predominant figure of the period—and of all time—in sculpture was Phidias (c. 490-417 B.C.), but there were other famous names, such as Polycletus (fl. 452-405 B.C.), Agoracritus, Alcamenes, Colotes, Callimachus.

The subjects of this fifth-century sculpture are gods, heroes or ideational entities such as Victory or Nemesis. But the perfect technique is visual. The same can be said of painting in which Polygnotus (c. 475-447 B.C.) won a renown as great as that of Phidias.

The characteristics of this great period of Greek art have often been described, and they will be briefly summarized here as the supreme example of what Sorokin means by his 'idealistic' mixed category or class of culture.

The idealistic artists of the fifth century B.C. used their excellent knowledge of human anatomy to depict human beings in their ideal or perfect form. There are, Sorokin reports, no realistic portraits, no ugliness, no defective traits or types. Before us are immortals or idealized mortals; old age is rejuvenated; the baby is depicted as grown up; the women have little that is specifically womanish but appear like perfect athletes; there are no concrete landscapes. The postures and the expressions are free from any violent or debased or too human emotion and distorting passion. They are calm, serene, imperturbable like the gods. Even the dead shine with the same calmness and serene beauty. All the statues have a 'Greek' profile; not because all the Greeks had such faces, as Winckelmann thought, but because it was the profile thought to be perfect. The hairdress is simple but well ordered; the drapery is perfectly adapted to the body, simple and

PLATE 3

MODERN SCULPTURE

HENRY MOORE: THREE STANDING FIGURES
Battersea Park, London. A.D. 1948

See page 31

PLATE 4

IDEATIONAL PAINTING
BOOK OF KELLS, folio 27
The Evangelical Symbols. *Circa* 9th century A.D.

See page 32

marvellous in its orderly beauty. Eyes are natural and perfect, and shine with calmness and serenity; the lips and mouth are ideally cut; the postures are dignified and idealized. (See illustration, Plate 2.) As Pliny pointed out long ago, it was an art which sought to make noble men still nobler. It is not that the artists could not or would not depict the lower passions, for these are shown on the vase paintings when the subjects are the creatures of the lower and inferior orders, such as slaves, centaurs, fauns and animals. Finally, Greek idealistic art was deeply religious, patriotic, instructive, moralizing and educative. It was created not only for its own sake, but also as a means for just such instruction and education. It was not separated from, but was the partner of, religion and of civic and social morality. After the resounding Greek victory over the Persians, there was a universal upsurge of national spirit, an ardent and enthusiastic desire to exalt their religion and their country; hence the unity, harmony, and marvel of the art of the period. Its horizons lay beyond common ordinary persons and objects, for it strove to create universal types of eternal and not merely of temporal value.

This great outburst of idealistic art was not sustained by more than about two generations of artists. By the end of the fourth century B.C. it had been replaced by the conspicuously sensate or visual style of Hellenistic art. From the historians of Greek art, Sorokin has summarized the main important characteristics of this later sensate Hellenistic art. Because the characteristics he enumerates are also common to the sensate mentality everywhere, they merit summarizing here.

In sensate art:

1. The figures of young women which before were rare, become quite common subjects of sculpture and painting, and they are represented as voluptuous, seductive, sexual figures often set off against realistic figures of old women.

2. A similar change occurs in relation to the figures of men.

3. Portraits of individual persons, especially of rulers and of patrons, become more common.

4. Real landscapes and dramatic historical scenes become more common.

5. Everyday life, crowds, mobs, the common run of people, especially pathological types, criminals, beggars, street urchins more and more replace heroes and ideal men, so that the emphasis is placed upon mortality instead of upon immortality.

6. Human postures and expressions lose their idealized patterns and

become realistic; serenity and calm are replaced by the pathetic, by passion and emotionality, including suffering, sorrow, pain, fear, agony and distortion. Dynamism and violent movement replace static immobility. There is no reticence about nudity or sex.

7. 'Art for art's sake' becomes the rule in order to give merely sensuous pleasure to the sensate man. No other ideal or value exists behind the art object.

8. Compensation for lack of quality is sought in mere hugeness, mere mass. The bigger a statue or building can be, the more impressive and the better it is supposed to be.

Roman artists fell so completely under the sway of the excellent Greek masterpieces that any native development they might have achieved was inhibited. There are unfortunately few extant examples of the earliest native Roman products, but there is some evidence that Italic art, the first source of Roman inspiration was rather ideational. The second source, the art of the Etruscans, was predominantly sensate or visual.

If this was the true state of affairs, it probably helps to explain, although Sorokin does not make the point, the intensity of early Roman distaste for the Greeks. By the time the Romans encountered them, they were already in what he would describe as a sensate decline which appeared deplorable and shocking to the stern and more ideational moralists of the Roman Republic in the second century B.C. Hence the resistance to Greek influences of Romans of the old school, such as Cato the Censor and his contemporaries, among whom was the grandfather of Marcus Tullius Cicero.

Sorokin classes the whole of Roman sculpture and painting from the first century B.C. to the fourth century A.D. as being predominantly visual (sensate) although he allows the Augustan period to be pseudo-idealistic. It was not a real idealism spontaneously springing from deep sources, it was rather a change of fashion, of the pattern for imitation, as a reaction against the imitation of the archaic Attic and of the overripe Hellenistic patterns of the preceding century.

Augustan pseudo-idealism barely survived Augustus, when it was succeeded by a more extreme visualism which endured until a change of style in the fourth and fifth centures A.D. paved the way for the Christian 'ideational' style.

The monumental remains of Imperial Rome furnish the evidence upon which this view is based. The Arch of Titus, the Column of Trajan, the vast palaces and colossal statues, the 'boudoir mythology' of Roman painting at Pompeii and elsewhere, all tell the same story of an overripe sensate visualism in art.

Then, in the fourth and fifth centuries of our era, a curious thing happened. All the artistic skill of the preceding centuries seems to have vanished. Instead we have in sculpture very rough 'blocks' cut apparently without any skill, very primitively, without showing any ability to render the individual traits of the persons rendered or even the anatomy of the head and other parts of the human body.

The usual explanation of this state of affairs is that it represents the decay, degeneration, death and end of Roman art. But, says Sorokin, this is to judge the matter by a very subjective evaluation, based on a mere assumption that there can be only one real style of artistic performance and that is the visual.

The development of sculptural art in our own day illustrates Sorokin's views. Many of the works of modern sculptors, Eric Gill, Henry Moore, Epstein and others, may have a crude and unformed appearance as the illustration in Plate 3 may indicate. They are anything but visual. Yet nobody can doubt that such masters of their craft could produce excellent works in the traditional visual manner if they wished. The same may well have been true of the sculptors of the fourth and fifth centuries A.D.

Just as many centuries before (see p. 28) the highly-developed Creto-Mycenæan art was succeeded by ideational Greek art, so now the Christian ideational art began to replace the sensate pagan visual art of the Roman Empire.

Christianity was an ideational cultural stream from its very emergence. Hence it necessarily gave rise to an extreme form of the ideational art, as any such culture must if it is truly integrated. And, indeed, the earliest Christian art, that of the Catacombs, was practically pure ideational art: symbolic and transcendental in form as well as in content. Symbols of a dove, an olive branch, an anchor, a fish, the cross, a good shepherd and a few others comprised its subjects. They meant not a fish nor an anchor but a transcendental value quite different from these visual signs. They were just the visible signs of the invisible world; in brief, it was 'otherworldly art' as Christianity itself was based on an 'otherworldly' mentality. In spite of that, it was still a form of art profoundly influenced by its Græco-Roman and Oriental past. Appearing in a small stream in the total Græco-Roman visual art, with the growth of Christianity it grew more and more, until in the fourth and fifth centuries it became practically a major stream. In this process of ascending to domination, Christian art lost something of its initial ideational purity by admitting an element of visualism. This ideationalism continues, however, throughout the subsequent centuries to the Middle Ages, almost up to the thirteenth century. Remaining examples of ideational painting are relatively few. The ninth century *Book of Kells* is one of the most remarkable. The reproduction of one of its pages in Plate 4 will give some idea of its quality but not of its colour.

During the period of this ideational otherworldliness with its extreme asceticism and radical puritanism there were numerous prohibitions against any art and any representation of religious topics in painting or sculpture, both in Byzantium and in Western Chrisitanity.

Any admixture of sensate visual art was felt as a taint so that the use of icons and iconography were very sharply discouraged. Sorokin quotes a typical pronouncement on this matter from a declaration of the Synod of Bishops in 754 A.D. in Byzantium:

'The sinful art of painting is an insult to the fundamental dogma of our salvation, Jesus Christ. . . . The ignorant painter, moved by the sacrilegious motive of profit, depicts what should be believed by the heart only . . . Christ was simultaneously God and Man.'

It was doctrine of this type which led Ruskin to make the plausible but misleading generalization that 'the religious passion is nearly always vividest when the art is weakest'. The Fathers of the Church, the Christian Orders and institutions who followed them, did not weary of protesting against or prohibiting any art or any element in it that was for sensuous enjoyment. This does not mean that they were indifferent to beauty. For them, beauty was essentially an object of intelligence. 'The beautiful,' said St. Thomas Aquinas, 'is the same thing as the good, differing only conceptually.' Whoever seeks the good by that very act also seeks the beautiful. An ideational culture is not therefore likely to bequeath a rich variety of art forms to posterity.

In Byzantium, with its peculiar synthesis of the Græco-Roman and Syriac-Egyptian styles, the development of the arts was also deliberately arrested. After the sixth century A.D., its (ideational) images were standardized and deviation from them was prohibited. Their characteristics have been described as 'iconographic idealization of attitudes; general kindness of the expressions of the visages; painting even the old faces rosy; exaggerated gracefulness of the body; forceful energy of movement and gesture, especially that of the foot stepping aside . . . poetically dishevelled head of hair (*chevelure*) "prophetic" or "Old Testament" lips; locks of small beards; an inspirationally directed look and a pupil turned profoundly to the corner of the eye.'

PLATE 5

IDEATIONAL SCULPTURE
FIGURE OF THE VIRGIN
Notre Dame de Bon Espoir. Eglise de Notre Dame.
Dijon. 11th century A.D.

See page 33

PLATE 6

IDEALISTIC SCULPTURE
PART OF A FIGURE OF THE VIRGIN
St. Amand-les-Pas. 13th century A.D.

See page 34 and
compare also Plate 2

For five or six centuries at least this style was maintained. Nevertheless, after the ninth century, sensate visual elements crept in, so that again a rare and harmonious synthesis occurred between the ideational and sensate elements, giving rise in the thirteenth and fourteenth centuries to Byzantine idealistic art. Akin in such respects to the art of Greece in the fifth century B.C. and to European art of the thirteenth, this new form has been styled the Byzantine Renaissance. Before it could develop into a more full-blooded sensate, visual art, the Byzantine Empire fell before the onslaught of the Turks in the middle of the fifteenth century.

The ideational character of Western European art during the same period was also strongly in evidence, although it took a slightly less uncompromising form, remaining more Greek and less affected by Egyptian and Syrian influences than was the art of Byzantium.

Sorokin suggests that it was this indirect Greek heritage, which had no important rivals, that helped to maintain in Europe a closer contact with the affairs of this world through the encyclopædic learning of the medieval schools of Europe based upon the seven liberal arts, the *trivium*—Grammar, Rhetoric and Logic; and the *quadrivium*—Music, Arithmetic, Geometry and Astronomy.

From about the ninth century also, as in Byzantium, sensate, visual tendencies became apparent in the Carlovingian Renaissance for example, but ideational characteristics continued dominant until the end of the twelfth century. The eleventh century sculpture of the Virgin Mary reproduced in Plate 5 may serve as an example and be compared for its otherworldly quality with the representation of the Hindu deity, Siva Nataraja reproduced as Plate 1.

Then one of those rare moments in the development of human culture again occurred. The rising tide of visualism and the ebb of ideationalism resulted, in the thirteenth and partly in the fourteenth century, in one of those sublime blends of both styles in the form of the supreme idealistic art of these centuries, an art in all its essential traits similar to the great idealistic art of Greece in the fifth and part of the fourth centuries B.C.

Sorokin stresses the interesting fact that such an idealistic art appeared when the dominant ideational style was declining and the moderate visualism was rising. Idealistic art does not appear when ideational art begins to replace sensate art. Instead there are fumblings for something new and strange to replace overripe visualism which may materialize as modernistic incongruities; cubism, futurism and other mixed 'isms' which are neither the fish of ideationalism nor the

c

flesh of visualism; nor are they a harmonious blend of both styles. Sorokin illustrates this generalization by reference to the transition from Mycenæan art to the Archaic Greek art or from the overripe Hellenistic Roman art to the Christian art of the fourth and fifth centuries A.D. and to the art of our own day in Western Europe. Whatever may be the reliability of such an apparent principle, Sorokin has no difficulty in establishing the singular correspondence in quality between thirteenth century Western art and that of Greece of the fifth century B.C. Both were ages of faith, refusing to derive their central values from this world or from earthly life. Thirteenth-century art was not an art for art's sake. Its grand Gothic cathedrals have often been described as the Bible in Stone. Its statues, in their postures, gestures, expressions, appearance, are all lighted by the sublime serenity of the religious and moral ideal. These great creations were anonymous collective works expressing a collective ideal. As in the Greek art of the idealistic period also, this new Western European form has calm and quiet and a lack of dynamism (the Platonic ideas do not change); there is no show and nothing *malerisch;* there is no patheticism, no sentimentality, no emotionalism and no disorder. It tended to convince but not to disturb emotionally. The parallel which Sorokin seeks to establish between the idealistic style of art in the fifth and sixth century Greece and of thirteenth century Europe will be better understood by comparing examples of each, such as those in Plates 6 and 2.

But, and again as in Ancient Greece, this period of idealistic grandeur was short. Already at the end of the thirteenth century the 'optimum' point was left behind, and the art of the fourteenth and fifteenth centuries already represents the period of transition from a waning idealism toward a full-blooded visualism.

The chief characteristics of sensate visual art, already described (see page 29), virtually all became manifest in a new setting and under different conditions. Sorokin thus has a new theory to account for the development of Renaissance art, the rise of Baroque and Rococo styles leading to the Impressionism of more recent times. He has no difficulty in supporting his own description of these art forms by quoting from the writings of historians of modern art and by reproductions of outstanding examples of the craft of painters and sculptors of the various schools and fashions which have succeeded one another since the fourteenth century.

Following one strand in the earlier period of transition from the idealistic to the visual sensate trend, he shows how for example the figure of the Virgin who, in the thirteenth century, was always shown as a noble lady, begins to be represented in more homely guise. Other writers have, of course, also drawn attention to the way in which the Virgin was given more of the nature of common humanity. Before long she was shown smiling at the gambols of her infant, and then as an ordinary peasant woman dandling or suckling her quite ordinary babe. She might also be depicted lightly veiled. Before long the execution of pious imagery assumed that commercial and industrial character it has not yet lost.

At the same time that idealized figures became more mundane, greater efforts were made to depict them as the victims of emotion, feeling and human passions. Unflinching faith having been lost, Sorokin says, and man being thrown upon himself, emotionality, passionateness, dolour, pessimism, suffering, side by side with the attempt to see salvation in pleasure, seized the Christian world. With the previous world (which seemed unshakable) falling to pieces and a new world not yet assured, such dolour and despair are rather comprehensible. Shall we wonder that exactly at that time such themes as Death in its ugliness, the dance macabre, corpses (including Christ) in all their reality, become as it were epidemic? Sorokin illustrates the matter by pointing to the fact that, beginning in the fifteenth century and continuing in the sixteenth, religious art became more theatrical, the images of corpses and death's heads and skulls multiplied in the churches, on church glass windows and in pictures.

Religious art, moreover, not only ceased to be the whole of art exclusively, but steadily fell away from being the main form of art. Secular art steadily became more visual, more realistic. Vasari boasted of having painted a strawberry plant so successfully that a peacock tried to eat the berries, thus paralleling the well-known story which testified to the greatness of the painter Zeuxis (c. 420-380 B.C.) by recording that one of his works was so realistic that a bird tried to pick up a grape he had painted. Both stories testify to the unquestioning acceptance of purely visual-sensate values in art. Generalizing, Sorokin says that when we study the change of technique, moving from the thirteenth century to the 'Primitives' of the fourteenth and fifteenth centuries, and from them to the 'Classics' of the Renaissance, and then to the baroque of the seventeenth century, we are immediately aware of the movement from less illusionism to greater, from the linear style to the *malerisch* style of painting. Sorokin's views absorb and complete those of other art historians rather than conflict with them.

Wölfflin, for instance, enumerates five fundamental pairs of the representational forms of art:

Linear	*versus*	Malerisch
Plane	*versus*	Recession,
Closeness	*versus*	Openness,
Multiplicity	*versus*	Unity,
Clearness	*versus*	Unclearness.

Sorokin says that the first elements of all these pairs are mutually interconnected, and that this is also true of the second. Wölfflin's first categories approach the ideational, while his *malerisch* with its related forms is nearer the sensate visual style. Now the linear appeals to the sense of touch, the 'painterly' (*malerisch*) to the eye only. In fact, says Sorokin, generally the shift from the ideational to the visual art (and culture) is marked by a great stress on the value of the *eye* among the organs of sense, and of the sight among all the senses.

These considerations, he holds, help to make it easy to understand how Western European painting and sculpture from the time of the Renaissance passed from the clear-cut linearism of the Primitives of the fifteenth century, through the Classics of the sixteenth century, to the baroque of the seventeenth, which is a pronounced *malerisch* art (i.e., from the linear classics, like Leonardo da Vinci, Piero della Francesca, Botticelli, Dürer, Raphael, Holbein, Michelangelo (partly), etc., to the *malerisch* Frans Hals, Van Dyck, Rembrandt, Velasquez, Bernini, Rubens, Vermeer, Ruysdael and so on.

However different are the various painters and sculptors in the fifteenth century in various countries of Western Europe, the trend toward visualism is common to almost all of them and to all countries. It cannot, of course, be maintained that the tradition of the Middle Ages and ideationalism were completely replaced, but their influence was waning. Instead there was a growth of individualism, dynamism, emotionalism and of portrait and *genre* painting. A secular spirit rises both in subjects and in manner. As in the Greek art of the fourth century, sensualism, voluptuousness, eroticism make further headway. The pretty woman begins to become more and more a common subject of art, even the saints were depicted nude.

It was against developments of this type that reformers, such as Savonarola, raised their voices, but in vain. Such was the undoubted broad tendency, despite individual painters, like Fra Angelico (1387-1455), who in the seclusion of their cloisters were more faithful to the earlier idealistic style. Piero della Francesca (?1416-1492) maintained it in the following generation as plate 7 will indicate.

PLATE 7

IDEALISTIC PAINTING

PIERO DELLA FRANCESCA. THE QUEEN OF SHEBA
WORSHIPPING THE TRUE CROSS

Part of a series of frescoes illustrating the story of the True Cross,
in Arezzo. Painted between A.D. 1452 and 1466.

See page 36

PLATE 8

SENSATE OR VISUAL PAINTING
JAN STEEN. THE ARTIST'S FAMILY
Netherlands. *Circa* A.D. 1626-1679

See page 37

Sorokin puts the complete triumph of sensate visualism in the sixteenth century. The Flemish school, beginning with the two van Eycks, grew in visualism and became entirely visual, and undilutedly naturalistic. As Taine pointed out, art fell from heaven to earth and began to serve human affairs almost to the exclusion of the divine. The Dutch school, as everybody who has visited the art galleries of the world will know, confines itself, again to quote Taine, 'to reproducing the repose of the bourgeois interior, the comforts of shop and farm, outdoor sports and tavern enjoyments, all the petty satisfactions of an orderly and tranquil existence'. The illustration in Plate 8 provides a characteristic specimen of this style of art.

No other country went so far as the Low Countries in this respect, although the classic painters of Italy kept close to an earthly idealism of the empirical world and of the sensory human body, of landscape and of visual form generally. The main thing in the art of design, according to Cellini, was cleverly to fashion a naked man or woman. Other countries, France, Spain, Portugal and England, midway some of them between the Italian and Flemish types, showed the same tide of rising visualism.

The Reformation and the Counter-Reformation may appear to have produced a reversal of this trend but, Sorokin holds, sensate visual art was in reality gaining all the time. Protestantism in its iconoclasm would not and did not have a religious art, a few religious pictures notwithstanding. After the Council of Trent of 1563, the Catholic Church imposed a stricter censorship on religious pictures and sculpture, but it proved powerless to resist the trend of the times. At best a simulated religiosity, a more or less mechanical standardization of the figures, postures and scenes depicted was all that was achieved. Such artificiality is easy to distinguish from the depth of genuine belief by which the best idealistic art is obviously inspired. Sorokin points to several factors which help to illustrate and explain the contrast.

In the first place the violence of the politico-religious struggle with the Protestants meant that the spirit of calmness, untroubled faith and serenity was gone from Catholic art. Then, as an index to the pronounced sensate visual nature of such art, he points to its pathological, sadistic and terrifying emotionalism. Religious pictures show the tortures and sufferings of martyrs, while secular art revelled in imagining the most violent scenes of ancient history. There is a great multiplication of the scenes of death and of death itself. The skull of death is a common adornment of tombs, rendered with a terrifying naturalness. Particularly noteworthy also is the change from the use of symbolism in the Middle Ages to that of the sixteenth century. Dante followed St. Thomas Aquinas in believing that the visible universe and human society were images in the mind of God. The persons in his poems are actual, but they symbolize some invisible form of existence. By the sixteenth century this was changed. The persons or actors were for the most part hypostazied intellectual abstractions—Justice, Prudence, Memory, Intellect, Liberty, Friendship, Sleep, and so on—usually with an effort not only to make the meaning of the allegorical figure naturalistically and intellectually justifiable but pleasant and enjoyable sensually as well, in a way quite foreign to the transcendental symbolism of an ideational epoch. As often as not the allegories of the sixteenth century failed to achieve their purpose and remained strange, artificial and cold.

Religious art in the sixteenth century was now being dwarfed by the more extensive secular art, a change which became yet more pronounced in the seventeenth century. Sorokin collects from the art historians of Western Europe a string of adjectives used to describe the conspicuous visual art of this sensate period collectively labelled, as a style, baroque: 'theatricality, illusionism, illusionistic artificiality, showiness manifest in the ostentation of art, sumptuousness, pomp, luxury, overabundance of decoration, impurity, latent or open sensuality and sexuality, paganism, dynamism, patheticism, twisted and convulsive exaltation of ecstasy, and other strong emotions, imitative, purely cerebral and chilly Academism, pseudo-idealism'. Particularly notable in the exterior of baroque buildings these qualities are present inside also, gluttony for mirrors, damask flowers, gilt, stucco, garlands, even pretty angels which are hybrids between the angels of religion and vulgar cupids. In complete contrast with the ideational or idealistic styles, baroque is at once recognised as the world of theatrical and ostentatious visualism, as a purely illusionistic world created only for the eyes as a mere show but with the intention to pass this show for a genuine world.

The somewhat later rococo style of the eighteenth century is the direct outcome of the baroque and belongs to the same family of theatricality and show, but the decorations are changed for the sake of variety. The rococo world is the same illusionistic, artificial world of seen surfaces and appearances, but they are now made in an effeminate, enfeebled, idyllic pastoral, coquettish fashion. It is the 'boudoir' world with artificial and illusionistic rocks, waterfalls, gorges, fountains, idyllic shepherds and pastorals, cupids and nymphs, with other exotic freaks and illusionistic devices of an enfeebled, weary, bored, overripe and half-senile society. Such art, originating in France, penetrated and became dominant in Germany, the Netherlands, and Italy, in Spain and Portugal; only England escaped its influence to any considerable degree.

In discussing other aspects of eighteenth-century art, Sorokin deals with the series of waves of imitation of other forms of art, a phenomenon also observable in the Hellenistic, sensate period of Greek art and in Roman art after the Augustan era. In this sequence of various fashions and imitations the previous idealistic form was never successfully achieved, all the imitative waves remaining generally in the visual stream and the change consisting in a variation of different visual forms in spite of the efforts to attain a real idealistic or even ideational art. How visual and sensate ecclesiastical art could be at this time is shown by the reproduction in Plate 9 of a female head then added to the altar in the Cathedral at Chartres.

Sorokin holds that the Renaissance saw the first imitative wave of the idealistic art of Greece, for which the over-ripe stage of Hellenistic and Roman art was copied by mistake. It produced instead, he says, a brilliant but pseudo-classic and psuedo-idealistic visual art. Then came as a reaction the purely naturalistic visualism of the Flemish school, the baroque of the Italian with Academism as its offshoot and as the second imitative wave of a pseudo-classicism. In spite of their differences, they all happen to be not less but more visual than the art of the Renaissance. Toward the end of the seventeenth and the beginning of the eighteenth century, the baroque as well as academism were worn out, and gave place to the rococo style on the one hand, and to the Flemish 'sweetened' naturalism on the other. Both by their very nature are fully visual and sensuous, each in its own manner.

About the beginning of the second part of the eighteenth century, the rococo style was practically worn out, and again, for the third time, there were signs of a return to classicism. This return was an accomplished fact in France at the end of the eighteenth century, with painters such as David and Ingres. Thus, within one century, art made a whole circle. That domination of the third imitation of classicism was short, however; around 1825 it was almost over, and it was soon replaced by the romanticism of the second quarter of the nineteenth century, typified in the works of painters such as Delacroix Daumier, Corot and the brothers Maris. Romanticism did not last longer and within one-quarter of a century was also outmoded. It was replaced by something like 'naturalism', and several other currents, one of which developed into the colourful impressionistic school of the last quarter of the nineteenth century, led by Manet, Monet, Renoir and others. In it visualism reached its most extreme and purest form: there was, and there is, no possibility of going farther along that line. The triumph of Impressionism was again short and, toward the end of the nineteenth century, its fashionableness was already on the decline. 'Expressionists', and especially 'cubists', 'futurists', 'symbolists' appeared as the opponents not only of the impressionistic school but of the visual style itself.

Sorokin adds to this summary account the following remark upon the art of our own times. At the present moment, we have a most diversified conglomeration of many schools and currents, among them those ready to challenge the visual style generally, and the first symptoms of the search for something akin to an ideational style. But these symptoms as yet are weak; the searchers look, but have not yet found what they desire. It is clear, from the often heated controversy which such efforts arouse, that innovation in style, particularly in the sensate visual style, is not merely difficult but also a most ungrateful task, rarely rewarded by sympathetic encouragement. Here, probably, is a fundamental reason why the position of the artist in contemporary life is felt to be a social problem. Sorokin amplifies his summary account of his three main 'logico-meaningful' (see page 11) forms of human cultural mentality by his effort, already stressed in Chapter Two as one of the distinctive characteristics of his work, to present some accurate statistical basis on which his conclusions not merely rest, but from which they may seem inevitably to arise.

To establish statistics as fully and as accurately as possible over the whole field of the available paintings and sculpture of Western culture since the Græco-Roman period was Sorokin's aim. With the assistance of others, he undertook this 'Egyptian load of monotonous work', an 'almost appalling quantitative study'. For each country and each period, all the pictures and all the sculptural works known in the history of art were analysed as far as possible, regardless of whether they belong to great or small or anonymous artists. For the early periods, particularly for those of which so much has vanished, such an analysis, however painstaking, cannot include more than a very small part of the actual production. It is, however, a much larger and more representative sample than has hitherto been used in any other study of art history.

The difficulties, apparently insuperable, of assigning the correct date and place of origin to all these artistic productions have been overcome as far as possible by classifying them in periods of two centuries or more, except that the impossibility of dating what remains of the earlier medieval period compelled Sorokin to relegate to one single class all the pictures and sculptural works studied (5,032 units) into one class 'before the tenth century'. The result is a collection of a great number of facts about the nature of works of art and the numbers of them in the following several distinct classes:

Whether religious or secular.
Whether landscape, everday *genre* or portrait.
Whether portraits are of men or women.
Whether the subject is royalty, the aristocracy, the clergy, *bourgeoisie* or the labour class.

These points are easily determined. Special precautions were taken before Sorokin's investigators dealt with questions such as the quality of paintings of the nude; whether ascetic, sensuous (erotic) or neutral or how any picture not obviously sensate (visual), ideational or idealistic, should be classified according to its predominant style. Studies in one place could to some extent be compared with those elsewhere. In Prague, 32,299 pictures and sculptures were studied by one team. In Cambridge, Massachusetts, 16,679 were studied by another worker. Reviewing the resultant discrepancies in classification by half-centuries since 1200 A.D., Sorokin reports that his results may not be completely reliable, but they are more reliable than any other data presented up to the present time, so far as the general course of art fluctuation is concerned. And this verdict relates to a particularly difficult series of analyses and classifications in which subjective valuations might be expected to differ widely.

In an introductory volume such as this, it is naturally impossible to present in detail either Sorokin's whole range of statistical investigations or his candid and full review of their limitations and implications. The information sought under the various subject classifications mentioned above is given as far as possible separately for Russia, England, Central Europe, Holland, France, Spain, Italy, Ancient Medieval Christianity and Islam. The range of the statistical material assembled and presented in the first volume of *Social and Cultural Dynamics* is best indicated by the following list of some of the charts and diagrams to be found in that volume:

Religious and secular art by countries.
Main styles of art by countries.
The visual and ideational in art by countries.
The extremely spiritual and sensual in art by countries.
Fluctuation of nudity in art by countries.

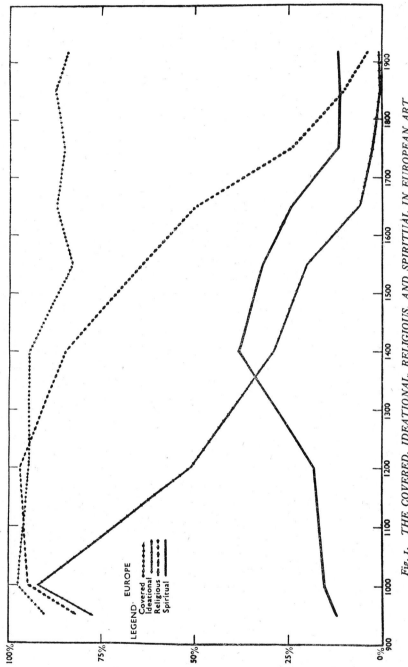

LEGEND· EUROPE
Covered
Ideational
Religious
Spiritual

100% 75% 50% 25% 0%

900 1000 1100 1200 1300 1400 1500 1600 1700 1800 1900

Fig. 1.   THE COVERED, IDEATIONAL, RELIGIOUS, AND SPIRITUAL IN EUROPEAN ART

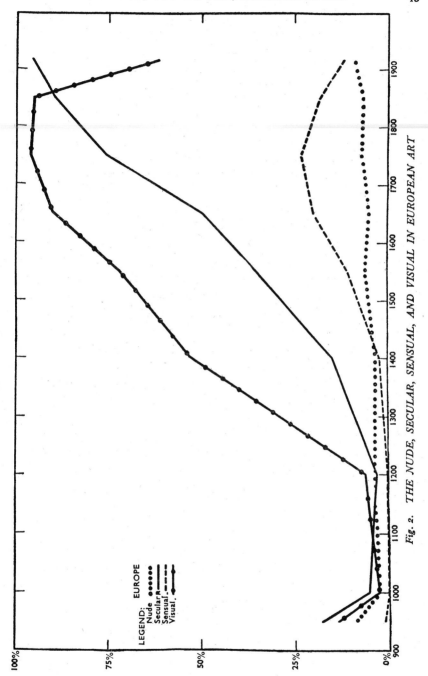

Fig. 2.   THE NUDE, SECULAR, SENSUAL, AND VISUAL IN EUROPEAN ART

Animals, still life, and *paysage* in art by countries.
Genre and portraiture in art by countries.
The fantastic and antique in art by countries.
Aristocracy, clergy and *bourgeoisie* in art by countries.
Intellectuals, military and lower classes in art by countries.
The sexes in portraiture by countries.

The several charts in which these and other facts are presented are too numerous for reproduction here, as is the lengthy appendix listing in nearly sixty long columns of small print the names, dates of birth and death of all the artists of whom any record exists for all countries of Western Europe.

It is important to note that Sorokin worked over the material from several directions. Otherwise it might be suspected that the results were inevitably predetermined by the way in which the material was classified and presented. If, for example, all pictures had been placed in three or four well-marked classes: sensate, ideational, idealistic and other mixed styles, it would not alone prove more than that such a fourfold classification could accommodate a number of paintings. Other classifications might serve to group paintings also and then seem to support the value of the classification employed. Sorokin's facts themselves first establish the necessity for his threefold classification at the same time as they demonstrate its value as an interpreter and guide.

The following brief statement summarizes the findings relating to European art as a whole, beginning with the Creto-Mycenæan and Græco-Roman cultures and ending with the present day. Accompanying them are two charts giving in diagrammatic form some of Sorokin's statistical findings upon the decline of ideational and the rise of sensate art, reproduced here as Figs. 1 and 2.

Period	*Dominant Style of Art*
B.C. 12th-9th centuries ..	Visual art.
B.C. 8th-6th centuries ..	Ideational with a possible transitory non-visual but not ideational reaction in the ninth century.
B.C. end 6th-beginning 4th centuries	Marvellously mixed idealistic.
B.C. end 4th century to A.D. 4th Century	Hellenistic and Roman visual art with several smaller, shorter and shallower ripplings of ideational, idealistic and visual fluctuations upon the main long-term tide of the main style.

PLATE 9

SENSATE OR VISUAL SCULPTURE

HEAD OF AN ANGEL

Chartres Cathedral. 18th century A.D.

See page 39

PLATE 10

IDEALISTIC ARCHITECTURE

THE PARTHENON, ATHENS. 447-432 B.C.

Above: Restoration, Metropolitan Museum, New York
Below: Present condition

See page 47

Period	*Dominant Styles of Art*
A.D. 4th-6th	Non-coherent, anti-visual reaction looking for something new and different from visualism but not having found it.
A.D. 6th-12th	Ideational, with several slighter fluctuations: slight return to visualism in Carolingian Renaissance and rigorous ideationalism in 10th, 11th and early 12th centuries.
A.D. end 12th to early 14th	Idealistic.
A.D. 14th-20th	Visual with secondary fluctuations.
A.D. 20th	Reaction against visualism.

On the basis of this study, of its development and succession of various forms of painting and sculpture, Sorokin claims that, by holding resolutely to his 'logico-meaningful' (page 11) method of study, and with the aid of his integrating principles of the ideational and sensate mentality, he has been able to contribute usefully and practically to the better understanding of the history of one branch at least of human cultural activity.

If this is true, he has already gone a long way towards establishing the value of these concepts of 'ideational', 'sensate' and 'idealistic' as true operational concepts. That is to say, they are able to group and classify a whole range of facts whose nature and necessary connexions would be imperfectly understood without their aid. They help to 'place' a work of art in its period; they throw light upon the nature of the mentality or outlook on life of that period. The clues they provide to the various distinctive characters of works of art help to show how and why they are related and in what way they change. By establishing such facts about forms of art, they help to place works of art in their true class or category, and also to show how far those classes and categories are coherent well-knit distinctive wholes with their own proper style and characteristics in the sense referred to on page 11. They help, says Sorokin, not only to discern between what variables in art we should expect the existence of the functional-causal relationships, but help to establish them in fact and to decide the integrated or unintegrated nature of a given compartment of culture, in this connexion, the compartments of art in painting and in sculpture.

Architecture

It remains to apply the scheme so developed to other branches of human endeavour. Sorokin next takes architecture. Here, however, he provides no charts or statistical tables, but it is clear that he has used a large body of facts in framing his theory. The best illustrations and the most detailed source of reference to the facts of architectural development which he describes are to be found in any good history of architecture, such as the well-known manual by Sir Banister Fletcher.

Briefly, Sorokin's findings are that Egyptian architecture throughout its history was predominantly ideational. It was mainly religious architecture producing pyramids and temples. Internally, therefore, it served ideational purposes. Externally, on many of its buildings there is not the slightest ornament. There were, it is true, waves of visual art. Under the Fifty Dynasty and towards the end of the Old Kingdom there appears a circular column with palm leaves already notably complicated and ornamental. It will be recalled that in the later stage of the Old Kingdom its paintings and sculpture seems also to have become more visual.

There were similar incursions and regressions of visual art at later periods. The beginning of the Middle Kingdom shows a very simple style of column which became more complicated later. Under the New Kingdom or Empire, there were the inverted bell-shaped columns which were followed, particularly in the Saito and the Roman periods, by overloaded decoration and a mixture of various architectural styles. It was then that a new type of capital with a human head beneath each face of the abacus appeared. This movement towards greater and more fanciful ornamentation and decoration became much more marked under the Ptolemies and the Romans. The form and especially the size of buildings over all these succeeding periods also showed corresponding changes from ideational to visual styles, or the reverse, in their painting and sculpture.

Similar developments occurred in Greece, where the architecture was predominantly ideational up to the fifth century B.C. The Doric order was an ideational style; simple even in details, modest in size, with a minimum of sculptural ornament. In the fifth century B.C., and for most of the fourth century B.C., idealistic styles with the Ionic order are characteristic. The buildings of this period, of which the Parthenon at Athens (447-432 B.C.) is the most renowned, were distinguished by marvellous harmony and proportions, striking just the right balance between ideational otherworldliness and visual beauty.

Ornament was indeed by no means shunned, as the eternally famous sculptured frieze of the Parthenon so well demonstrates (see Plate 10). At the end of the fourth century B.C., a long period of visualism set in, lasting until the fourth century A.D., although shallow, short-lived reactions and minor fluctuations occurred, not however affecting the main stream. The 'visual' revolution affected the inner character of buildings no less than their external appearance. Great size, profusion of ornamentation, luxury, costliness, visual magnificence, increase of illusionary devices, mixtures of all styles are among the characteristic marks to which Sorokin calls attention in the architecture of this sensate period. The Corinthian order and still more the composite columns and capitals of the later Roman style, notably such examples as those furnished by the Arch of Titus (A.D. 81) and the Arch of Severus (A.D. 204), provide good illustrations of the visual style as it developed in the Roman Empire.

The few extant ruined remains make it possible to imagine the sense of grandeur and magnificence with which these buildings were designed to impress the onlookers. Until the heyday of Augustus and of the Emperors who succeeded him, Rome had not been notable for architectural splendour. Under the Republic it was indeed a dull and somewhat mean city until the first century B.C., when the increase of wealth with new ideas of building brought about a change.

Augustus boasted that he had found a city of brick and had left a city of marble, but the change had begun before his time, and it would probably have occurred without his intervention. Had there been no Emperors, the houses of Rome's leading citizens might yet have come near to rivalling the huge imperial palaces built on the Palatine Hill of Rome, whose ruins yet remain to suggest something of their vast scale.

Apart from a temporary reaction towards simplicity and austerity under Trajan and Hadrian (A.D. 98-138), the sensate wave gathered momentum and carried everything before it. The Great Temple (about A.D. 131-161) and the Temple of Jupiter (A.D. 273), both at Baalbek in the distant Syrian valley, the colossal baths of Caracalla in Rome (A.D. 211-217) and the baths of Diocletian (A.D. 302), are among the many mute but exceedingly effective witnesses to the strength of visualism in late Roman imperial times.

The downfall of the Roman Empire in the fifth century A.D. meant the eclipse not merely of the sensate style but of architecture as well. Where it survived, as it did in Byzantium, it took a notably different course. There the wave of ideational Christian architecture was indeed based upon Græco-Roman skills and traditions, but it did not follow their styles. The manner in which external decoration disappeared from Christian architecture is one striking sign of change. The basilica and the Byzantine dome show their technical antecedents clearly enough, but their manner leaves no doubt that their true nature and purpose was something radically different from that of the buildings on which they were modelled. The illustration of the Church of St. Vitale in Ravenna (A.D. 526-547) in Plate 11 indicates the new note struck by early Christian architecture. The difference was further accentuated when the Romanesque and Gothic styles were elaborated. Sorokin points out that exteriors were plain, but ample compensation for the dull exterior of the basilica was made by the gorgeous polychromatic decoration of the interior for the greater glory of God. Quite as important as the decoration was the symbolic form of the Christian churches. The great dome of the basilicas was regarded as representing Christ, the four adjacent domes were the four Evangelists. The later churches were built in the shape of a cross, facing eastwards towards the Holy Land.

Sorokin points out how in medieval towns and cities, the great cathedrals and churches dominated the skyline, completely overshadowing the civic buildings, the houses of the wealthy, or the palaces of the great, as some of them, notably the Cathedral at Chartres, still do. It was not until the fifteenth century that the grand architecture becomes more and more secular. The palace, the Rathaus, the mansion, the commercial edifice, the parliament buildings and so on then began to command attention by their size and magnificence.

Before that occurred, there was the marvellous blend between the visual and ideational elements which reached its climax in the second half of the thirteenth century, after having inspired and created cathedrals such as those at Noyon (about 1157-1228), St. Denis (1144), Sens (1144-1168), Notre Dame at Senlis (1155-1185), Chartres (1194-1260), Reims (1212-1300), Amiens (1220-1288), Beauvais (1225), Canterbury (1174) and Salisbury (1240).

These glories were not sustained as the spirit of the age continued to change from ideationalism to a sensate character. From the end of the fourteenth century until the Renaissance, Gothic architecture became more decorative and flamboyant. By the sixteenth century there seemed no hope of further progress from this style of building and decoration, and it was then that some effort was made at the Renaissance to revive the older styles. Columns, pilasters and entablature were revived in Roman fashion, but for decorative rather than for structural purposes.

PLATE II

See page 48

IDEATIONAL ARCHITECTURE

ST. VITALE, RAVENNA. A.D. 526-547

PLATE 12

SENSATE OR VISUAL ARCHITECTURE
PAVILION OF THE ZWINGER PALACE
Dresden. A.D. 1711

See page 49

Despite an effort after simplicity and its very considerable success at the hands of a genius like Brunelleschi, it remained a new wave on the strong sensate tide which was sweeping all before it. That is to say emphasis continued to be put on appearance rather than upon structural merit. In the seventeenth century, possibly as one result of the attempt to combine classical with Gothic styles, or as a reaction against a narrow interpretation of the canons of Vitruvius, Western architecture assumed the so-called baroque style. All the emphasis went upon visual, illusory show; the search for effect through the arrangement of light and shadow; a taste for contrast and movement; a search for theatrical effects and a distinct appetite for the colossal. It was a quest by no means unrewarded, as anyone can testify who saw Dresden before it was obliterated (see illustration on page 12).

The rococo in architecture as in painting was still more visual, erotic, futile; reduced almost entirely to puerile decorations. Sorokin calls it a confectioner's sweet and toyland architecture.

In the late eighteenth and in the nineteenth centuries, several waves of neo-classic, romantic and classic architecture with attempted revivals of Gothic and Renaissance prototypes followed one another, but none succeeded in creating an ideational style, or any original style at all.

Sorokin will not lightly concede that skyscraper architecture represents a new and real style. It is, he admits, undoubtedly a trend toward structural simplicity but hardly ideationality. It resembles modern cubist painting in being a reaction against extreme visual art. It is not ideational, because nearly all its buildings are secular. They do not pretend, says Sorokin, to symbolize any transcendental reality. They serve instead the most material, the most commercial, the most empirical and the most visual needs. Among the merits claimed for them are indeed that they are 'functional'. They are machines in which to live and work. Desperate efforts are made to combine maximum size with maximum profits and dividends. Hence they are too cerebral, mathematical, commercial, scientific and planned, quite regular and deadly correct.

On the basis of his rapid survey, Sorokin is able to amplify his provisional conclusion (see page 45) by claiming that his ideational, sensate and idealistic categories fit the world of architecture as satisfactorily as they do the two branches of the arts, painting and sculpture, which he had previously examined in much greater detail. By 'fit the world of architecture' is meant not merely that buildings bear obviously a distinguishing hallmark of their age which corresponds sufficiently

D

accurately with those categories, but that the categories themselves
help to suggest the hallmark or distinguishing characteristics.

It is easy to see how such a claim might seem dangerously like
begging the question in the manner most 'philosophies of history' beg
it, namely by imagining a 'law', or a 'principle', or series of 'laws' or
'principles' of historical change and then looking for facts to 'prove'
the laws; such inescapable facts that seem either not to fit or indeed
to disprove the laws are then given some special interpretation to
make them fit the theory. Nobody has more trenchantly exposed this
inherent fallacy in the writings of others than Sorokin. It will occur
at once to every reader that he also faces this pitfall. He puts his hope
of avoiding it in his strenuous efforts to look at each main branch of
human activity separately; assessing the facts by as objective an interpretation as he can and seeing whether they conform fairly to the
ideational-sensate-idealistic principle.

This is the task he sets himself throughout, and it remains to see
how far he succeeds with it. At the outset he has established his three
main logico-meaningful cultural mentalities—ideational, sensate (visual) and idealistic—by a very full statistical sampling of thousands of
paintings and many sculptures. Without any similar statistical enquiry
he has given a summary survey of the main trends of style in architecture which fits plausibly into the pattern provided by the history of
painting and sculpture.

He has shown how his interpretation of the history of art brings
order and sequence into art history over many ages and epochs in a
way that challenges and supersedes all previous theories on the subject. The proposal of Sir Charles Holmes, for example, in *A Grammar
of the Arts* (1931), to divide all art into representative art, decorative
art, and constructive art can at once be seen to be inadequate. Sorokin
mentions some, but does not by any means survey all these rival
theories. The inadequacy of many of them, already revealed by the
succinct survey of Ogden, Richards and Wood in the *Foundation of
Aesthetics* (1925), will it is believed, be shown with greater clarity when
they are again reviewed in the light of Sorokin's principles which, as
the following chapters will show, are by no means merely views about
art, but relate, as rival theories seldom pretend to do, to the entire
range of cultural life as a whole.

Will the history of the other human arts and sciences confirm or
upset Sorokin's provisional conclusions?

CHAPTER FOUR

Music Drama
Literature Criticism

I s there such a thing as ideational music or sensate music? To the majority of those who have been trained by long familiarity with the great tradition of music developed in Europe since about the middle of the eighteenth century, this may well sound a strange question. Music for them probably means the production of outstanding and renowned composers, such as Handel, Bach, Mozart, Beethoven and their successors up to our own time.

It is true that some new kinds of music bearing scant resemblance to the works of those classic composers are now apparently giving satisfaction to many, but for the most part these novelties are little better understood or appreciated than are similar efforts to create new styles in painting, sculpture and architecture.

In the Middle Ages music was also something very different from either classical music, or the works of modern composers. There is a definition of music by the philosopher Bœthius at the beginning of the Middle Ages which Sorokin quotes to bring out this difference: 'Human music is that which is understood by anyone who descends into himself (or sinks into himself)'. By these mysterious words, Sorokin considers that Bœthius thought that a knowledge of music should impart to the mind an understanding of its true principles, and that this was very much more important and valuable than the mere practice or performance which brings music to the ear. It is merely another example of the general principle that the mind is superior to the body. Consequently the real musician is the man who knows a chant by force of reason, not the man who has learned it by practice. The testimony of the ear, in other words, is of no significance and should be ignored.

Such a doctrine, which sounds so strange to us, was, however, the theory supported by most of the Greek philosophers. It was supported by the thinkers of the Middle Ages, and it reigned supreme for almost one thousand years. Strange as it is, it is no stranger than the concept of ideational painting. Bœthius and his famous predecessors and followers meant by it what Sorokin styles the ideational or symbolic form of music, in contradistinction to the sensately audible. Just as in ideational painting, the visual impression through the eye plays a secondary role, and the aim of the picture is to give the idea of the object as it exists in the mind; likewise in ideational music, the main thing is not how it sounds—pleasant or unpleasant—but to grasp that which is beyond the sounds and for which they are mere signs and symbols. This hidden meaning beyond the sounds is only to be grasped by intuition, reason or mind, by 'descending into oneself', as Bœthius put it. Such music need not be harmonious, pleasant or enjoyable; indeed the combination of sounds perceived by the ear may be ugly, but if to the mind it means something great for which it is a mere symbol or 'symbolic' stimulus, then it is great, 'heavenly', ideational music.

Sensate music, on the contrary, is judged by its sheer 'audible beauty', regardless of any hidden meaning. It takes sounds at their face value and it is an end in itself.

In more detail, Sorokin analyses the difference between the two classes under the following main characteristics:

Ideational music tends to be 'inner'. Like the silent communion of the soul with God, it employed the simplest means: no orchestra, no musical instruments. The voices sang in unison. There was no polyphony and the melody was all within one octave. At the time of St. Gregory, the Roman school had only seven singers. In all the luxury of the Sistine Chapel, there were but thirty-seven, and this number was reduced to twenty-four in the year of Palestrina's *Mass of the Pope* (1565). This, however, was one of the early monuments of polyphony. Sensate music tends to be theatrical and external. It has to be interesting, enjoyable, entertaining, successful and popular. It seeks effect by the massing of voices, from their wide range, their modulations; by all kinds of consonances and especially dissonances; chromatics; contrasts of rhythms and of intensity. It demands enormous choruses and concert halls. With the aid of commercial advertising and publicity, it seeks to be the richest, loudest and biggest in the world.

Ideational music tends to be and is comparatively pure in style. Sensate music is not and cannot afford to be pure. Sorokin refers briefly to some of its adjuncts: the lowest forms of vaudeville and musical comedy with their mixed styles, including everything from classical music to jazz, dancing, athletics, comedy actors, complicated by light effects, scenery effects, and sound effects. As though the spectacle were not enough, it is accompanied by the sale of ice cream and sweets for the unoccupied mouths of the audience. Not, of course, that this is a nineteenth-century novelty, for Aristotle observed two thousand years ago that the sale of sweetmeats in the theatre was greater if the performance was poor. Higher in the scale perhaps, but essentially similar in type, is the musical drama of Richard Wagner with its mixture of music, poetry, dancing, stage, popular topics and legends, which Sorokin describes as the most magnificent incarnation of impurity, in the noblest forms of sensate art.

Ideational music, in complete contrast, consists of audible signs for great inaudible values which are and have to be the values of a collectivity. The values of an individual are too weak, fragile and uncertain to be great enough to become those of a collectivity. Ideational music, therefore, requires a fairly well-knit homogeneous society to sustain it. Sensate music does not need such support. It is music for the buyer, and it satisfies heterogeneous societies. Ideational music, as self-communion or communion with God, has no pride of authorship. Sensate music has to be individualistic and its author is concerned to protect his rights and to insure that his name and authorship figure as prominently as possible in public performances.

Ideational music does not give rise to any special æsthetic theorizing by critics. It is controlled by religious and moral censors whose concern is with its relations with the values lying behind the sound symbols. Sensate music, by its nature, calls for a criterion of its beauty and perfection, and hence stimulates theories of beauty and æsthetic theorizing by musical critics.

The principal mixed class of music, the idealistic type, seen in the works of Palestrina, Vittoria, Orlando di Lasso, Bach, Handel, Mozart and Beethoven, also has a considerable purity of style, but it is not so pure as that of the ideational epoch. Yet its values are perfectly blended with sensual beauty.

Sorokin holds that the beauty of the music of the great composers of the idealistic period is immediately appreciated by all who hear it, and that it stands in no need of critics to bring forward reasoned proofs that it is great and beautiful or to tell people to admire it.

So much for preliminary definition and description of the three main contrasting forms of music. Have they historically the reality which Sorokin supposes? He points out that just as ideational and sensate painting are found in most primitive, as well as in most civilized, cultures, the same is true of music. After referring briefly to some other views of musical development, he says that it is reasonable to suppose that primitive peoples sing when they are excited, when they have an abundance of energy or merely because they enjoy it, because music and singing are pleasant and biologically useful. All such chant- ing and singing are merely forms of sensate music. Side by side with it there is an ideational form. It has two main varieties, the music of magic and that of religion. Both of these forms are in their essentials ideational music, not sensate. The use of music in performing magical acts and in religious societies is universal and is found even among the most primitive societies. But it is not confined to primitive peoples nor need it be assumed that all primitive peoples practice it. Those that do so believe that with the magic chant everything is possible. Incan- tations exist for various vitally important purposes, for obtaining rain or fine weather, for appeasing evil spirits, or for curing disease in men or animals. The sense and the importance and influence of such music, therefore, derives not from its sounds as such, which may to the sensate ear be repellent, but to the magical, mystical or religious value lying behind them.

Ideational symbolic music has existed in Egypt, China, India, in Greece, Rome and in Europe during the Middle Ages. It was owing to its mystical or symbolic meaning that it became one of the most important responsibilities of government, and this is why the sages, thinkers and statesmen, such as Confucius, Pythagoras, Plato and Aristotle, gave so much time and thought to it.

The difficulties of illustrating changes in the vogue of ideational, sensate and idealistic music are very much greater than those arising from the similar treatment of painting and sculpture. Sheer lack of knowledge makes it impossible to trace the exact way in which changes occurred in the predominant music of Ancient Egypt, Assyria, China, India and Palestine. That both the ideational and sensate forms existed and that one form followed the other in the history of these lands is the most that can be established. Sorokin believes that the same is true of the earlier period of Græco-Roman music and certainly of Creto- Mycenæan music, despite the fact that not a single note of music has survived from these early periods, nor unfortunately from the period of Terpander, his contemporaries and successors of the eight, seventh and early sixth centuries B.C., when Sorokin considers ideational Greek music reached its highest development. Some of the names of these musicians are known, and the forms and styles of their music are indi- cated by surviving references. It was a grand music, bound up with religious ceremonies and religious civic performances which took place in temples and religious theatres. Being an integral part of important public functions, it was jealously protected. From a speech of Demosthenes of 349 B.C. against Midias, it is evident that the death penalty could be demanded as late as the fourth century B.C. for a supposedly unlawful interference in the functions of the man in charge of the chorus in the festivals. The terms used in referring to this music all indicate its religious character. *Nome* meant a religious chant in honour of one or other of the gods of a given province; *dithyramb*, a lyric hymn to Dionysos; *paean*, a chant to Apollo; other terms like the *prosody*, the chants of the march of the religious cortege to the temple, and the *threnody* are equally of religious or magic significance.

It was an essentially simple music. The instruments were poor and must have lacked variety of *timbres*; the performers were few, since sixteen to twenty-four voices at most made up the chorus in the lyrical dramas of Greece.

Sorokin believes that in the course of the sixth century B.C. the sensate form of music began to be heard. Towards its end and in the fifth century B.C., roughly speaking, the decline of ideational music and the rise of sensate music balanced to produce the marvel of the idealistic music of the fifth century. This idealistic music seems to have reached its point of maturity or a perfect equilibrium between religion and pure art in the music and, associated with it, in the poetry and drama (tragedy and comedy) of Pindar, Æschylus, Sophocles, Euripides (partly), Aristophanes, Simonides of Klos, Agathocles, Melanippides of Melos (master of counterpoint), Bacchylides, Damon and others. In its essential parts it still remained ideational and kept the forms of the hieratic music and drama demanded and sanctified by traditional beliefs. But elements of sensate music began to creep in. If the tragedies of Æschylus (525-456 B.C.) exhibit these but slightly, they are already in considerable evidence in the works of Euripides (485-406 B.C.), and this is the reason why most of the thinkers who immediately succeeded him, like Plato, take Euripides as the boundary line of what they styled decadence.

Sorokin summarizes the characteristics of the transition from ideational to sensate music and drama with which music became increasingly involved as follows:

(i)   Progressive abandonment of the purely sacerdotal art in favour of music to please.

(ii) Increasing substitution of destiny for the gods and other metaphysical abstractions.

(iii) Complication of the technicality of music intended to make a greater impression and to please more.

(iv) Increase of the purely 'human' theme of music and drama associated with it.

(v) Increase of the comical, satirical and sarcastic veins in ridiculing and satirizing human affairs and events and relationships (Aristophanes and the increasing number of comedies).

(vi) Decreasing role of the chorus and increasing role of individual performers. Likewise an increasing individualism characterizes the authors also. They begin to be more and more individualistic and less and less ready to sink their own personality in the anonymous collectivity.

(vii) Progressive permeation of the profane spirit in art.

(viii) Progressive loss of calm serenity in music in favour of its increasing passionate, pathetic, individual emotionality.

(ix) Introduction of the feminine element on the stage.

After the fourth century B.C., sensate music, already strong, continued to grow and to dominate the ideational music of the preceding period. The marvellous balance of the fifth century was disrupted in favour of sensate music.

Euripides, Melanippides, Phrynis and his disciple Timotheus of Miletus were denounced as the corrupters of taste, but their successors, such as Philoxenes of Cytherea (436/5-380/79 B.C.), Telestes (*b.* 420 B.C.), Agathon (*d.* 401 B.C.), and a crowd of parodists, continued this tendency. The essential traits of this music are its increasing profane, sensual, human, individualistic interest, its increasing striving after effect through greater mass and quantity and its new professional character. Then began the monster concerts with hundreds and thousands of artists and the craze for the biggest building, the biggest orchestra and chorus and the greatest noise to be achieved by the power of instruments, by contrasts of consonances and dissonances and the concentration upon pure technique generally.

The status and functions of the music-maker also underwent a fundamental transformation. From being a moral and social leader, a prophet, magician or priest, he became a professional and an individualist seeking personal renown, fame and fortune by his art. Through it he sought to make his living—and a most luxurious one—to be famous, to be popular, to be the idol of a crowd of emotional and half-hysterical followers. The cult of many of them, says Sorokin, was hardly less than that of Richard Wagner with the enormous crowd of half-crazy Wagnerian devotees throughout the world. The cities of Greece vied for the honour of having a famous musician among their citizens: some of them were named after artists; statues were erected to composers; enormous sums were paid for their concerts. In brief, the popular musician was a manufacturer of an important sensual pleasure, and as such he was paid well by sensual values, from applause and fame to wealth and sensual and sexual love. In this way the situation continued, with slighter ups and downs, until the victorious ideational music of Christianity put an end to this sensual music, great in a way in its initial stages, but, Sorokin believes, completely degenerate during the Alexandrian, Pergamene and the Roman period.

Roman music suffered, as did other forms of Roman art, by being completely eclipsed by the earlier maturity of the Greeks. Early Roman music was probably of a rather low-grade ideational form, but, before it or a Roman sensate music could develop, the Roman world was flooded by what Sorokin describes as the superannuated and overripe sensate music which was imported from Greece. The intermediate stage, the classical miracle of idealistic music was almost unknown to Rome, as it was unknown in painting, sculpture and architecture, except by imitation. By the end of the first century B.C., the Roman world was avid for musical festivals on a gigantic scale. Music to be sure was by no means the sole attraction at these spectacles, but it was nevertheless tremendously popular as a source of social distinction. Nero and his fiddle may typify the popularity of music from the emperors to the *bourgeoisie*. Children were taught music which became a lucrative profession, and great was the vanity of its virtuosos. There were also many critics and theorizers about music.

In such a period of sensate art, there appeared, says Sorokin, a crowd of grammarians, rhetoricians, philosophers and art amateurs, art critics, art reviewers, evaluators and educators, most of whom were neither artists nor did they know anything about art except beggarly superficialities. But they occupied the front stage, became noisy, influential, authoritative, and they wrote innumerable texts and compendiums, not to mention articles, in which and through which they crushed many talents and created successes out of nullities. Even when a moralizing voice like Plutarch's is heard in this noisy crowd it is a voice crying in the wilderness. Moreover, his preaching is not spontaneous, not otherworldly or mystic or ideational, but entirely reasoned, rationally calculated and based not so much upon ideational principles as upon very earthly, very utilitarian, noble but sensate considerations.

With the Middle Ages in Europe, the scene is entirely changed. During almost nine hundred years, from about the fifth century A.D. to the fourteenth century, music was either exclusively ideational or predominantly so, and the ideational character of this music was of the purest and most sublime. Its central form was the Gregorian chant which, says Sorokin, from the standpoint of a sensually audible criterion is no music at all but something queer, unenjoyable, primitive and dry, lacking what we now consider to be the elements of music; for it has neither measure nor harmony nor polyphony and it divides words without any regard for their sense and unity. Its predecessor, the Ambrosian chant, was yet more extraordinary, having had as many as 332 notes to one syllable. It was not music intended for listeners but for performers, and all those in church chanted it. Its value arose solely from its symbolic nature. We may be helped to appreciate this fact by remembering music which we ourselves value not for its æsthetic quality, which may indeed be poor or absent, but for its association and meaning. Sorokin enumerates school and college songs and national anthems by way of illustration.

The religious grand music of the Eastern Church was very similar to the Gregorian chant, which consisted roughly of about three hundred introits and communions, one hundred graduals, one hundred Alleluias, twenty tracts and one hundred offertories, all characterized by a spirit of gentleness, humility and resignation and possessing a curiously ethereal, static, timeless quality.

It was not achieved as a whole all at once, but represented the results of continuing efforts by the Fathers of the Church over two centuries, notably by St. Augustine, St. Benedict, St. Jerome, Clement of Alexandria and others who opposed instruments and instrumental music, which were excluded from churches after the fourth century.

The classic expression of ideational music in the Byzantine Church occurred in the fifth, sixth and seventh centuries. Sensate elements began to creep into the grand religious music from the tenth to the twelfth centuries, gaining in power and influence to produce the great idealistic music of Byzantium in the thirteenth, fourteenth and fifteenth centuries, somewhat earlier therefore than in the West.

There, the first signs of its mixture with the sensate music occurred in the twelfth century with the rise of the troubadours, *trouvères* and *Minnesingers*. Slowly secular motets, madrigals and symphonies grew from these beginnings. In spirit and character this music was different from the chants heard in the churches. Love and the affairs of this world are its themes. Its monodies were sentimental and gallant with instrumental accompaniment. No doubt the new style perpetuated a traditional secular folk music which continued during the great period of ideational music, never however enjoying such prestige or respect among the leaders or 'the bearers' of the predominant culture. Nevertheless it and the songs of the troubadours continued to be much influenced by the ideational music of their age, and they were not fully sensate in quality. Profane love and worldly affairs were still idealized. A modified idealistic Platonic spirit reigned. Gradually the sensate trend showed itself in new developments. After the thirteenth century music became measured, it developed polyphony, produced and developed counterpoint, which reached its Golden Age in the fifteenth century. A richer variety of rhythms was introduced and cultivated. Harmony and 'vertical' scoring instead of 'horizontal' marked another major development, and new complications were introduced by varying the volume and intensity of sound: *piano, forte*, for example. The use of chromatic consonances and dissonances was mastered and perfected and so was instrumental music, which was blended with the human voice. It then remained to develop choruses and orchestras, and to enlarge their scale and finally to combine the sound impressions, thus rendered infinitely more varied and expressive, with visual impressions through form, colour and motion. This trend was general in Western culture, particularly in France, Flanders, Italy, England and Germany from the thirteenth to the sixteenth centuries.

It is, of course, unfortunate that, over the vast period from the ancient World to the Middle Ages, not a note of music has survived. Sorokin's conclusions, like those of all who write or speculate on the nature and development of early music, are necessarily hypothetical, supported solely by literary references. Statistical evidence to illustrate such conclusions is therefore entirely lacking for the major part of musical history. From the sixteenth century onwards, Sorokin has made two collections of statistics, one of the number of composers and the second of the number of their works, each being divided according to whether the composers and compositions were religious or secular.

Sorokin recognizes that it is impossible to get an accurate picture from either of these sources. Are the Gregorian chants, for example, to be counted as one work? Is a madrigal of a few bars to be regarded as quantitatively balanced by a complete Mass? Are composers of many works such as Palestrina to be equated with those of more slender output? These are the elementary difficulties of any effort to apply quantitative measures to cultural history. All that can be established by such enquiries is the direction of the main trends of development. Imperfect as the results may be, they at least claim to be based upon as complete a survey of the whole field of effort as it is possible to make. To that extent they are not less reliable than casual summary judgments based upon varying degrees of familiarity with musical history. On the contrary, they are probably more reliable than the best critical opinion which had not also attempted a similar quantitative comparison.

It is, at any rate, in the light of such a survey, and on its authority, that Sorokin's main conclusions on musical evolution since the sixteenth century are based. The broad trend, as would be expected, is one in which the proportion of religious music tends to decrease, while that of secular music tends to increase.

In the sixteenth century, the number of known musical works (those mentioned in the standard histories of music) were 44 per cent. religious and 56 per cent. secular. The number of religious composers was 53 per cent.; of secular, 47 per cent. In the nineteenth century, the religious composers accounted for 24 per cent., the secular 76 per cent.; while the religious compositions were only 21 per cent. against 79 per cent. of secular works.

Statistics of this sort do not show how the ostensibly religious music of the later periods became itself increasingly secular in character. If some parts were religious in spirit, says Sorokin, the other parts were sensate, the music of opera or symphony.

During this change, from ideational to sensate music, which became increasingly evident between the sixteenth and nineteenth centuries, there again occurred a manifestation of the mixed or blended idealistic type of music. What is remarkable is that, in comparison with painting, sculpture and architecture, the idealistic form in music seems to have been delayed until the sixteenth, seventeenth and eighteenth century. Here Sorokin encountered the first striking discrepancy or lack of synchronous correlation in the development of a form of art; for the perfection of the idealistic phase of European sculpture and architecture occurred in the thirteenth and fourteenth centuries. At its greatest period, with Bach, Handel, Mozart, Beethoven, there is little difference in style between idealistic religious and secular music. It was music still inspired by sublime ideals and idealistic values, although these influences had waned in other cultural fields.

From the time of Palestrina (A.D. 1524-1594) up to Beethoven's Ninth Symphony and his last quartets, music reached great heights of purity, nobility, idealism and sensuous perfection. Some muddy streams of lesser music, no doubt, are also to be found during this long epoch, but they were of small account in comparison with the prevailing tone. At the outset, during the period of Palestrina-Vittoria-Lasso-Bach, religion continued to provide the inspiration and main value of music. In the development from Lulli-Rameau-Gluck-Mozart-Haydn, although the religious quality is less evident, the music, Sorokin observes, is a fresh, pure, spontaneous song of youth; idealistic, imaginative, with silvery laughter; without any burden of sin or tragedy or worry or 'dirt of daily vulgarity'. The idealistic period culminates with the music of Beethoven, the music of a sage to whom all the ecstasy of wisdom and all the tragedy of reality are known; its pain and pleasure, its noble and its vulgar aspects. He has fathomed all this and has not been seduced by it.

The steady growth of sensate music during these centuries is shown not merely in the relative decline of religious music, but by the increasing theatricality of music, oratorio, opera and comic opera. Richard Wagner epitomises this evolution. Sorokin quotes with approval a description of him as 'neither a musician who made poems, nor a poet who made music, but a theatricalist who made both whenever he wanted them'.

By Wagner's time, another mark of sensate art characterized music also; the growth of colossalism. Monteverdi's Orpheus (1607) was scored for about thirty instruments. Orchestras did not get very much larger until after the end of the eighteenth century. Bach and Mozart wrote for orchestras of thirty to sixty instruments. By 1830 the *Fantastic Symphony* of Berlioz was scored for more than a hundred instruments. At the same time there has been a steady increase of the brass, woodwind and percussion instruments in orchestration. This sign of rising sensualism is emphasized in what Sorokin calls the field of vulgar music, where it appears in the domination of the brass band and the saxophone, which have driven out the more delicate music of the strings of the eighteenth and previous centuries.

Then there has been the complication of the texture of music and the deliberate creation of technical difficulties. It is a feature, Sorokin thinks, of decadent periods, whether in art, science or religion, to look to technique to make good the absence of genius.

The increasing professionalism and individualism of composers is another aspect of the same degenerative process, and so also is the enormous development of musical education, musical criticism, musical discussion and musical æstheticism. These characteristics have often been explained as being due in whole or in part to the fact that sensate art is created for a market. Artists are, therefore, inevitably tempted to adapt their work to the prevailing taste of the largest class of consumers who will usually also be the poorest. This leads directly to the danger that art, being forced to search for cheap sensation, will become vulgar and commercial, subject to incessant change under the continuing pressure for increasing variety and the effort to popularize new and contrasting fashions. Sensate music, like sensate art in general, is therefore committed to a search for all that is striking, extreme, exotic, picturesque and monstrous. Its themes, therefore, tend to be perverse, exotic and dramatic, as will be seen to be especially true of literature and the drama. The rise of musical comedy, which was quite unknown in a period of ideational art, further emphasizes the ridiculous, stupid, perverse and criminal aspects of life.

Another source upon which sensate music relies for novelty is also one neglected by ideational art: that of ordinary everyday life. Examples are musical compositions on themes such as the railroad and aeroplane by Honegger, the factory by Molotov, Noises of London by Elgar, and the *May First Symphony* of Shostakovitch. More popular themes, however, are those portraying life as something exotic and, like cocktails, detective stories and thrillers, providing a contrast with the habitual routine of life. They are usually woven around sex. Sorokin lists *Samson and Delilah*, *Aïda*, *Oberon* and the whole Wagnerian series of the Ring, *Tristan and Isolde* among many examples of this type of sensate music.

He points also to a general tendency running through all sensate art, including music, towards pathos, dramatism and emotion, of which he notes 'moronic and sentimentally sad crooning' as a recent example in the field of contemporary vulgar music. He points also to the rising proportion of music written in a minor key. From Aristotle onwards, the minor key has generally been considered sad, dolorous and lamentable. In the sixteenth century it was still regarded as something painful and abnormal. Since that time it has been increasingly used. Sorokin has made a calculation showing that from the eighteenth century, when about 22 per cent. of the works of the main composers were in the minor key, the figure increased to 25 per cent. from 1800 to 1850, and to 38.5 per cent. from 1850 to 1900.

From the same sources, Sorokin provides a rough index of the types of musical composition according to their content divided into seven main classes. These are:

Mythology and Pseudo-history, e.g., the operas of Lulli, the aristocratic operas of the Venetian School and the *galant* operas of Rameau, the *Prometheus* of Beethoven, the *Œdipus* of Stravinsky, etc.

Comic and *Genre* Music, e.g., classical comic operas: Rossini's *Barber of Seville*, Smetana's *Bartered Bride*.

Revolutionary and War Type, e.g., Tschaikovsky's *1812*, Beethoven's *Leonora* and *Fidelio*, Rossini's *William Tell*.

Animalism and *Paysage*, e.g., Debussy's *Clouds*, Rimsky-Korsakoff's *Scheherazade*, Wagner's *Siegfried's Idyll*.

Historical, e.g., Moussorgsky's *Boris Godunoff*, Wagner's *Meistersinger*.

Exoticism, e.g., Beethoven's *Ruins of Athens*, Weber's *Oberon*, Strauss's *Salomé*.

Urbanism and *Nature Morte*. These are works reflecting industrial, urban, mechanized or still-life phenomena, examples of which by Honegger and others have already been quoted.

It is significant that, until the eighteenth century, musical themes were apparently drawn solely from the first two of these seven classes, and that no more than eleven works were devoted to war and revolution during the eighteenth century, while those eleven works all date from 1780 to 1800. The remaining four classes were yet slower in developing. Sorokin's statistics are summarized as follows:

TABLE I—TYPES OF MUSICAL COMPOSITIONS

Period	Mythology Pseudo-History	Genre Comedy	Revolution War	Animalism Paysage Folk Legend	Historicism	Exoticism	Urbanism Nature Morte
600-1700	123	24	—	—	—	—	—
1700-1800	112	97	11	—	—	—	—
1800-1820	14	26	3	—	—	—	—
1820-1840	14	14	5	2	4	—	—
1840-1860	14	12	4	16	5	8	—
1860-1880	9	40	15	20	10	13	12
1880-1900	12	14	3	25	8	20	8
Total 1800-1900	63	106	30	63	27	41	20
1900-1920	15	15	6	19	6	11	20

From his analysis of musical history in the light of his general principles, Sorokin sees little hope for contemporary music. Inner emptiness and the most complicated and brilliant technique are the destiny to which it is doomed until it is replaced by the ideational music which has still to appear, but, he thinks, will eventually probably grow. Sorokin detects the first hesitant signs of it in some of the modern 'isms'. In the works of composers like Stravinsky and Honegger, he sees the modernism or 'cubism' in music and a revolt against sensate music, notably similar to the reaction of the anti-visualists in painting. Such modern composers, he holds, are still searching, but they do not know what they are looking for, since they remain the product of a sensate age unable to transcend its sensate mentality.

This brief and necessarily imperfect summary survey of the history of music indicates that, despite minor fluctuations in style, there seem to have been major 'tidal' waves of ideational and sensate music. They do not correspond point by point with similar movements in painting, sculpture and architecture. Music became classically ideational in the fifth and sixth centuries A.D., while the ideational period of painting, sculpture and architecture began two or three centuries later. The idealistic phase of music lagged in comparison with that of the other arts, all of which had attained it by the thirteenth century. The idealistic phase of music dates from the fifteenth to the beginning of the nineteenth century.

Literature

It will be unnecessary to devote much space to a description of the nature of ideational and sensate literature, because the preceding summary characterizations of similar forms in painting, sculpture, architecture, music and drama should sufficiently have indicated their quality.

Sorokin provides fewer statistics for this aspect of his study, which is devoted to a brief summary of the evolution of literary forms in a few of the chief countries of the Western world, confined to those inheriting the cultural traditions of Greece and Rome.

Regarding as ideational those literary works dealing with super-empirical and transcendental matters and the invisible world, and as sensate those concerned with empirical phenomena in their sensory aspect where words and images have nothing but their empirical meaning, Sorokin lists productions ranging from hymns, dithyrambs, prayers, odes, narratives, proverbs, incantations up to Dante's *Divine Comedy*, as examples of ideational literature, and the purely realistic and naturalistic novels, dramas, plays and lyrics as typically sensate literary productions. He acknowledges that, in a rough or highly developed form, both of these types of literature seem to have co-existed in virtually all cultures at all periods. They occur, however, in different states of purity and in different proportions.

Among primitive tribes, both forms, and especially the ideational, are to a large extent impure, with the ideational and sensate elements interwoven. Most of the early epics are of this class, such as the *Maha-bharata* and *Ramayana*, the *Gilgamesh* epic, parts of the Bible, the *Iliad*, the *Odyssey*, the *Edda*, the song of *Beowulf*, or the Russian folk epics about the great heroes, Iliya Murometz, Dobrynia Nikititch, Sviato-polk and others. Nevertheless it is probable that to those who first heard them, these epics appeared very much more symbolic than they do to us to-day. Some were idealistic in Sorokin's meaning of the word.

The question therefore arises, do the ideational-sensate-idealistic categories offer the same aid in reviewing the history of literature that they have appeared to bring to the study of sculpture, pictorial art and music? Sorokin holds that they do, because it is possible to dis-tinguish different proportions of the two extreme types at a given moment in literary history, and he further holds that these propor-tions do not remain constant but fluctuate in a manner closely parallel-ing similar fluctuations in the fields of painting and sculpture. It is a view which he illustrates by referring to selected examples derived from a comparative study of the leading histories of literature and of literary criticism, beginning with the earliest surviving literature of Greece.

The exact dates at which Homer and Hesiod wrote are unknown, but it was possibly in the eighth century B.C. To the Greeks before the fourth century B.C., the *Iliad* and the *Odyssey* were regarded as religious, moral and educational works rather than as works of art. What, how-ever, is more significant of the predominantly ideational trend of the literature of that period is the fact that most of it was practically insepar-able from music and was religious, magical and symbolic in character. Such were the Doric choral lyrics of religious nomes, dithyrambs, pæans, prosodies and threnodies (see also page 55).

Side by side with the ideational stream, there was sensate literature, especially the Ionic stream represented by Theognis, Sappho, Anacreon and the Sicilian comic but moralising poets of the sixth century B.C. It was a minor and subordinate current permeated also by ideational-ism and idealism. The fifth and sixth centuries B.C. were the period when the great ideational-idealistic literature of Greece flourished, in which both sensate and ideational elements were marvellously balanced, in con-tent and in form. With Pindar, Æschylus, Sophocles and to some extent Euripides and Aristophanes, the literary art of Greece reached its peak.

The increasingly sensate character of the literature and literary criti-cism which followed this period, particularly after the end of the fourth century B.C., is indicated by all the symptoms already noted as charac-terizing Greek painting, sculpture and music. The chief are:

Less religious and more secular subject-matter.
Gradually heroes and even gods are depicted as mortal, while common, vulgar, sub-social and picturesque types become more popular as themes.

E

Description becomes more realistic and scientific.

Symbolism practically disappears.

Tragedy gives way to comedy, to satire, to burlesque and to the picaresque.

A false archaism in the attempted revival of archaic forms in more 'modern' guise.

Increasing sensualism, eroticism and concentration upon pleasure as the only objective.

Development of 'art for art's sake,' æstheticism, art criticism, art education, art appreciation.

Growth of individualism among writers with an emphasis on their professional character, mannerisms, vanity and influence marked also by improvement of their social and material position.

All these developments are seen in the progressive evolution of Greek literature. The Old Comedy with Aristophanes, which developed after the death of Euripides, was in its origin and early stages also religious, but, as the Middle Comedy and New Comedy succeeded it with Menander and Philemon, the gods and heroes disappear, and with them went all mythological, religious and heroic quality also. Surviving fragments indicate that practically all these later comedies dealt with very ordinary people; morality was at a low ebb and sexual themes were frequent.

With the later literature of the Hellenistic period, the sensate type reaches its extreme point. The main characteristics of the literature of this period are compactly summarized by Sorokin as including imitative epics in which contemporary potentates and patrons assumed the place of the gods and heroes in whom all belief had vanished; pedantically learned and super-scholarly poetry of the rococo type, thoroughly technical and scientific and therefore perfectly mediocre even in the works of its greatest representatives, such as Callimachus, Apollonius of Rhodes; bucolic and pastoral poetry of Theocritus, with his sugary shepherds and shepherdesses; mystery stories, epigrammatic and satirical literature, the riddle and figure of poetry of Lycophron and others, and the whole permeated by notorious Alexandrian eroticism and indecency.

Literary Criticism

Sorokin finds his views confirmed by the development of literary criticism among the Greeks. Other writers have been surprised that there were no literary critics before Plato and Aristotle, and some have concluded that the Greeks had no æsthetic consciousness or feeling for and appreciation of beauty until the Peloponnesian War.

Plato's attitude is characteristic. All readers of the *Republic* will recall the striking passages in which he proposes to censor poetry and to banish artists in order to ensure that literature should serve religious, moral, social and political values. Aristotle also, although he does not ally himself uncompromisingly with such views, is as Saintsbury said 'doubly and triply ethical' in his appraisal of artistic effort.

After Aristotle, the development of rhetoric and the rise of the sensate school of literary critics is marked. Menander, Theophrastus, Pausanias, and Athenæus are among the best known, but there were dozens of guides, manuals and text-books, and scores of professional critics during the third and second centuries B.C., especially in the Pergamene and Alexandrian schools. Commentary after commentary was compiled on the classical works of Greek literature, such as those of Homer, which were analysed from every conceivable point of view. As the mass of verbal criticism and technical rhetoric grew, so creative ability declined. There are few better illustrations than that provided by the literary productions during the late sensate age of the truth that artistic perfection is not a thing in itself, not something to be pursued in abstraction, but rather a quality achieved in devoted self-forgetful search for other values, desired for their own sake. The art of this later period of Greek literature, says Sorokin, became separated from other values— religion, morals, idealism and philosophy—and, freed from their tutelage, turned into a mere source of sensual pleasure, ceasing to produce anything comparable with the works of Homer or Hesiod, Theognis, Pindar, Æschylus, Sophocles, Euripides, Aristophanes or even of the lesser creators in literature.

He might have added that æsthetic values are not singular in this respect. There are other desirable qualities which share the fate of æsthetic values if they are consciously pursued as ends in themselves. Beauty, peace, happiness and other great qualities are like the bloom on the peach. They have no existence apart from that of the healthy organism by which they are sustained. They are, as it were, a by-product generated by the organism's own health-giving activities which are undertaken usually with little or no consciousness of self-seeking, but always with reference to some ends or values transcending the self with which the self can be identified and submerged. Health, happiness, love itself are among those abstract qualities which, like literary creativity, elude the over-eager pursuer.

Roman literature, like Roman art in general, as Sorokin has already pointed out, suffered from an irresistible invasion relatively early in its own development by the whole weight of the Greek artistic and literary tradition, comprising almost all the works of all the famous Greek painters, sculptors and writers from the early ideational period, as well as those of the later sensate decline. The full splendour of this tremendous heritage, available to the Romans in its entirety instead of in the fragmentary form in which it has reached us, must indeed have been overpowering. Efforts were made by the Romans, as late as the middle of the first century B.C., to protect their native culture, but in vain. Cato the Censor (c. 234-149 B.C.) and Cicero's grandfather have been mentioned as typical of the strict Republicans who, throughout their lives, had set their faces against Greek influences. How completely the situation had changed by the first century B.C., in two generations, may be seen in the activities of Cicero himself. Nobody strove more energetically than he did to introduce Greek civilization and culture into Roman life. He was able to do it openly without apology or the danger of censure from which, in an earlier generation, men as renowned and as able as Scipio Africanus and Caius Gracchus had by no means been immune.

Before the influence of Greece carried everything before it in Rome, art and literature remained archaic but sincere and predominantly ideational or idealistic, being mainly religious, magical and moral. At the same time there was a strong undercurrent of rugged naturalism and rough but subdued sensatism which must have been immensely stimulated by the impact of sensate Hellenistic models. For this reason the idealistic period of Roman culture was cut short. It was compressed into the first century B.C. and the beginning of the first century A.D., and it is exemplified in the writings of Cicero, Sallust, Lucretius, Livy, Seneca, Virgil, and, to some extent, of Horace.

The strength of the purely sensate stream, Sorokin says, is evident in the idealistic materialism of Lucretius, and still more in the poems of Catullus and Ovid. Sorokin rightly omits any reference to Plautus and Terence, despite the fact that their plays antedate the works of these later writers, because they were but translations and adaptations of the Greek comic dramatists. He might however have referred to Ennius as an example of the early Roman ideational period.[1]

By the second half of the first century A.D. Roman society had become highly literary and æsthetically-minded, as the works of Persius, Petronius, Seneca the Younger, Juvenal and Martial show. There were many bookish æsthetes like Pliny the Younger and his friends. Quintilian well illustrates the vogue of criticism and the refinements

[1] The author may here perhaps refer also to his own study of the various fields of Roman Literature from 243 B.C.—44 B.C. included in diagrammatic form to illustrate "The Lost Literature of Rome" in *Cicero and the Roman Republic*, 1948 p. (67).

of æsthetic theory. Despite the intensity with which it was cultivated, literary inspiration eluded the Romans in the most flourishing centuries of their vast Empire, the greatest and best organized that the Western European world has ever known. Aulus Gellius, Macrobius, Statius, Longinus are surviving examples of the barrenness that then pervaded life.

The most virile and cultivated literary form was that of satire, represented by Lucian, Petronius, Juvenal, Martial, Persius and others. Tacitus was perhaps the greatest of them all, and he was as much a mordant critic of his age as he was a pure historian. Toward the end of the fourth and the beginning of the fifth centuries A.D., the sensate wave of Græco-Hellenistic art had run its course and was dead. A sterile æstheticism lingered into the following century, of which Sorokin quotes one specimen provided by an extract from a letter of Sidonius Appollinaris, a bishop, count, poet and critic, complimenting his friend Claudian on a new book he had just produced.

'O book multifariously pollent. O language, not of a thin, but a subtle mind! He feels like Pythagoras! He divides like Aristotle! . . . He "suades" like Cato, dissuades like Appius, persuades like Tully. . . . He is instructive like Augustine. He soars like Hilary, and abases himself like John, reproves like Basil, consoles like Gregory' and so on.

It was from a low ebb such as this that the ideational Christian literature rose. Despite some survivals of the outmoded, outworn and artificial sensate style, the ideational stream was dominant by the end of the fifth century A.D., and it remained dominant for the following seven or eight hundred years. When again sensate cultural influence gained in vigour in the thirteenth and fourteenth centuries, it gave rise first to a mixed idealistic style, soon swept away by a marked sensate literature which has endured with minor cross-currents until our own times.

In Italy, France, Germany and in England before the thirteenth century, there is practically no writing of consequence that was not devoted to religious themes. The rare exceptions are heroic poems like the *Hildebrandslied* in the ninth century and *Beowulf*. All the literary effort of these centuries went into the production of commentaries on the sacred books, the lives of saints, religious poems such as those of Cynewulf, and translations such as those of Bede, Orosius, Bœthius, St. Gregory and others.

Sorokin calls attention to the way in which symbolism during this period became a fundamental category of human thought dominating

all the thinking and writing of the early Middle Ages. The Fathers of
the Church—Gregory the Great, Dionysius the Areopagite, Cassio-
dorus, Bœthius, Scotus Erigena, Isidore of Seville, Bede, and other
writers, all show a determined search to find, expound and interpret
hidden meanings whether in the Bible or in the works of pagan writers
such as Cicero and Virgil. Everything in the world was forced to serve
as symbols, signs and imperfect indications of the real world, the World
of God, lying beyond and above this world.

The writers of such a period reveal in their choice of themes and
manner of treatment the same exclusiveness that has already been
mentioned as characteristic of the painting, sculpture and music of
an ideational age. Sorokin points to another feature distinguishing ideational literature in general that is also apparent in medieval literature,
namely, its lack of perspective or sense of historical space and time.
This feature, so strangely evident in the medieval treatment of classical
and biblical figures who were regarded apparently as belonging to the
same epoch as contemporary or recent medieval heroes and heroines,
appears also in the highly ideational Brahmanic writings of India. The
reason for it, says Sorokin, is evident. Ideational literature deals with
and is moored to the eternal unchangeable world of Being, not to the
fleeting and changing world of Becoming. History, as we know it, as
a separate branch of thought and learning, cannot develop in a highly
ideational society, as will be explained in more detail in the section
on Being and Becoming, page 106.

Just as Sorokin has noted that great attention to literary techniques
and the elaboration of critical standards are characteristic of a developed sensate age so he remarks upon the absence of literary criticism
during almost the whole of the Middle Ages. This is no new discovery
of his. What is new are the reasons he advances to explain it by means
of his analysis of what he regards as the main forms of human culture.
Lacking such a comprehensive historical perspective of the rise and
fall of systems of culture, other writers have sought to account for this
lack of literary criticism in the Middle Ages by advancing various
theories, some of which seem plausible and true up to a point. Some
explain the matter by reference to the rule of the Roman Church
'having imposed the fetters of religious dogma on the medieval mind';
or by biological analogy 'the age, being one of intellectual childhood,
it was incapable of detachment and reflexion which all critical thought
demands'; or by 'the intellectual isolation of the Middle Ages and the
prevailing ignorance of much that was best in the teaching of antiquity'. These quotations are not from Sorokin but from J. W. H.

Atkins' review of the problem in *English Literary Criticism: the Medieval Phase*, 1943.

The manner in which the early medieval ideational form of culture was succeeded under the growing impulse of sensate influences, first by a mixed idealistic phase and subsequently by unmistakably dominant sensate styles, will be evident to all acquainted with the nature of the national literatures of Western Europe. A brief summary survey listing some typical works is all that Sorokin attempts, and it is necessary still further to abridge it here.

In France, Germany and England the proportion of religious among major writings, which was about 95 per cent. in the ideational period, fell in the thirteenth and fourteenth centuries to about 30 to 55 per cent. The growing secular literature was however still permeated by the religious point of view so that it remained heroic, positive, ennobling and moralizing. In France, *La Chanson de Roland, Tristan et Iseult*, the *Roman de Renard*, the histories of Joinville and Froissart and the *Roman de la Rose* are outstanding. In England, there were the Arthurian romances and epics, and Langland's *The Vision Concerning Piers Plowman*, leading at the end to Chaucer and the dawn of a new age. To deal in any detail with the special characteristics of national literatures would upset the scale on which Sorokin had to plan his work. Its broad scope and universal range compel him to deal in generalities which may not always fit particular epochs and specific countries. It is as though he is mapping whole continents: others must fill in the provinces and the counties. His readers will be able to compare his general analysis with that arising from their own reviews of the infinite detail of national cultures and national literatures.

English literature, for example, provides a special case in the survival of an English prose style of remarkable beauty and power until the fifteenth century, preserved and developed in the devotional literature of the English people during a period in which Norman French was the language of their rulers. Both because this is an aspect of English literature which has only recently received adequate recognition, through the work notably of G. R. Owst and of R. W. Chambers, and because it aptly illustrates the theory advanced by Sorokin, it deserves mention as one aspect of literary history and of the vitality of a culture; in this case the ideational culture of pre-Conquest England.

If one work had to be selected as a pre-eminent example of the idealistic literature of medieval Europe, it would undoubtedly have to be Dante's *Divine Comedy*. Although it is still read and studied, it is not surprising to find it to-day, in a new and very different age, regarded as being among the waning classics. During 1950, for example, it, with other products of ideational and idealistic periods, was prominently placed in a list of boring works by students at Columbia University, New York.

The transition to the more sensate style is typified in the *Roman de la Rose*, probably the most popular work of its period. Sorokin points to the difference between the first and the second parts of this work. He considers that the first part, by Guillaume de Lorris, provides an allegorical treatment of sensate love at its sublimest, noblest, most decent, in a most delicate and most romantic form, according to the chivalric code of love. Somewhat later, Jean de Meung composed the second part, more fleshy, more sensate, partly cynical, erotic and scoffing. He satirises chastity, the clergy, kings, nobility and the monastic orders. He provided the motto *Fais ce que tu voudras* taken over later on by Rabelais. From a literature in which the sex of a saint is rightly regarded as immaterial, to one in which a woman is distinguished sharply from man but reverenced and idolized, we move in the fourteenth and fifteenth centuries to a *bourgeois* attack on women as untrustworthy, sensual creatures, a necessary evil and a pest. Chaucer, who died in 1400 A.D., typified this transition for English readers, notably in his 'Canterbury Tales,' in which the contemporaneous existence of an ideational and grosser sensate culture is admirably portrayed. Romance and romantic love, belief in magic, the farce and comedy of everyday life are portrayed together with a reverence for things holy which typify a mixture of cultural influences and indicate at the same time that new influences and tendencies were abroad. Later writings accentuated this development. Sorokin reports that an (unpublished) study of the number of occasions in which adultery or illicit sex relations are described in the literature of the period, indicating whether they are condemned, praised, or left without comment, gives statistical confirmation of the trend indicated. Similar results are forthcoming if search is made for other traits of sensate culture. The economic argument, for example, which has to-day become so much of an obsession that it is sometimes supposed to be a kind of key able to solve all problems of art, philosophy and social science, is virtually absent in literature before the twelfth century. In the idealistic period, it comes out in a religious guise, in complaints against moneylenders and, in the fourteenth century, especially after the Black Death, in references to the evils of avarice and speculation, the shortage of labour and the over-taxation of the labouring classes.

Another theme is that of duty *versus* revolt, the obligation to persevere even in painful and uncomfortable conditions in ways of life recognized as obligatory. Ideational literature invariably regards religious and moral duty as absolute, as being the only category which counts. Homage was still given to this requirement in idealistic literature, but some measure of flexibility in its observance was regarded as excusable in particularly difficult circumstances. At the same time patriotic and chivalrous duty began to be recognized, and proportionately to weaken the emphasis upon religious duty. In the fourteenth century, self-interest and material convenience grew much more powerful at the expense of a sense of duty; one clear symptom of an increasingly sensate cultural system.

Other symptoms include greater attention to the affairs of everyday life, to landscape and nature, to the common man and the lower classes, to real historical persons and the adoption of an increasingly dramatic, emotional and pathetic tone. Ideational literature is simple, serene, calm in an unfaltering faith in God and His providence. By the fourteenth century, a very melancholy, sad and pessimistic tone becomes evident, particularly in France. In England also the *Vision of William concerning Piers the Plowman* by a contemporary of Chaucer, the later *Piers the Plowman's Crede* (about 1393), and the works of Wyclif testify to an increasingly sombre outlook on life.

So it almost always happens, says Sorokin, when one major cultural system comes to an end and the next has not arrived. When the new form has come, the sadness will be replaced by the most optimistic assurances of progress and by a refreshing joy of life. If Sorokin is right, then it is wrong to suppose, as many critics and historians of literature have done, that a sufficient explanation of the cultural climate or temper of an age is to be found by reference to purely material conditions, even although they are as catastrophic as the Black Death of 1348-9. Sorokin holds that it is the cultural temper that determines the manner in which material things exert any influence. His theory seems to have greater reason and plausibility than the view he contests, for if the melancholy tone of literature during the last half of the fourteenth century is to be attributed to the Black Death, it would be natural to suppose that all such calamities would always provoke a similar melancholy. But this is not a sequence which can uniformly be detected in history.

The transition from the ideational to the idealistic phase of culture is seen, Sorokin claims, in literature when symbolism yields to allegory. Sorokin is careful to emphasize the significant difference between the two. Symbolism attempts to indicate by signs taken from the actual everyday world, the transcendental realities of the world beyond the senses. Allegory tries to endow abstractions, mostly taken from the sensory world, such as love, beauty, youth, liberty, hope, reason, purity, innocence, and so on, with a semblance of existence as though they were persons. In the *Roman de la Rose*, for example, such characters abound: Dame Leisure, Sir and Madame Wealth, Liberality, Frankness, Courtesy and Youth and others. Such a strange outmoded literary style is easier to understand if it is regarded, as Sorokin suggests, as a compound of the sensate and ideational aspects of reality, and typical therefore of idealistic art.

Interesting also is the suggestion that as this allegorical literature broke down, it survived in modified form in morality plays (such as *Everyman*) and mystery plays, but degenerated in the sixteenth century into euphuism and other artificial literary mannerisms which lingered on until the eighteenth century, when allegory practically disappeared.

The idealistic period was also the beginning of literary criticism, although it by no means attained any great development; Dante's *de Vulgari Eloquentia* and some parts of the work of St. Thomas Aquinas are probably the most notable critical works of this period.

Sorokin dates the domination of sensate literature and criticism from the fifteenth century up to the present time. He allows for minor fluctuations of sensatism and ideationalism, but holds that they were merely ripplings upon a fairly continuously rising tide of sensatism that showed no signs of being halted until the end of the nineteenth century.

This trend is first noticeable in the increasingly secular nature of literature. Religious writing declined in quantity. For France, it may roughly be regarded as 100 per cent. of all literature up to the twelfth century, 55 to 30 per cent. from the twelfth to the fourteenth centuries, 25 to 20 per cent. in the fifteenth century, 25 to 35 in the sixteenth, seventeenth and eighteenth centuries, and about 10 per cent. in the nineteenth and twentieth centuries. Ten per cent. of the literary production of the nineteenth century meant, of course, vastly more works than 55 per cent. of the total product of the fifteenth century. More significant than this purely percentage decline, which is obviously a merely relative and not an absolute measure, is the far more important qualitative change in the nature of religious writing which became increasingly controversial, and, in the eighteenth century, increasingly irreligious. The quarrels between Protestants and Catholics, the quarrels of Protestant sects among themselves, the search for a more empirical matter-of-fact view of religion such as that undertaken by the Deists, not to mention the sceptical undermining of religion by the Encyclopedists and the openly ironical, satirical and slanderous attacks on asceticism, otherworldliness and religion and the priesthood, must all be included under the general heading of books on religious matters, but their style and content are quite foreign to that of an age inspired by ideational values.

Merely to mention some outstandingly popular works illustrating these tendencies would require many pages. Boccaccio's *Decameron*, de la Salle's *Cent Nouvelles nouvelles*, many of the works of Rabelais, Molière, Diderot, Swift, Lesage and Voltaire may stand as typical of an outlook which was later to be perpetuated and accentuated in France alone by writers such as Zola, Flaubert and Anatole France among the better known.

Love as a theme of literature has shared the fate of religion in being progressively stripped of its idealistic character in order to be exhibited in a more sensual guise. The transition, says Sorokin, was from the idealistic love of Dante for Beatrice, to Petrarch's love for Laura, still delicate but permeated by sensate motives, to the sensual gallantries of Boccaccio, and thence to the obscenities of Aretino, Beccadelli, Lorenzo Valla and the buffooneries of Poliziano.

Where the tendency did not run to extremes, as in some of the works of the authors just cited, and when reticence and deference to etiquette are better preserved, as in the works of Castiglione, Poggio and others, there is little trace of idealism, still less of ideationality. In brief, says Sorokin, love as it is treated in literature, changed within two hundred years from a purely platonic, almost ideational form devoid of sensuality, to a mere bedroom affair of crude sex physiology not unmixed here and there with perversity. Logically and in practice, there can thereafter be no possibility of going farther along this road, the end of which had already been reached in Italy and France at least by the sixteenth century.

All that could be attempted by way of a search for novelty thereafter was to apply the same treatment to more and more classes of society on a wider range. It was a development aided by the technical improvements in printing and publishing which continually cheapened production and put books and periodicals within the reach of vaster masses of people whom compulsory free education was teaching to read and write.

The result, seen notably in French literature of the nineteenth and twentieth centuries, says Sorokin, was that sensual and sexual love, both normal and pathological, became the dominant theme: love of the old and the young, of the poor and of the rich, love bought, love granted, love in this way and love in that—but love always hovering near the bedroom and rarely if ever idealized and never ideationalized. Chateaubriand, Mme. de Stael, George Sand, A. de Musset, Stendhal, Balzac, Hugo, Merimée, Baudelaire, Zola, Maupassant, Verlaine, Daudet, France, Flaubert, Goncourt are among those included in his comprehensive enumeration of the sensate school from which their admirers will be hard put to it to extricate them. Sorokin is not, of course, concerned, as his language may suggest, for he makes no secret of his preference for idealism, if not for ideationalism; to draw up an indictment on puritanical lines, such as Robert Buchanan's well-known attack on 'The Fleshly School of Poetry' in England in the 1890's. His purpose is to place the writers quoted in the broad context of cultural development to which he considers them to belong.

He admits that he overstresses his case in the interests of brevity and clarity, and he realizes that all countries do not show the same developments at the same time, although the tendency in all of them is to move in the same direction. In England, for example, he does not allow Chaucer's 'Canterbury Tales' any trace of ideational or idealistic inspiration, which seems rather hard on the Prioress, although he acknowledges that Gower, Sir Thomas Wyatt and Roger Ascham, among others, maintained the earlier quality. It would not be difficult to add names, such as those of Sir Thomas More and others, to these perpetuators of idealistic traditions.

Preoccupation with economic questions is another unmistakable sign of sensate culture. Certainly it has developed on an increasing scale since the fifteenth century. Almost entirely absent, as was noted on page 72, during the ideational period, economic considerations and problems emerge in the idealistic period when, however, they receive scant treatment and are by no means to the fore. By the nineteenth and twentieth centuries, the most important themes of literature were either economic questions or economic interpretations of almost all forms of human endeavour. Love itself was not immune. Economic matters, such as food, drink and material possessions, make the strongest appeal to all the organs of sense, so it is self-evident that the more the sensory nature of reality is emphasized, the more prominently will economic interpretations and considerations seem self-sufficient as a key to human thought and behaviour. It is easy to see why literature became increasingly preoccupied with the generosity or wickedness of the rich; with the exploitation and the wrongs of the poor; with crimes attributed to the poverty, greed, hypocrisy, unfaithfulness and self-seeking of all manner of people in various social groups. The further and deeper that authors were able to carry such analyses, the greater was the degree of insight and wisdom attributed to them. Hence not literature alone, but psychology and other human and social studies were invaded in the nineteenth and twentieth centuries by attempts to provide an economic interpretation for every manner of human activity.

It is in the light of considerations such as these that Sorokin is able to claim that his explanation of the rise of capitalism is more satisfactory, because it is a more fundamental explanation than that provided by writers such as Max Weber, Ernst Troeltsch or R. H. Tawney who have tried to find the impetus for the nascent economic enterprise of the sixteenth and seventeenth centuries in the theological and religious doctrines of the Protestant reformation. Without in any way detracting from the sound scholarship and great learning of these writers, Sorokin is nevertheless able, by relating both economic capitalism and Protestant ideas to the newly emerging sensate culture, to supersede the argument which sought to establish some cause-and-effect relationship between the two.

A third great distinguishing mark of a rising sensate literature is that the classes of people whose activities, thoughts and aspirations are made the themes of literary efforts in the sensate age include as broad a range of the common run of everyday folk as possible. The wide canvas filled by Chaucer has continually been enlarged, so that, after the fourteenth century, merchants, peasants, courtiers, artisans, servants, rogues, criminals, prostitutes, failures, derelicts and the wretched become the subjects of literature, and to these are added, as time goes on, other plainly pathological types: murderers, swindlers, exploiters, hypocrites, scoundrels, profligates, idiots, and any other picturesque personalities. In this way among others, a sensate cultural epoch becomes an Age of the Common Man.

Shakespeare is a writer whose standing in Sorokin's scheme of cultural standards many readers will wish to have explained. Sorokin does not specifically include Shakespeare as a sensate writer, although he quotes others who have pointed to Shakespeare's naturalism. There are other unquestionably sensate qualities in his poems and plays, yet it is impossible to deny the idealistic insight and inspiration that characterize his work and are among his enduring titles to fame as an unrivalled interpreter of humanity. Sorokin recognizes Shakespeare's idealistic character by pointing out that his heroes, like those of most Elizabethan dramatists, are still in the main truly heroic figures.

The same is true of the epic poems and romances, whose heroes in the fourteenth, fifteenth, sixteenth and part of the seventeenth centuries were still drawn on a grand scale, paying little heed to the mediocre, the vulgar, the everyday and the banal. Ariosto's *Orlando Furioso*, Tasso's *Gerusalemme Liberata*, Camœn's *Lusiad*, Ronsard's *La Franciade*, Spenser's *Faerie Queen* and Milton's *Paradise Lost* are outstanding examples of the vitality of the idealistic tradition in epic poetry.

Romance and novels, particularly those such as Malory's Arthurian romances and the innumerable *Amadis* stories, flourished until the seventeenth century, despite the gibes of Rabelais (*Pantagruel* and *Gargantua*, 1535-1552) and Cervantes (*Don Quixote*, 1605-1615). These stories of more exalted personalities and their adventures, which can often seem exceedingly boring and tedious to a modern reader, lost their popularity in the eighteenth century, when tales about heroes and heroines of a very much more matter-of-fact and everyday type rose in popular favour. It is not difficult to add to Sorokin's general account of the progress of this tendency in Western Europe a few details of its development drawn from the history of English literature.

There was no lack of idealistic influences in seventeenth-century England after the death of Shakespeare, and it is not necessary to do more to establish the fact than to add to Sorokin's general review the names of some pronouncedly idealist writers, such as Henry More (1614-1687), George Fox (1624-91), John Bunyan (1628-88), Sir Thomas Browne (1605-82), Izaak Walton (1593-1683), Jeremy Taylor (1613-67), Richard Baxter (1615-91), John Milton (1608-74), George Herbert (1593-1633), Richard Crashaw (? 1613-49). Nevertheless such men stood out in strong contrast to many writers of the time. The underlying sensate culture evident in other aspects of life is made plain by careers such as those of John Donne (1573-1631), whose later piety and religious devotion atoned for a youth in which such qualities were very little in evidence.

After the Restoration of Charles II, the comedies of Aphra Behn (1640-89), William Wycherley (? 1640-1716), William Congreve (1670-1729), Sir John Vanbrugh (1664-1726), George Farquhar (1678-1707) and Thomas Shadwell (? 1642-1692), gave the most convincing evidence of the profoundly sensual character of the stage before Jeremy Collier delivered his attack on plays and playwrights in his famous pamphlet *A Short View of the Immorality and Profaneness of the English Stage* (1698).

Sorokin draws attention to another fundamental difference between sensate and ideational literary forms which is revealed most clearly by the drama. Sensate drama is essentially a show, an illusion, a temporary substitute for some reality. The ideational mystery and miracle plays were not of this order. They were not frequently performed and never for mere entertainment, amusement or pleasure. The very development of the theatre is in itself a highly important symptom of the growth of the sensate culture. It therefore helps to explain why the reaction against the theatre should be violent in a society loyal to ideational standards.

The forty years which separated the end of the Puritan regime in England from the beginning of the eighteenth century were sufficiently full of vigorous life and thought to render hazardous any attempt to sum up or to label the true characteristics of the period, so varied and so complex were its manifestations in many spheres of life. The *Mayflower* expedition to the New World in 1620 may symbolise the Puritan reaction to worldly excesses which remained a vigorous force in the minds of men for many generations after it seemed to have lost the battle politically and socially. It is not surprising, therefore, that the Puritan tradition survived to guide the life and conduct of vast numbers of men and women who were not born until long after it had apparently vanished away. Vital as this tradition has been, and indeed yet remains, both in the United Kingdom and in the United States of America, it did not survive unblemished. It is sufficient to recall the prevailing temper of the age revealed in the lives of Charles II and his Court, in which characters like Samuel Pepys could pass as exemplary by comparison with the majority, to realize the increasingly sensate nature of English society. Sensate influences had far less opposition after the disappearance of the Revolutionary generation of Puritans. 'Never before in this country,' says an historian of English literature, 'had men written so much about religion and practised it so little' as in the eighteenth century.

The rise of the English novel dates from this period. Daniel Defoe (? 1661-1731), 'a pioneer novelist of adventure and low life', was the first to write entertaining fiction about the lives of soldiers of fortune, pirates, prostitutes and a deaf and dumb conjuror. It will be unnecessary to follow the development of the novel up to our own times through the work of Samuel Richardson (1689-1761), Henry Fielding (1707-54), Tobias Smollett (1721-71) and Laurence Sterne (1713-68), remembering that Sterne was a priest of the Anglican Church, in order to add a few more English examples to illustrate Sorokin's conclusions. To-day the majority of bookstalls and commercial lending libraries with their high proportion of best-selling thrillers, detective stories and novels notable only for their more or less skilful variations upon the theme of sex, offer a daily incontrovertible demonstration of the victory of sensate cultural standards.

Stage entertainment has followed a similar course to arrive at the same end. The theatre critic of a London newspaper, *The Evening Standard*, on 21 July, 1950, summed up the character of a popular stage show then running as 'another example of the ruthless technique of Broadway in which a formula is rigidly prepared and relentlessly carried out. The basis of the play is Sex, Sadism and Sentimentality. To this is added some adolescent humour, a spice of idealism, a drop or two of patriotism and a quart of pretended innocence,' concluding that 'we are passing from art to photography while the undiscerning mob shout their joyous approval'. At about the same time in 1950, another stage entertainment was being advertised by a single word coined by the same critic and triumphantly repeated in bright red letters by those promoting the show: 'Sexcess'.

The annual reports of the Public Morality Council provides chapter and verse for any who may be in doubt about these persistent sensate trends, notably in its recent complaints about nudism on the London Stage.

Not merely has this concentration upon abnormality and low life characterised the novels and drama of the nineteenth century, but, Sorokin contends, it has effectively killed the capacity to depict heroic, positive social types. They have to be sought now in queer and abnormal personalities, such as Tolstoi's Pierre Bezoukhy or Dostoevsky's Raskolnikoff and Prince Myshkin, most of Ibsen's and Hauptmann's characters, the heroes of Zola, Maupassant or even the best types of Charles Dickens. The alternative is to create what he describes as quite unreal purely 'paper-made' synthetic *resonneurs* like Romain Rolland's *Jean Christophe* or to present a positive social type of a very cheap, very ordinary or doubtful quality like some of the proletarian characters of socialist-communist literature.

The reason, says Sorokin, is plain. The sensate, realistic mentality concentrating upon sensory perception sees human beings empirically as physiological entities moved by instincts, reflexes, complexes and drives, often of the lowest animal order. Any attempt to soar from this low level and to create a real hero is frustrated. Sensate writers have their wings clipped and are forced, says Sorokin, to crawl over the surface of the earth. Earthbound, their vision is limited to very ordinary and very evanescent mortal beings. The vogue of the satirical, ironical and comical in literature in general, and in novels, stories, or plays in particular, is another aspect of this same prevailing tendency. As we move into the eighteenth, nineteenth and twentieth centuries, the range of such satirical writing has widened to include all the fundamental values of the ideational and idealistic cultures until, Sorokin concludes, there is nothing left which it has not slandered, ridiculed or debased. Religion, God, the saints, the Virgin, angels, devils, sacraments, Paradise, Inferno, the Creed, the State, the Government, aristocracy, nobility, talent, genius, sacrifice, altruism, marriage, the family, asceticism, idealism, chastity, faithfulness, loyalty, science, philosophy, moral duty, property, order, truth, beauty, righteousness, man himself; everything and everybody is slandered, satirized and defiled. Not a single value, Sorokin concludes after this comprehensive list, has escaped.

The 'debunking' biography, a relatively recent innovation, is symptomatic of the same trend. Froude's *Life of Thomas Carlyle* (1884) was an early precursor of a style that has attained a great vogue in recent years, particularly since the First World War. Lytton Strachey (1880-1932) led the way with a brilliant set of essays on four very diverse characters of the generation before his own, whose only common quality, significantly enough, was their outstanding attachment to religious experience and to a quest for spiritual certitude which dominated their lives, as it also dominated the lives of very many of their contemporaries, in a period which clearly showed an idealistic reaction or ripple upon the prevailing sensate tide. Strachey's four 'Eminent Victorians' were the first martyrs of an acid bath in which less skilful imitators have sought to devour established reputations. Hardly any intimate or shameful details have been regarded as irrelevant by this new school of biographers dismissed by Sorokin as 'dirt painters'.

They may stand as examples of the tendency of literary criticism to follow the same sensate evolution as literature itself. The lack, in an ideational period, of criticism as an independent intellectual exercise valuable in its own right has already been stressed. Using the findings of historians of literary criticism, such as David Sauvageot and George Saintsbury, Sorokin shows how its rise occurred in the fifteenth century and how by A.D. 1600 it had become a recognized department of literature. Criticism then, as between the fourth and third centuries B.C. in Greece, still had religious and moral values as well as purely æsthetic standards as its criteria. With the sixteenth and subsequent centuries, the non-æsthetic ideational criteria became progressively less relevant. By a writer like Montaigne, literature and art are valued largely as a means of amusement and enjoyment and, not solely, of

F

knowledge. In some countries, in France particularly, an effort was made through academies to codify the principles of æsthetic criticism which, had they been long respected, might have delayed the free development of sensate attitudes.

Sensible, moderate, rational, even scientific, this academic authority was powerful in the seventeenth century, and it survived into the eighteenth century, particularly in France, to sustain the fading light of idealism for two or three generations. How important criticism became is evident from the standing in the world of letters and of polite society of figures such as Addison, Johnson, Voltaire, Schiller, Lessing, Diderot, Gœthe, all of whom were notable for their critical opinions. The social and literary standing of the professional critic is now well established. Sorokin thinks that now, as in Rome during the later Roman Empire, most of their criticism is empty, ignorant, thoughtless and negligible so far as its inner content is concerned, although it is powerful in other respects. For it is able to exercise a great influence upon the taste of the general public toward the good or bad, and to determine the success or failure, fame or tragedy, the poverty or fortune of artists and writers. He notes also the inevitable tendency towards linking critical opinions with the quantitative success of the work criticized so that books which sell in large quantities or plays with long runs are those praised by critics. At the same time these great successes have a short life, the best seller of one season being rapidly replaced by another. These conditions are reacting upon criticism itself, which is being replaced, Sorokin thinks, as an effective agency for creating public demand for books, by merely commercial forces: the skill of advertisers and public relations experts who are able to help publishers in the fierce competitive scramble for markets. Such agencies symbolize the bankruptcy of contemporary criticism, being anonymous and merely profit-making, not always administered by critics or connoisseurs of art or literature. Sorokin had contemporary tendencies in American publishing in mind, but similar complaints are not lacking in the British Isles. At the occasion of the Edinburgh Festival in August, 1950, Sir Stanley Unwin called attention to the danger that the same pressures might produce the same results in England also. Criticism of the critics by futurists, symbolists, surrealists and other modernists provides additional evidence of the crisis in sensate criticism, although it does not yet point to paths leading to a new and greater kingdom of art and literature and criticism. It will be evident that Sorokin's theory of the kinds of cultural activity briefly summarized above is based in the main upon the history of Western European civilization. He is chary of claiming that it is also adequate as a key to the art of the Middle and Far East, although he believes that it will be found to be equally useful as a guide to their cultural development. Sorokin's analysis of the evolution of artistic and literary values has the merit not merely of providing a workable historical frame of reference, according to which changes in style can be grouped and explained, but it also serves to illuminate some difficult problems of philosophical æsthetics. He is able by its means to confirm the view he had already taken (page 22) on the vexed debate whether 'pure art', 'art for art's sake', is or is not the true æsthetic ideal, superior to the opposite notion that art is only art if it worthily serves some purpose other than that of providing mere æsthetic satisfaction. The answer is plain. Those who champion 'art for art's sake' have really been fighting for the sensate form of art, the direct and main function of which is to give sensate gratification, delight, pleasure, joy. To the extent that art is thereby separated from great values of society or of culture it may be said to have been 'freed', but it is then simultaneously enslaved to sensations. So the true difference between 'pure' (sensate) art and 'impure' ideational art consists not in the fact that the one is free and the other is not (because it is the 'handmaid of religion' for example), but in that they are subordinated to two quite different masters: one to hedonism, to emotions and sensations; the other to the ideational and idealistic values of religion, morals, civics, science and philosophy.

The apparent greater freedom of the sensate artist is, moreover, an illusion as long as he is dependent upon finding someone to hire him and to give him the highest material or money value for his work. In a free market, or to use Sorokin's words which however have become almost an abusive slogan, in a capitalist society, the highest bidder will be the rich and the powerful; the captains of industry and commerce. In a totalitarian society, everything must obey the dominant gangsters, whether military, demagogic, fascist, nazi or communist. These classes are able to dispense with bids for support; all they need do, and they usually do it fairly quickly, is to silence, eliminate or liquidate any writers or artists who do not support them. The sickening sycophancy of the tolerated performers with the brush or pen who remain and are allowed any activity in such a community is a quality vastly different from the genuine single-minded devotion of ideational artists.

The ostensible servitude of artists in an ideational society is not felt as subservience, since no consciousness can arise of the separation of art from the other values which that society cherishes. Religion, philosophy, science, morals, civic patriotism, art, were organically one in

Greek culture up to the end of the fourth century B.C. The same was true of the ideational medieval period in the West. Sensate culture can also be an integrated culture, despite its principle of diversity and the independence of its main values and activities. Its æsthetic category for instance seeks to be autonomous and separate from the other categories of truth, wisdom, religion and moral principles. The task of integration is therefore doubly difficult because it is not felt to be essential.

Sorokin's account and analysis of the slogan 'art for art's sake' is but one example of the way in which he is able to offer wider, more inclusive, yet self-sufficient standards of judgment than any provided hitherto in the history of art. He also has the merit of being able to show the strength and weakness, the degree of validity and effectiveness of the views and theories of other writers upon the history and appreciation of art. He briefly examines some of them. The theory of the German writer, Paul Ligeti, in his book *Der Weg aus dem Chaos*, for example, is shown to be fallacious, because it attempts to see what Sorokin describes as ideational art only in architecture, idealistic art only in sculpture, and sensate art only in painting. Frank Chambers attempted, in his *Cycles of Taste* (1928) and *History of Taste* (1932), to account for the lack of art education, æsthetic theory and art criticism in Sorokin's ideational period of Greek and medieval art by supposing them to be times when æsthetic consciousness and the appreciation of art did not exist, a supposition which Sorokin considers to be indeed strange if it is to explain Homer's *Iliad*, the Parthenon or the Cathedral at Chartres with its ten thousand pieces of sculpture. Not only, he holds, is such a view clearly untenable but the theory deduced from it, that creativeness in art falls as the development of art appreciation and art criticism rises, is equally false. There were critical standards in the days of Phidias, and before him, and also among the Fathers of the Church, but they were concerned with the extent to which art-forms were in agreement with, and able to express the main non-æsthetic ideational values. Saintsbury is nearer the truth when he wrote that 'no constant ratio exists between periods of creation and periods of criticism'.

Sorokin considers the correct view to be that which recognizes different forms of art, ideational and sensate, each with their masterpieces. With some reservations he claims that one of the greatest periods of creativity in art usually occurs in the idealistic periods, when art is not yet divorced from the ideational world, and at the same time dresses itself in the noblest forms of sensate reality. So it was in the fifth century B.C. in Greece and in the thirteenth to the fifteenth century A.D. for architecture and sculpture; to the seventeenth for painting; and to the eighteenth and nineteenth centuries for music.

The strength of Sorokin's position in comparison with previous attempts to describe and explain the development of human culture clearly rests upon his insistence that it is essential to regard the main cultural systems as existing in their own right. When this fundamental doctrine is accepted a great number of earlier views become untenable. They can be seen to be the source of errors which Sorokin is able to avoid, because he refuses to use criteria appropriate to one cultural system in appraising the value of another. The fact that the ideational mentality is absolutist and centred upon a fixed value, makes it inevitably opposed to diversity and variety. For this reason it appears from a sensate standpoint, to be monotonous, poverty-stricken and boring. Those condemned to endure it are pitied as creatures living in the Dark Ages, as though, as Charles Lamb objected, they were crawling about in a world which knew no sunshine. It is more probable that they were, or many of them were, illumined by an inner light which has now vanished from the earth.

The one cultural system cannot, therefore, yield principles by which the other can be condemned or praised, because the strong and marked differences between them are fundamental and cannot be brought into relation by terms common to each. Their basic major premises, says Sorokin, are incommensurable. If this is so, there is, or may be, no other ground for choosing between them than that of purely personal preference.

Readers acquainted with the philosophical views of R. G. Collingwood, whom however Sorokin does not quote, will recall Collingwood's remarks that the analysis which detects absolute presuppositions may be called metaphysical analysis; that all metaphysical questions are historical questions and that all metaphysical propositions are historical propositions. This insistence that metaphysical systems, as they succeed one another in the history of philosophy, must be understood as wholes and within their own frames of reference is a view common to both writers despite their differences in other respects.

Sorokin's provisional conclusion, therefore, that there can be two or three equally valid solutions to the problem of æsthetic values may stand until the history of other forms of cultural life, science, philosophy, law and ethics and forms of social, political and economic organization, has also been reviewed. On them also Sorokin has new insights to offer.

CHAPTER FIVE

Philosophy

If the nature of any historic period of cultural development is to be understood as a whole, it is obviously impossible to stop short after reviewing its paintings, sculpture, architecture, music, drama, literature and criticism, despite the evident fact that many eminent students and investigators would consider it to be a very considerable performance to provide half as much, or less. After his comprehensive survey of all these subjects, Sorokin proceeds to devote a further volume of some seven hundred pages to the main trends in the development of philosophy, logic, scientific knowledge, ethics, legal systems and the theory of the State in the history of Western European culture from its early Græco-Roman foundations to our own day.

Again he attempts, at the cost of an extraordinary amount of laborious research, to provide, wherever he can, as sound as possible a statistical basis for his own conclusions. The doubts and criticism excited by any effort to apply statistics to the history of art and literature are likely to become very much more serious when their subject-matter is philosophy, ethics and law. Yet, as it was pointed out in Chapter One, and must be repeated elsewhere in this work, just as the refusal to be interested in the philosophy of history is itself a philosophical position, so the refusal to attempt to give greater precision and clarity to ideas about size, quantity and number, relying instead upon rough estimates or vague guesses, is also to make quantitative judgments, although they will probably be crude, unreliable and not really very enlightening.

A great deal depends obviously upon the philosophical ideas selected for quantitative study. The only way in which Sorokin has found it possible to bring so vast a field as philosophy, religion and science under ordered examination in this way has been by selecting as the basis for his comparative study one or two of the critical major themes or special topics upon which philosophers and thinkers generally have been divided in successive cultural epochs in the history of Western thought.

These themes are idealism and materialism; being and becoming; realism, nominalism and conceptualism; society and the individual;

86

the nature of personality in law; determinism and indeterminism; the idea of progress; optimism and pessimism; crime and punishment; the nature of space, time, number and casuality and of scientific thought generally.

Sorokin's main findings on this vast field of human speculation will therefore next be reviewed and summarized.

Theories of Truth

There can be few more critically revealing aspects of the inward nature of any period of cultural development than the fundamental factor of the doctrine of truth and knowledge adopted by each system as its ultimate guide or goal. For it is clear that unless religions, philosophies and sciences acknowledge the same standards of ultimate truth, there cannot very well be any presumption that they belong to the same type of culture. When, however, such common standards of truth distinguish two or more cultural systems, or their component elements, those systems must be linked in a very definite manner. Sorokin describes such a common property as evidence of 'a basic logico-meaningful identity' (see page 11).

Now to hold that there can be more than one logico-meaningful cultural system is to assume that there can be more than one standard of truth and knowledge. This is an assumption which does not occur naturally to the great majority of people, who accept without question the values and norms they find ready-made by the society or the culture into which they are born.

At the end of Chapter Four, it was seen that Sorokin arrived at the idea that there can be two or more systems of truth and value as a result of his study of the evolution of styles of painting and other arts. This conclusion may be provisionally accepted as a basis for Sorokin's descriptive analysis of the main cultural systems in the expectation that an effort will later be made to review and reformulate it (see pages 240 to 242). When therefore, on this provisional basis, he asks, 'What are the main systems of truth and knowledge?' it is not surprising to find that he expects an affirmative answer to the further question 'Are the categories ideational, idealistic and sensate applicable to truth generally?'

For he can logically expect that the truth of the organs of sense will be most unlikely to play a dominant or important part in an ideational culture in which the truth of faith inspired by God through revelation, intuition or mystic experience will be thought to be the sole valid and certain guide.

A third possible source of truth is that to be gained by human reason and logic. Those who put their faith in human reason are willing to examine both the evidence of the senses and what is offered as the testimony of revelation or intuition, trusting that the human intellect will succeed in judging how far each is valid. This mixed ideational-sensate outlook is characteristic of the idealistic culture.

There are, as Sorokin has been careful to emphasize, several other forms of mixed cultures beside the idealistic. There is also the attitude of extreme scepticism and unbelief, and there is also the despairing state of mind which desperately wants to believe but cannot, which Sorokin describes as Fideism.

The three main systems with some samples of the subject-matter of each and the way in which each considers truth to be attainable are summarized by Sorokin as follows:

IDEATIONAL TRUTH OF FAITH

Subject Matter:

Supersensory and superrational: God, devil, angels, spirits, soul, immortality, salvation, sin, redemption, resurrection, purgatory, paradise, inferno.

Sensory and empirical phenomena are studied incidentally only, not for their own sakes, but as visible signs of the invisible world, as symbols of supersensory reality.

Theology is the supreme study. Exposition of the truth is based upon general principles (apodeictic) and is symbolic.

How Truth is Reached, or the Method of Validation:

By reference to the sacred source or Scripture with which statements must be in accord. New truths must be shown to be due to the same divine inspiration or, in less theological language, to intuition. Purely logical reasoning and the testimony of the senses have a merely subsidiary role and are allowed only in so far as they do not contradict the truth of the revealed Scripture. Otherwise they are rejected as invalid or inspired by the devil, when they become heresy, blasphemy or black magic.

IDEALISTIC TRUTH OF REASON

Subject Matter:

Partly supersensory, partly sensory and empirical. Knowledge about sensory reality is not so highly valued, but it is sought and included as far as the scientific development of the time allows, and it is embodied in a total system of knowledge which usually takes the form of idealistic rationalistic philosophy. The ultimate reality is thought of as knowable, to be reached by reasonable argument based upon self-evident or agreed foundations or premises (i.e., the exposition is dialectic and deductive).

How Truth is Reached, or the Method of Validation:

Mainly by logical reasoning but also by reference to the testimony of the senses. The findings both of reason and of sensory perception are supported by reference to sacred writings and revealed truth with the aim of including them all in an harmonious body of knowledge.

SENSATE TRUTH OF THE SENSES

Subject Matter:

Mainly the world revealed by sensory perception. Any matters not easily reducible to sensory-material forms (such as thought, feeling, values) are dealt with either by concentrating upon their sensory aspect (e.g., as in behaviourism) or by disregarding their non-material aspect, which may be treated as subsidiary, irrelevant, unknowable, or non-existent (e.g., as in agnosticism, positivism). The natural sciences are then regarded as providing a pattern for the study of all other subjects.

Truth is to be reached by concentrating upon the facts, especially those to be reached by experiment (e.g., exposition is inductive).

How Truth is Reached, or the Method of Validation:

Mainly by reference to the testimony of the senses reinforced by their extension through instruments or apparatus, such as microscopes, telescopes and balances, supplemented by logical reasoning, especially in statistical and mathematical forms. All such findings remain provisional as hypotheses and are not accepted as proved until tested by the sensory facts. Hypotheses contradicted by the facts are unhesitatingly rejected. Sacred writings and faith in revelation have no place and are rejected as superstitious and as valueless. They are dismissed in much the same way as the findings of the senses are ignored by those who uphold an ideational system of knowledge.

After this preliminary survey of the specific characteristics of the three main logico-meaningful cultural systems from the standpoint of their system of truth, Sorokin proceeds to look at the historical record to see how far each is in evidence in the works of the leading thinkers in Græco-Roman and Western cultures from 580 B.C. to A.D. 1920.

He is careful at the outset of this historical investigation to point out its inevitable limitations. The sheer lack of information about the actual opinions of the great majority of people on such questions in the Middle Ages and in ancient times is the first, most obvious and critically serious of these limitations. The problem how to use what information we do possess is particularly difficult, because it is not a question of merely counting up the expressions of opinion on the nature of truth but of attempting some assessment of their relative influences.

Sorokin, with the aid of two leading Russian professors of philosophy, set about this task. They adopted a scale of 'marks' or 'credits' from one to twelve, and sought to credit every known thinker with his appropriate rating or weight in this scale. It is not a question of assigning marks according to the scientific or any other value of the various thinkers, but solely of the extent to which their work and example influenced others. Everybody who writes or reflects upon the history of thought is led to make such estimates. Sorokin seeks to make them as thoroughly and as scientifically as possible by boldly trying to devise a scale of magnitude to show such influences. The history of culture obviously has much to gain from a sound judgment in this first step of judging the relative *influence* of leading thinkers. The criteria used in preparing this rough measure of the comparative influence of great philosophers are listed as the following:

(*a*)   The number of special studies or monographs devoted to a philosopher.

(*b*)   The approximate number of times the philosopher's name has been mentioned in the works of his contemporaries and later philosophers and thinkers.

(*c*)   Whether he was a founder of a school of philosophical thought.

(*d*)   Whether his name is mentioned in elementary textbooks on the history and the theory of knowledge.

(*e*)   The number of his disciples and followers.

(*f*)   Whether his works have been translated into foreign languages.

(*g*)   Whether his works have been frequently republished.

(*h*)   Whether he was the creator of an original and complete system of philosophy and epistemology.

Sorokin and his collaborators claim to have considered almost all the relevant facts under the above eight headings. After doing so, they assigned to each thinker the value between one and twelve which seemed to them adequately to indicate his status and influence in the particular branch of the history of human thought they were attempting to review. The merit of such a procedure is to reduce the influence of subjective elements in estimating the standing of thinkers. Some sample valuations of the thinkers listed under their various schools of thought will best illustrate the procedure followed. Sorokin's lists contain many more names than those given in the following pages which merely list some of the better-known writers.

RATIONALISM, 560 B.C.-A.D. 1920

Anaximander	5	Thomas Aquinas	12	Tillotson	2
Heraclitus	7	Copernicus	8	Kant	12
Pythagoras	8	G. Bruno	8	Swedenborg	4
Parmenides	7	Descartes	8	Lessing	6
Zeno	5	Comenius	7	Goethe	8
Socrates	9	Pascal	7	Hegel	8
Euclid	3	Malebranche	7	V. Cousin	4
Plato	12	Guelincz	6	Whewell	6
Aristotle	12	H. More	4	Rosmini	6
Alcuin	4	Leibniz	9	Boole	4
Photius	3	Spinoza	8	Bradley	7
Adelard of Bath	2	Cudworth	5	Bosanquet	4
Abelard	4	Bossuet	6	Michelet	2
R. Grosseteste	4	Fénelon	6	McTaggart	5
Albert the Great	8				

MYSTICISM, 360 B.C.-AD. 1920

Plato after 385 B.C.	12	Comenius	7	Schelling	8
Xenocrates	3	H. More	4	Schopenhauer	8
Nigidius Figulus	4	Malebranche	7	W. Blake	4
Philo Judaeus	8	Arnauld	4	Hegel	8
Plutarch	8	Nicole	4	Shelley	6
Plotinus	12	Cudworth	5	Schleiermacher	4
Macrobius	4	Shaftesbury	5	F. Schlegel	4
Maximus Confessor	6	A. Collier	5	Emerson	6
John Scotus Erigena	8	Berkeley	8	Ruskin	6
Anselm	7	J. Edwards	1	J. Erdmann	4
Bernard of Clairvaux	5	Sam Johnson	1	Bergson	8
Eckhart	8	Rousseau	8	M. Eddy	4
Thomas à Kempis	4	MASONS:		Michelet	2
Paracelsus	4	English Masons	4	Dostoevski	8
St. John of the Cross	4	French Lodge, The		E. von Hartmann	8
G. Bruno	8	Great East	4	Bradley	7
Cardan	6	Russian Masons	4	Soloviev	6
St. Theresa	6	Jacobi	6	Steiner	4
Jacob Boehme	6	Herder	6	Tolstoi	8
Pascal	7	Fichte	8	Nietzsche	9
Spinoza	8				

FIDEISM, 400 B.C.-A.D. 1920

Antisthenes	5	Seneca	8	Jacobi	6
Diogenes	5	Lucius Annaeus Cornutus	4	Fichte	8
Crates	4	Musonius Rufus	5	Lammenais	4
Zeno	8	Epictetus	6	Hamilton	6
Cleanthes	5	Dio Chrysostom	6	Mansel	2
Menippus	5	Marcus Aurelius	6	McCosh	4
Chrysippus	7	Peter Damian	3	Khomiakov	4
Panaetius	5	Loyola	8	Gratry	1
Q. Mucius Scaevola	1	Pascal	7	Cousin	1
Posidonius	7	Reid	4	Sigwart	5
Cato	2	Beattie	2	Renouvier	7
Cicero	8				

SCEPTICISM, 460 B.C.-A.D. 1920

Protagoras	8	Sextus Empiricus	6	Diderot	6
Gorgias	5	John of Janduno	3	Hume	8
Critias	3	Nicholas of Autrecourt	4	L. Feuerbach	6
Thrasymacus	3	Montaigne	6	J. Stuart Mill	8
Hippias	4	Charron	2	Kierkegaard	4
Aristippus	6	La Rochefoucauld	1	Renan	6
Pyrrho	6	Glanvill	2	Nietzsche	9
Timon	3	Bayle	6	Pierce	1
Carneades	5	D'Alembert	5		

EMPIRICISM, 580 B.C.-A.D. 1500

Thales	4	Lucretius	8	Manichees	3
Anaximenes	2	Asclepiades of Prusa	4	John Chrysostom	5
Diogenes	3	Celsus	1	John of Salisbury	3
Empedocles	6	Galen	7	Alexander Neckham	2
Democritus	8	Tertullian	6	Roger Bacon	6
Xenophon	7	Longinus	2	William of Ockham	8
Epicurus	8	Diogenes Laertius	3	Buridan	2
Apollodorus	2	Eusebius	3	Nicolaus (Oresme)	2
Zeno	2				

EMPIRICISM, A.D. 1500-1920

B. Telesius	6	Brown	4	Helmholtz	6
Bacon	7	D. Stewart	4	Hamilton	6
Herbert of Cherbury	4	Gauss	4	Du Bois Reymond	5
R. Boyle	4	James Mill	6	Galton	6
Newton	9	Bentham	6	Binet	4
Locke	8	Cuvier	8	Baldwin	5
Leeuwenhoek	5	H. Spencer	8	de Roberty	3

Hooke	5	J. S. Mill	8	F. Brentano	4
Buffon	6	A. Comte	8	Meinong	3
Voltaire	7	Purkinje	6	Tönnies	4
Montesquieu	6	Buckle	5	Croom Robertson	4
Hutcheson	4	Lafitte	5	G. Gomperz	4
Condillac	6	G. Grote	2	Masaryk	4
Reid	4	C. Darwin	8	Mach	6
Pestalozzi	8	Liebig	4	W. James	7

The above, it must be repeated, are merely a selection of some names according to one of the many classifications used by Sorokin. His full lists occupy seventy-five pages of small print in double columns.

Such catalogues obviously present a very plain target for criticism, and long arguments might range around almost any of the valuations, apart from any questions about the validity of the basis on which they are made. That Rousseau, Locke, Fichte and Darwin should be equated in their influence, for example, may seem a surprising result. So is the equation of a world figure such as Voltaire with the relatively little-known Renouvier both with credits of 7. The temptation to dismiss the whole elaborately constructed tables of evaluation because of disagreement over a point or two in the marks or ratings of various individual thinkers, may appeal to critics in a hurry to discredit a novelty, but to yield to it would be to overlook the fact that discrepancies of this order of magnitude have little or no effect on the broad trend and cumulative results. Like the multitude of small dots which collectively make up each pictorial illustration in a daily newspaper, the individual ratings contribute to a general effect which would not be noticeably different even though here and there one or two, when seen through a magnifying glass, may be slightly larger or smaller than they should have been. The rating assigned to some thinkers varies with the classification under which they appear. Thus Jeremy Bentham, whose influence may have seemed undervalued by being listed as 6 among empirical thinkers, is given a rating of 7 when classified among the upholders of the theory of determinism. Samuel Johnson, assigned only 1 as a mystic, gets 6 as an upholder of the ethics of principles. Despite the length of the lists and the large number of thinkers included in them whose names will be unfamiliar to any except specialists, there are one or two omissions of which the more notable for English readers will be Richard Rolle of Hampole (1290?-1349); Joseph Butler, on whose famous *Analogy of Revealed Religion* (1736), generations of English clergy have been trained; William

Law who through his *Serious Call to a Devout and Holy Life* (1728) has also had a wide influence; and William Wordsworth (1770-1850). This is a small matter in comparison with what has been included to illustrate Western cultural development by showing as concisely as possible the influence of any given thinker, the number of thinkers in a given movement of thought and the strength of that movement.

Sorokin recognizes and emphatically rejects the objection that cultural matters cannot be weighed and measured in this way. The very people who object themselves do it all the time, but they do it vaguely and without committing themselves too far. They use such generalizations as 'it was the epoch of the rise and triumph of . . . materialism . . . nominalism . . . socialism . . . or the Gothic style of architecture'; 'Kant was one of the greatest philosophers'; 'the period was marked by an increase in riots, revolts and disorders'. Statements of this kind used to give some rough indication of the comparative influence, popularity, magnitude, value, size, frequency, or the increase or decrease, growth or decline, rise or fall of various cultural phenomena may be called *verbal quantitative* propositions in contrast with Sorokin's resolute effort to substitute *numerical quantitative* propositions for them. There can be little doubt that, as well as being vague, the *verbal quantitative* description is a lazy way of comparing magnitudes. One of the dangers of trying to substitute numerical quantitative descriptions for it arises from this laziness of readers who may be tempted to take on trust and without examination the hard work of others, such as Sorokin. It is a danger increased by the natural inclination or the necessity to make some numerical estimate upon what may often be inadequate grounds. The figures might then seem to lay claim to greater precision and certainty than the real state of knowledge would warrant. The aim must be to guard against such dangers without giving excuses to those who would prefer to cover up their disinclination to grapple with a tough problem by adopting an attitude of general scepticism about the possibility of achieving any reliable estimates at all.

The search for clear and distinct ideas in this field cannot be held up by such fears and hesitations. Sorokin would be the first to welcome greater precision, and his work remains a standing challenge to those able either to prove its invalidity or to organize co-operative research so as to investigate with greater intensity and accuracy the rise and fall of systems and types of human culture in whose detailed history and quantitative assessment he has sought to pioneer.

The first task was to assess the individual contributions of distinguished and representative thinkers and writers by devising a scale of significant influence from 1 to 12. Then Sorokin grouped the thinkers in their various schools of thought to indicate the fluctuations in the main systems of truth. Here he departs from his broad three classes of the truths of faith, of reason, and of the senses. Instead he uses the following six classes:

A. Empiricism,
   the truth of the senses.
B. Rationalism :
   (a) Religious or ideational rationalism, the truth of faith.
   (b) Idealistic rationalism, the truth of logic; of the human mind, its laws, categories and concepts.
C. Mysticism,
   a less rational and more esoteric brand of the truth of faith than religious rationalism.
D. Scepticism,
   methodical doubting of the possibility of human knowledge.
E. Fideism,
   logically connected with scepticism in that it believes that the truth of the most important principles and facts cannot be obtained through mere cognition, empirical or rational, but is to be achieved through the act of volition, the will to believe or instinct. Related to mysticism, and not merely negative like scepticism.
F. Criticism or Agnosticism
   contends that the phenomenal or empirical world alone is accessible to our knowledge, while the ultimate or transcendental reality, whether it exists or not, is inaccessible and need not be known. It thus occupies a somewhat middle position between empiricism, rationalism and scepticism, but is closer to empiricism.

On the basis of his numerical assessments already described above, he then calculates the way in which the influence of these six main systems of truth has fluctuated between 580 B.C. to A.D. 1920. The results are shown first in a table of changes for every twenty years, and secondly in another in every hundred years in these twenty-five centuries. They have also been shown in graphic form on page 96.

Sorokin draws attention to one or two conclusions suggested by the results of this statistical study.

The first is the absence of any single line of advance or progress. None of the main systems has steadily increased, decreased or remained constant. The popular notion, therefore, that there has been a progressively increasing acceptance of the empirical truth of the senses

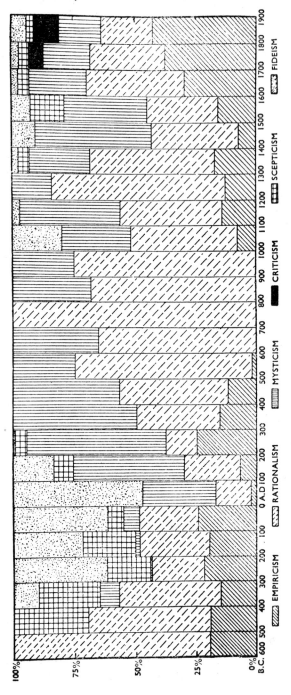

Fig. 3. FLUCTUATION OF THE INFLUENCE OF SYSTEMS OF TRUTH (BY CENTURIES)

at the expense of a continually declining loyalty to the truth of faith (religious rationalism, mysticism and fideism) or to the truth of reason (idealistic rationalism) is shown to be false. Such a movement is indeed characteristic of the last five centuries and is additional evidence of the predominantly sensate character of their culture. It is evident that a similar progress of empiricism was not maintained after its early beginnings in the sixth century B.C., when it grew only to decline once more in the third century B.C., thereafter remaining almost non-existent from the fifth to the eleventh century A.D.

The notion popularized by Comte that mankind passes from the theological to the metaphysical and then to the positive stage, which has been called the law of three stages, does not fit the facts. It seems plausible, because it gives pre-eminence to the empirical sensate system in which we are living and to whose values therefore those of the theological and metaphysical stages appear as preparatory and inferior.

Similarly, Herbert Spencer's theory that society and culture moves from a less differentiated and integrated to an increasingly differentiated and integrated system is also contradicted. Since the Middle Ages, it is true that such a development has occurred, but the Middle Ages themselves showed, says Sorokin, a recession to simplicity after the complex society on whose ruins they were established had passed away. Spencer might conceivably have retorted that his theory stands up a good deal better if continuity in the history of the Middle Ages is looked for in the story of the Germanic tribes who broke the Græco-Roman cultural pattern. The fact that the pattern broke would, however, remain to indicate the occurrence of fundamental change or of weaknesses of which many other symptoms abounded, all of which demand explanation. This is a question which will call for further consideration in Chapter Eleven in studying Sorokin's views about the nature and causes of fluctuations in cultural systems.

The difficulty of measuring cultural trends is illustrated at the outset of Sorokin's historical survey of the first of his six systems of truth and knowledge. On the basis of the work of but one thinker, Thales, about whom very little is known, it might be concluded that the period from 580 B.C. to 560 B.C. was absolutely dominated by empiricism, although there are plausible grounds for regarding him as very similaɪ to the religious rationalists, idealists and believers in a divine providential control of the universe. Later Greek thinkers about whom more is known, show that up to about 460 B.C. the truth of faith, represented by ideational or religious rationalism, amounted to about 90 per cent.

of all the systems of truth. Thereafter the truth of senses, empiricism, grew, remaining strong with minor fluctuations. From 460 B.C. to 400 B.C, the nature philosophers, Empedocles and Democritus, the Sophists and others, brought about the development of the natural sciences in Greece which were further developed, especially between 320 B.C. to 260 B.C., the period of the Epicureans and the disciples of Democritus.

It was a movement which had its echo in Rome, particularly between 120-20 B.C., the epoch of Lucretius, the Græco-Roman materialists and Epicureans. In Rome also there were some discoveries in the natural sciences at this time. The empirical way of thinking then seems to have weakened and remained low until about A.D. 200-360, the time of the Epicureans, of Gallienus and the Peripatetics, as well as of some of the empirically inclined of the Church Fathers and Manicheans. Then it flared up and remained comparatively high until about A.D. 480. After about A.D. 540 it disappeared, submerged by Christianity's rising truth of faith, and it did not again come into evidence until about A.D. 1100. Gaining influence fairly steadily in the twelfth, thirteenth and fourteenth centuries, empiricism was not yet dominant, and indeed it disappeared in the first half of the fifteenth century. The following notable short upward waves of empiricism occurred around

A.D. 1100　　Roscellinus and others;
1180　　John of Salisbury, Alfred of England, Alexander Neckham;
1220　　Michael Scott, Roland of Cremona;
1230-1250　　Bartholomew Anglicus;
1260　　Roger Bacon;
1320-1340　　William Ockham, Buridan, Nicholas of Oresme, Albertus of Saxony;
1460-1500　　Gabriel Biel.

After about 1460, when empiricism re-emerged, it rose rapidly, especially in the sixteenth century and, after minor fluctuations, reached the extraordinary and unique indicator of 42 per cent. for the whole of the nineteenth century, and the still higher figure of 53 per cent. for the first twenty years of the twentieth century. High as these percentages are, many readers will probably be surprised that they are not very much higher. Sorokin does not, however, belong to the 'all or none' school of sweeping generalizations, and his method reveals the complex nature of the reality he seeks to portray.

Recessions in the forward surging wave of empiricism occurred in the second half of the sixteenth century, in part of the seventeenth and at the beginning of the nineteenth century.

Discoveries and Inventions

Sorokin supports the conclusions arrived at by his statistical survey of the number and influence of empirical or sensate philosophers and thinkers by an independent investigation of the number of discoveries and inventions in the natural sciences. Nor merely were the computations upon which this second investigation was based taken from entirely different sources, but they were provided by another set of workers who were unaware of the first enquiry. It is not surprising to find that the development of natural sciences and of inventions aid each other and therefore occur at the same time. Both are products of a sensate mentality.

Using as a foundation the co-operative chronological survey provided by twenty-six German scientists in Darmstädter's *Handbuch zur Geschichte der Naturwissenschaften und der Technik*, Sorokin and his collaborators constructed statistical tables to show for nine main branches of science (mathematics, astronomy, biology, medical science, chemistry, physics, geology and technology), the number of inventions in each by 100-year periods from 800 B.C. to A.D. 1500 and by 25-year periods from 1501 to 1908. From these tables, a series of graphs were drawn, of which that reproduced as Fig. 4 may be regarded as summarizing the main conclusions reached.

Lack of data unfortunately makes it impossible to extend the chart to include Egypt and the ancient civilization of the Near East.

When the study is pushed into an investigation in greater detail of the contribution of various countries to the sum total of inventions and discoveries in more modern times, it becomes evident that no continuous or single line of development has occurred in the progress of discovery. This fact is interestingly brought out by Sorokin in another chart not reproduced here. By these means, Sorokin succeeded in showing that there has been a positive correlation between periods in which the truth of the senses was dominant and a correspondingly high rate of discovery and invention. 66490

He is also able to show that the domination of the truth of faith is negatively correlated with the progress of discovery and invention, as a comparison of Fig. 3 and Fig. 4 will show, despite the combination in Fig. 3, under the heading 'rationalism', of both ideational and idealistic rationalism. Looking at the evidence respecting the dominance of religious or idealistic rationalism, mysticism and fideism it is evident from Fig. 3 that, throughout the period from the beginning of our era to the end of the fifth century A.D., these three currents of the truth of faith were dominant. Mysticism and fideism were then strongly in evidence, as they were not before the fifth century B.C. or after the sixth century A.D., when the pure ideational truth of faith completely dominated the scene, driving out empiricism and scepticism

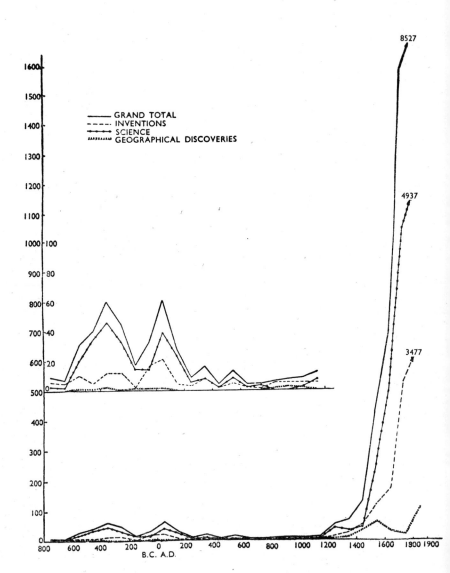

Fig. 4.   NUMBER OF SCIENTIFIC DISCOVERIES AND INVENTIONS, 800 B.C. TO A.D. 1900 (BY CENTURIES)

and so removing the main source of both mysticism and fideism. In the sixteenth century the last desperate effort was made to maintain the influence of the truth of faith before the steady decline set in which has continued ever since.

Neither mysticism nor fideism is a movement likely to achieve any considerable popular following, and it seems rather unnecessary to single them out for special treatment in an introductory survey. It is interesting to note, however, that the main periods in which mysticism appeared to provide a satisfactory source of truth were about the middle of the fourth century B.C. (Plato after 385 B.C., Xenocrates and others); around the beginning of the Christian era (Philo, Nigidius Figulus and others); the fifth to seventh centuries A.D.; the ninth century; a high point in the twelfth century (Erigena, Maximus Confessor and others); the fourteenth century, remaining high in the sixteenth century although not so high as previously. There were slight crescendos from 1660 to 1720 and between 1780 and 1840.

Atheism may logically be expected to show movements opposite to those of the truth of faith, but parallel with the truth of the senses. Thus before the fifth century B.C., there is scarcely a single case of atheism, but thereafter criminal condemnation of impiety appears. By the second century A.D., the decrease in atheism becomes evident. It disappears in the Middle Ages.

Idealistic rationalism was prominent between 540-450 B.C. (Pythagoreanism, Heraclitus and the Eleatic school); in the second half of the fifth and first half of the fourth century B.C. (Socrates, Plato, Aristotle and others); again about 200 B.C.; about 80 B.C.; from the twelfth to the first half of the fourteenth century, which was its climax in the history of Western culture; the first half of the fifteenth century; the sixteenth and first half of the seventeenth centuries; the end of the eighteenth, and the beginning of the nineteenth centuries, after which time its trend has been downward.

It remains to note that scepticism, although not a system of truth; reached its highest points from 460 B.C. to 380 B.C.; 180-120, B.C. about 20 B.C. and in the second century A.D. It reappeared in the sixteenth century, since when it has existed as a minor stream of thought, especially notable in the periods 1520-1540, 1560-1600, 1740-1780. Scepticism therefore emerges when the truth of faith declines and when the truth of reason, and particularly truth of the senses, find more followers. As empiricism triumphs, scepticism retreats; but not to vanish as it does when the truth of faith is dominant. When scepticism fades, so also does fideism, since fideism is the desperate reaction which scepticism provokes. Looking ahead to Chapter Nine, some connection may be noted between the growth of scepticism and social upheavals.

Criticism, as a distinct development in philosophy, was a late manifestation at the end of the eighteenth century, seen especially in the work of Hume and Kant. After a temporary recession it resumed its growth after 1860 to become, next to empiricism, the most powerful current in philosophical thought. Its movements being almost opposite to those of scepticism, suggest to Sorokin that it fulfils functions which scepticism is unable to perform at certain periods in the history of thought.

Summing up the totals provided by his system of indicators for the whole period studied, he records the following relative weights. It may here be pointed out that the combined totals of the 'weights' of influence of all the thinkers in the various schools of thought corrects the bias shown by the percentages of such thinkers at any one time, such as that noticed on page 97. Thales produced a record of 100 per cent for materialism in the period 580 to 560 B.C., but his contribution to the total weight of that school is only 4.

Truth of Faith,
    composed of mysticism, fideism and religious rationalism   1,650

Truth of Reason	1,292
Truth of Senses, composed of empiricism	1,338
Scepticism and Criticism	476

From these results Sorokin concludes that religious and idealistic rationalism has so far been the most powerful system of truth; empiricism being next in importance. The record suggests, says Sorokin, the principle of self-regulation of cultural processes and their automatic tendency to balance one another. Possibly also, he thinks, each form of truth has its own part to play in the life of the mind and of society and that each may be equally necessary. Such in outline are the main features of Sorokin's views on the main trends in one significant aspect of the history of philosophy. His many quotations illustrating his conclusions cannot be reproduced here, but may be followed in the second volume of *Social and Cultural Dynamics*.

Every reader will no doubt test Sorokin's theories for himself in the light both of his own conceptual framework, resulting from his own independent study, and of his own detailed knowledge of special periods in the development of human thought.

Idealism and Materialism

Before leaving philosophy and the history of thought, Sorokin examines the varying fate of other first principles or fundamental concepts during the time that has elasped since they were first discussed by the Ancient Greeks.

The first such additional principles are the well-known opposing schools of thought of idealism and materialism and the mixed theories based on each. Idealism maintains that the ultimate or true reality is spiritual; that it is God, spirit, soul or mind, or Platonic ideas. According to these views, reality is immaterial, spiritual or psychical in essence. Two main types of idealism may be distinguished. *Monistic Idealism* regards all individual and separate systems of immaterial and spiritual reality as being but the temporary manifestation of One ultimate, all-embracing spiritual being, whether it be thought of as God or the Absolute: Absolute Idea for instance; Mind or Spirit. *Pluralistic Idealism*, still believing in the immaterial nature of reality views it as being made up not of one fundamentally simple system but of a multitude of independent centres or systems of spiritual reality, such as souls, spirits or monads, which together constitute the ultimate reality.

In striking contrast to the two types of idealism stand the many varieties of materialism. Sorokin singles out two as the main and most important types. The first form regards ultimate reality as living matter capable of sensation, of striving and to some extent possessing consciousness. This form he calls *Hylozoistic Materialism*. Hylozism, from two Greek words meaning 'matter' and 'life', was a word used by Cudworth in the seventeenth century. The second form, *Mechanistic Materialism*, is materialistic in a more thorough-going way, since it regards spiritual and immaterial phenomena such as mind, if indeed they can be said to have any true reality, as a passive product of matter and of mechanical motions of material stuff or particles.

Mixed forms of idealism and materialism include scepticism, agnosticism and critical philosophy.

In order to assess the relative influence of these various attitudes towards fundamental reality, Sorokin and his collaborators again classified all the thinkers who have written about them, assigning to each an appropriate weight on the scale of 1 to 12, in the manner already described in the treatment of the various systems of truth. The results have been embodied in a series of statistical tables which are shown in graphic form in Fig. 5.

Sorokin again explains that the years 580-540 B.C. are misleadingly

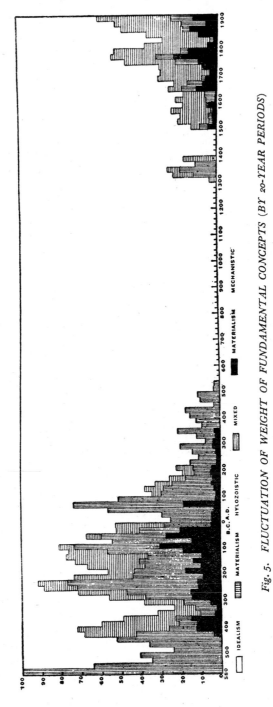

Fig. 5. FLUCTUATION OF WEIGHT OF FUNDAMENTAL CONCEPTS (BY 20-YEAR PERIODS)

classified as completely under the sway of hylozoistic materialism, owing to the fact that only two names, Thales and Anaximander, are known. The probability is that the period was in fact predominantly idealistic. Making due allowance for this necessary adjustment, Sorokin is able to show that idealism is correlated closely with the truth of faith and materialism with the truth of the senses. If not in all the minor fluctuations, then at least in the main waves, the empirical system of truth of the senses shows itself as being positively associated with materialism. The truth of faith is similarly associated with idealism, especially in its pluralistic form. The truth of reason is linked less with religion and more with dialectical idealism, especially with monistic idealism. Significantly enough, reliance upon the truth of reason began again to manifest itself in the thirteenth century. Sorokin describes the more intellectual, argumentative, idealistic systems of the twelfth and thirteenth centuries as *dialectical*, to distinguish them from the simple, purely religious idealism of earlier centuries.

It follows that the empirical system of truth, materialism and scientific discoveries are closely associated. They are negatively related to the truth of faith and to pluralistic idealism. Such results are not very surprising, and indeed are, as Sorokin points out, logically to be expected. They reinforce the view already become familiar, that the predominant form of culture in Greece in the sixth, fifth and fourth centuries B.C. was mainly ideational and idealistic. In the centuries from the third to the beginning of our era, culture was mainly sensate. From the first to the sixth centuries A.D. there was a decline in the sensate and rise in the ideational culture. From the sixth to the twelfth centuries the Ideational culture prevailed virtually to the total exclusion of all other forms. The twelfth, thirteenth and fourteenth centuries were mainly idealistic, but the tide of sensate culture was rising. A desperate reaction against its onset was made during the fifteenth century, but it did not succeed in damming back the sensate tide which has steadily gained, with minor fluctuations, ever since it again began to rise in the sixteenth century.

Sorokin's views may be illustrated by the contrast at the end of the seventeenth century between the newer materialism and the older idealism summed up in the controversy between John Locke and Leibniz. The mind, said Locke, is a blank until actual experience imprints impressions upon it. He believed the old maxim *nihil est in intellectu quod non prius fuerit in sensu.* Leibniz also admitted the truth of this remark as far as it went, but he pointed out that the senses do not receive external impressions in the form of ideas. The active work of the mind is necessary before external sense impressions can create internal ideas. Leibniz therefore vindicated the idealist view by adding to that maxim the deeply significant words *nisi ipse intellectus* to emphasize the all-important creative activity of the human mind in building up knowledge. But the work of Leibniz, which he was too generous to publish after Locke's death, was little known, and for two generations it lay buried among the mass of his manuscripts at Hanover.

The sensate tide rolled on. It is manifest to-day in the contemporary tendency to interpret man, culture and history mechanically. It is to be seen in the emphasis now put upon reflex actions, upon the influence of endocrine glands, upon psycho-analysis and upon economic conditioning as determinants of behaviour. Spiritual, idealistic influences are rarely allowed any operative power. Far otherwise was the situation over the many centuries in which ideational and idealistic forms of culture prevailed. Yet, as Sorokin notes once again, neither the ideational nor the sensate cultural stream can claim continuous development. There are no periodic or wave-like movements. There are no rises or falls every hundred, three hundred or six hundred years, as some writers have plausibly tried to suggest. Likewise there is no adequate evidence to support famous theories of periodicity in cultural progress, such as that of Hegel with his three-beat rhythm of 'Thesis-antithesis' and resulting 'higher synthesis'.

Being and Becoming

Other philosophical first principles, in addition to the notions of idealism and materialism examined by Sorokin, are the twin notions of being and becoming or of permanency and change. He describes these as the eternalistic and temporalistic mentality, and he points out that they are the basic principles underlying hundreds of more specific theories in science, philosophy and religion.

The philosophy of pure Eternalism was paramount in the thought of Brahmanic India and of Taoism in China. It has characterized the thought of several Western philosophical systems, such as those of Parmenides and Zeno. The famous paradoxes of Achilles and the tortoise, and of the arrow, by which Zeno sought to prove that motion and change are unreal, are outstanding examples of the philosophy of being. Although not part of the religious thought of the Middle Ages, it reappeared in Christian literature with Pascal. Among others holding such views, Sorokin notes Cervantes and J. Boehme, and among relatively very few modern thinkers, Schopenauer.

The opposite school of thought regards reality as a constant state of becoming. It holds that everything is in a state of incessant change and flux. The little that is known of the pre-Socratic philosophers of Greece already shows the force of this thought at an early age. The often-quoted remarks of Heraclitus that 'all things are born through opposition', and 'are in flux like a river', is typical. In our own time, the same doctrine has had powerful advocates in David Hume, Diderot, Feuerbach, Bakunin, J. S. Mill, Renan, Nietzsche, William James, Vaihinger and Spengler.

Mankind has found, however, that neither pure being nor pure becoming can alone satisfactorily explain their world and their experience. Those who attempt to rely solely on one of these theories have always failed, for they have been compelled to bring in, however surreptitiously, the other to help to give their doctrine a semblance of truth. The idea of process must seek meaning from the idea of being, whether it be in the form of 'the ultimate reality', cosmic rays, matter, energy, God, the Universal Spirit, or the Unknowable.

The effort of idealistic thought to realize and express the truths of both the notions of being and of becoming has taken various forms. Among them, Sorokin enumerates the atomic theories of Leucippus and Democritus. According to this view, matter is regarded as stuff whose ultimate nature consists of unchangeable atoms. From the ever-changing combinations of these atoms the opposite notion of becoming is derived. In our own time, atoms are replaced in the theory of being by electrons, protons and neutrons.

Another form of the theory attempting to explain both being and becoming is that of Plato, of the Neo-Platonists, partly of the Peripatetic school, and of most of the medieval thinkers from St. Augustine, St. Thomas and the Scholastics to Spinoza. These thinkers regarded the realm of being as the supreme ultimate reality. The realm of becoming for them is that of the empirical world of sense perceptions subject to generation and corruption, process and change. This view Sorokin calls eternalism-temporalism, and he finds that by far the greatest number of thinkers incline to it. Outstanding are Plato (12), St. Thomas Aquinas (12), St. Augustine (10), Luther (8), Loyola (8), Spinoza (8), Berkeley (8), Hegel (8). The numbers after each name indicate Sorokin's estimate of the relative influence and importance of the thinkers mentioned from the standpoint of the development of this doctrine of eternalism-temporalism.

Sorokin notes a variant on this theme in which reality is graded into three or four classes; on a scale of an increasing 'being', and a decreasing 'becoming', as the lower forms of existence are overshadowed by increasing emphasis upon the higher forms. He does not mention the remarkable monadic theory of Leibniz in this connection, although he awards him a score of 9 out of 12 among the thinkers who sought to achieve an equilibrium between the two schools of eternalism-temporalism and of temporalism-eternalism. The few thinkers whose influence he rates about as high or higher in this respect are Pythagoras (8), Socrates (9), Aristotle (12), Zeno (8), Chrysippus (7), Cicero (8), Plutarch (8), Nicolas of Cusa (8), Leonardo da Vinci (8), G. Bruno (8), Kepler (8), Descartes (8), Galileo (8), Kant (12).

Yet another variant of the mixed types is that which concentrates upon the relationships of things, picking out the uniformities, regularities and causal relationships between them, which it then attempts to state as laws according to which changes take place. These laws then become the immutable, constant and unchanging factors in the universe. The whole effort of science becomes concentrated upon these uniformities and causal laws, so that a tendency arises to regard science and the scientific statement of laws as an end in itself, perhaps even as the refuge of the immutable being.

Social science, as well as natural science, has also become a field in which uniformities and laws are sought, but this has been a relatively late development in Western thought. G. B. Vico was a pioneer in the search for what he regarded as 'the ideal universal and eternal laws along which proceed all nations in the cycles of their appearance, development, decadence and end'. His words had very little immediate influence and, despite other beginnings on different lines, such as those of Montesquieu, it was not until the nineteenth century that the search for uniformities and laws invaded history to create a new branch of thought, the philosophy of history. From the standpoint of Sorokin's theories, the history of history as a separate branch of thought is specially revealing, since it can only develop during the prevalence of the sensate-temporalistic mentality. Hence it is not surprising that the Hindu ideational mentality failed to develop any historical sense or any reliable chronology. The same deficiency characterizes the Middle Ages in Europe and the heroic periods of Greece and Rome. History, in the modern sense of the word, did not properly emerge until the fifth century B.C. in Greece (Herodotus and Thucydides) and not until the second and first centuries B.C. in Rome. In European culture, history, as distinct from chronicles, such as the Anglo-Saxon Chronicle and others, first appears with Joinville and Froissart in the fourteenth century A.D., after which it steadily grows until, in our own time, every subject is treated historically. Life itself is controlled by time measurements. 'We cannot live without a watch,' says Sorokin. 'We go to bed winding it; we get up at the command of the hands or alarm of a clock, we move, work, act, eat, sleep, love, quarrel, study, pray, live by a watch and controlled by watch time.' This is all very new in the age-long experience of humanity.

There are therefore five main groups of theories on the subject of the nature of things as either process or reality or both. Sorokin lists them as

1. Pure Eternalism.
2. Eternalism-temporalism, where the aspect of becoming is present but is greatly overshadowed by the aspect of permanent being.
3. Pure Temporalism.
4. Temporalism-eternalism, where the aspect of becoming is far more stressed than that of being.
5. Equilibrium of Eternalism-temporalism, giving equal importance to both aspects which are regarded as equally important modes of reality.

In a statistical appendix of eleven closely-printed pages, Sorokin lists and classifies the various thinkers in these five main groups, giving each thinker a numerical indicator of his relative influence on a scale rating of 1 to 12 (*Social and Cultural Dynamics*, Vol. II, pp. 663-675).

After reviewing the various theories of being and of becoming, Sorokin summarizes his detailed findings in a series of statistical tables and in graphic form in Fig. 6.

The comparative strength of the various systems is set out in the following statistical table, which brings out the predominance of the

Table 2—FLUCTUATIONS IN THE DOCTRINES OF BEING AND BECOMING

Period	Eternalisms		Temporalisms		Equilibriums
	Pure	Mixed	Pure	Mixed	
500 B.C.-A.D. 100	18	75	179	136	317
A.D. 100-600	0	194	29	11	341
600-1500	0	284	0	4	324
1500-1900	149	1337	131	767	481
1900-1920	47	268	37	382	109
	214	2158	376	1300	1572

All Eternalisms 2372   *All Temporalisms* 1676   *Equilibriums* 1572

idealistic mixed eternalism-temporalism variety of eternalism in comparison with pure doctrines of being (eternalism), or of becoming (temporalism). At the same time the results testify to the continuing vitality of apparently quite outmoded ways of thought, showing once again the qualifications necessary before any age can be labelled purely sensate or ideational.

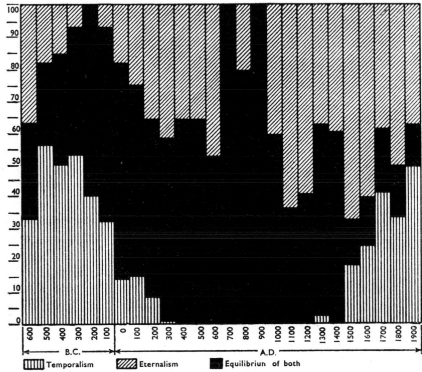

Temporalism   Eternalism   Equilibriun of both

Fig. 6.   TEMPORALISM, ETERNALISM, AND EQUILIBRIUM OF BOTH

Realism and Nominalism

More striking still is the illustration Sorokin brings to his study of philosophical development by analysing the relative importance and the number of thinkers who, at various epochs, took opposite sides on another fundamental theme. This is the great question started by Plato, about the true nature of the definitions, generalisations and concepts of human thought. Is it true that there is nothing in the real world that corresponds to our general abstract ideas about such subjects as society, the state, or justice, or about classes of things such as the horse; as the Nominalists believe, or are they themselves the true reality, the eternal truths, as the Realists such as Plato said they are?

Or is the third possibility correct, that concepts exist in the mind only and are real to the extent that we think with them and operate with them, but that they do not exist in their own right outside the mind, as the Realists contend they do? This third view is that of the Conceptualists.

The three schools of thought had several variants but they can be roughly summarized with the aid of a few Latin prepositions to indicate whether general ideas (or in Latin *universalia*) existed before and, apart from their manifestation in actual concrete form *ante rem*, before the thing of which they are the generalized expression. Such was the view of transcendental realists as Plato and those who followed him are often described. For them there is in every individual some real element common to all of them beyond their specific differences which makes up their essence or *universalia*. Beyond brown horse, black horse, white horse, there is the universal horse, without which horse A and horse B could not be put into the class of horse. There is, therefore, in our minds, and also beyond space and time, a real world of universals, in this example, horse. Plato called this generic essence the Idea of the single individuals in which it is exemplified. Another form of realism, still believing in the independent existence of general ideas or universals, regards them also as present in or immanent in the individual objects of the empirical world : *univeralia in re*, existing in the thing. Such is immanent realism, of which Aristotle's theory was an example. Many philosophers who accepted both these ideas also thought that we reach universals or general ideas through our knowledge of individual objects, after actual experience, by abstraction and comparison, *universalia post rem*. St. Thomas Aquinas held this view, but he believed also in transcendental and immanent realism.

Conceptualists are not willing to go beyond the idea that our knowledge of universals is gained after and through our experience of things. That is to say they accept *universalia post rem* but neither *universalia in re*, as the immanent realists do, nor *universalia ante rem* as the transcendental realists do. Universals for them are concepts in the mind. In the process of thinking about general ideas such as horse, a special non-sensory, but not supersensory, cognition of them enters in and transforms the singular impressions and images into abstract concepts.

The position of the nominalists is simple. They do not believe that there is anything in the external world corresponding to generalized concepts or *universalia*. Likewise they hold that there are no real concepts in the mind; nothing but individual images and impressions. The notion that we have concepts in our minds arises, they say, because we are deluded by words, because we use the same word or symbol for many single impressions of similar things. We experience white horse, brown horse, black horse, and then fallaciously assume that there is something real corresponding to the word 'horse'. Because philosophers of this school of thought argued that to look for any reality beyond the words or names, *nomina*, is a vain quest, they were called nominalists.

Sorokin emphasizes the fact that the battles between realists and nominalists are by no means things of the past. The truth of his contention is evident in the controversies occasioned by logical positivism which are still being vigorously debated and in popular works on the newly-christened subject 'semantics', such as that of Stuart Chase, on the nominalist side, *The Tyranny of Words*.

Again relying upon his statistical method, Sorokin and his collaborators classified all the main philosophers according to their stand upon this greatly debated question of the status of the general concepts, with the results shown in the diagram reproduced as Fig. 7.

Once more it is probably desirable to refer again to the various

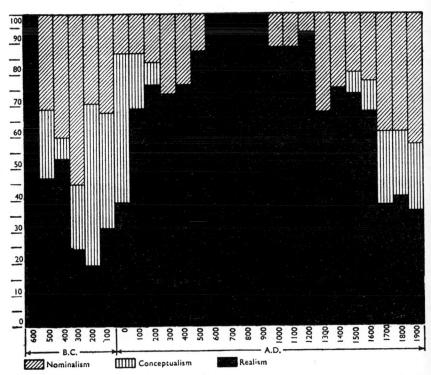

Fig. 7. MOVEMENTS OF NOMINALISM, CONCEPTUALISM, AND REALISM

limitations by which the accuracy of these statistical estimates and of their diagrammatic representation must be qualified in order to make it clear that minor adjustments may be thought necessary by some readers who may object to some of the classifications (e.g., the inclusion of Abelard among the nominalists), as well as to some of the assessments of relative influence relating to certain philosophers. Nevertheless the broad result is probably very similar to that which any other independent survey would produce.

The results show that realism is the doctrine of the ideational culture, conceptualism of the idealistic culture, and nominalism of the sensate culture. Again there is no clear progress in one direction or unilinear evolutionary trend, as Sorokin calls it. Again the results show how the influence of any one system of truth depends upon the prevalent culture, rising and falling with that culture. It is the rise of the sensate culture which has given nominalism its 'scientific' and convincing quality. Truth, or what appears to be truth to any individual human being, cannot be understood except as a manifestation of the culture in which it arises and functions.

Theories of the State

Philosophical debates about the nature of knowledge, particularly when they sound so technical as these discussions of 'the nature of universals' may seem remote from practical realities. Nevertheless they can and do illuminate difficult or baffling problems of everyday life. Subsequent chapters, particularly Chapters Seven and Eight, will provide further illustrations of the manner in which men's views about the true nature of universals have been reflected in their opinions upon many other subjects also.

One such is the relation of the individual to society. Must the individual always be sacrificed for society, or should the claims, rights and welfare of the individual always be put first? Already, before the World War of 1939-45, Sorokin could write that thousands of lives have been sacrificed and hundreds of thousands mutilated in the struggles resulting from passionate determination to uphold one way or another of answering such questions. The police state of the Fascists in Italy or of the Bolsheviks in Russia was followed by the atrocious police state of Nazi Germany, and we have by no means yet seen the end of the menace they represented. To be sure the Bolshevik, Fascist and Nazi doctrines about the nature of society were the hastily improvized rationalisations of political gangsters seeking to disguise their self-seeking, power-grabbing acts of violence with a respectable cloak

H

of pseudo-philosophical doctrine. They were not based upon philosophical reflection, nor upon those old political theories which regarded society as the true and primary reality and which thought of the individual as something altogether secondary and derivative. Sorokin labels that way of regarding society as *universalism*. Those who hold it are logically bound to regard society not only as the fundamental true reality but also as the source of values for mankind, so that corresponding to the philosophical idea about the true nature or being of society (the ontological aspect of the matter), there is also an ethical view as well, namely, that of ethical universalism. These are among the results of regarding human society as the realist philosophers do, and of believing that society is one of the 'universals' which has a reality of its own which cannot be reduced to the individual existences by which it is composed.

In complete contrast stands the view that the individual is the true and primary reality. Society on this view is of value only to the extent that it provides the individual with a richer life and helps him to achieve a fuller realization of his self-seeking impulses. This is ethical singularism. Clearly it is the view the nominalists must take of the matter in opposition to the ideas of the realists.

An effort to harmonize universalism and singularism can be made by regarding individual and social interests as two aspects of the same value, resulting in the doctrine of ethical harmonism. The philosophers and thinkers who have written on these questions do not, however, fall neatly into these three broad divisions of universalism, singularism and harmonism. Some writers did not always think or write consistently on the subject. After a patient analysis of their work, Sorokin distinguishes the three following main groups: singularism, with three sub-groups; universalism, with two sub-groups and the view believing in the mystic unity of individuals. The three types of singularism are:

PURE INDIVIDUALISM or, as Sorokin describes it, extreme or consistent sociological singularism. For this view the individual alone is real, he alone must be the source of value and his rights should be paramount. Social values are at best derivative, because society is of value only in so far as it serves the life and happiness of the individual. Extreme hedonists and anarchists are its products as well as moral individualists such as Stirner. This atomistic view of society as a mere aggregate of individuals is, of course, a sociological form of nominalism. Among some of the better-known of the writers listed by Sorokin as exemplifying this way of regarding society are the following, together with the index number or 'marks' indicating their approximate importance and influence in the history and development of thought.

Thrasymacus (3), Epicurus (8), Diogenes (3), Lucian (4), Mandeville (4), Rousseau (in his *Discours* only) (8), Diderot (7), Godwin (4), Proudhon (6), Bakunin (4), Dühring (6), Fourier (5), Carlyle (5), Nietzsche (9), Tolstoi (8), Stirner (6), Kropotkin (4).

MODERATE SOCIOLOGICAL SINGULARISM. Logically believing that none but individuals are real, this less extreme form of singularism is willing to look at the sum of all individuals, or society, as a supreme value, along with individual value. Sorokin gives a relatively short catalogue of the writers and thinkers who have taken this point of view. It includes Sir Thomas More (6), Campanella (7), Fénelon (6), Saint-Simon (4), Robert Owen (4), K. Marx (8), Engels (6), L. Blanc (3), W. Morris (4), Jaurès (5), S. Webb (4).

COLLECTIVISTIC SOCIOLOGICAL SINGULARISM is a form of singularism in that it does not regard the nature or essence of society as being anything more than the sum of the individuals it contains. Nevertheless it differs from the two more extreme forms of singularism in that it regards the whole body of individuals banded together as more important, or as ethically more valuable than any individual alone. In this sense it may be said to give priority and superiority to the collectivity and not to individuals. The welfare of the group is the supreme law. The utilitarian doctrine of the greatest happiness for the greatest number best characterizes this form of singularism and the liberalism of the nineteenth century was in many respects its best expression. In our own times, the Bolsheviks, Fascists and Nazis have taken this point of view with the utmost violence and in complete disregard for individual human rights not for theoretical but for solid practical reasons. If those in control can pose as some sort of collectivity, as representing the proletarian class, the Communist party, the Fascist, or Hitler party, the nobility, the religious collectivity, it pays them to adopt a theory which subordinates all other individuals to themselves in their collective disguise. This subordination can be of the most complete and drastic kind, involving the silencing or extermination of all who criticize or oppose those who take it upon themselves to decide upon the ethical or other purposes the collectivity is to serve. These purposes can often be nothing more than the crudest purely materialistic form of the ethics of happiness. Among the better-known of the writers and thinkers, whose doctrines support such a singularistic-universalist view, Sorokin lists, with the indicators of their relative influence on his 1 to 12 scale of ratings:

Socrates	9	*Montesquieu*	6	*James Mill*	6
Democritus	8	*Voltaire*	7	*J. Stuart Mill*	8
Empedocles	6	*A. Smith*	6	*H. Spencer*	8
Thucydides	8	*Hume*	8	*Buckle*	5
Protagoras	8	*Burke*	4	*de Tocqueville*	2
Xenophon	7	*Tom Paine*	4	*Cobden*	3
Demosthenes	4	*Helvetius*	6	*Grote*	3
Carneades	5	*Quesnay*	6	*Darwin*	8
Horace	6	*Condorcet*	6	*Freud*	4
Ovid	6	*Gibbon*	6	*Tarde*	5
Dion Chrysostom	6	*Bentham*	6	*Gobineau*	4
Marsilius of Padua	4	*B. Constant*	6	*Simmel*	5
Machiavelli in his		*Sismondi*	4	*Westermarck*	4
Discorsi	6	*Malthus*	6	*Galton*	5
Locke	8	*Ricardo*	5	*F. W. Maitland*	5
Bayle	6	*J. Adams*	3		
Hutcheson	4	*A. Comte*	8		

Needless to say these men would have shrunk from the lengths to which twentieth-century totalitarian states have gone in perverting their theories by bending them to their own ends.

SOCIOLOGICAL UNIVERSALISM is based upon an entirely different idea of the nature of society, which it regards as something existing in its own right beyond and apart from the mere aggregate of individuals of which it is composed. Society, according to this view, has its own organic life which cannot be reduced to any expression in terms of the existence of individuals. It is therefore from society, and not from individuals, that supreme values are to be derived. Such a doctrine is obviously one which would come naturally to anyone who believes in the true reality of supersensory phenomena, in other words, to the realists rather than to the nominalists.

Sorokin distinguishes two classes of the main varieties of sociological universalism.

Moderate Sociological Universalism, which while still maintaining the independent existence and value of society as its first principle, nevertheless recognizes some reality and value in the individual. In practice, therefore, although certainly not in theory, this moderate form of universalism approaches the doctrine of collectivistic sociological singularism just reviewed above. The following are some of the principal writers and thinkers adopting this theory:

Pythagoras	8	*Abelard*	4	*Kant*	12
Heraclitus	7	*Roger Bacon*	6	*Schiller*	8
Aristotle	12	*Duns Scotus*	8	*Fichte*	8

Chrysippus	7	William of Ockham	8	St. Simon	6
Polybuis	4	Wycliffe	3	Fourier	5
Nigidius Figulus	4	Petrarch	3	Macaulay	4
Cato (Utica)	2	Gerson	4	A. Comte	8
Caesar	6	Calvin	6	Lassalle	5
Varro	5	Zwingli	4	Renouvier	7
Virgil	8	Knox	4	Emerson	6
Philo Judaeus	8	Althusius	4	Le Play	7
Tacitus	4	H. Grotius	6	Fabian Society	7
Apuleius	6	Milton	7	Gierke	6
Clement of Alexandria	6	Harrington	4	Renan	6
Pelagius	3	Pascal	7	Tönnies	4
Dionysius the Areopagite	8	Comenius	7	Durkheim	5
Gregory the Great	4	Spinoza	8	Sombart	5
Bede	3	Rousseau Contrat Social	8	Stammler	5
Alcuin	4	Beccaria	6	Max Weber	5
Lanfranc	3	Herder	6		

Universalism, the complete expression of the realist idea of society, in which the individual is nothing and society or the state is everything, is exemplified by many others of whom some of the best known are:

Anaximander	5	S. Thomas Aquinas	12	Bossuet	6
Parmenides	7	Raymond Lully	5	Fénelon	6
Plato	12	Dante	8	Vico	6
Tertullian	6	Luther	8	Wolff	7
St. Augustine	10	Machiavelli (Prince)	6	Hegel	8
St. Anselm	7	Bodin	6	Schopenauer	8
Gregory VII (Hildebrand)	6	Campanella	7	Carlyle	5
Peter Lombard	4	Francis Bacon	7	Ranke	5
John of Salisbury	5	Hobbes	8	V. Soloviev	6
Albertus Magnus	8	Leibniz	9	Dostoevsky	7

Apart from these two major and opposite theories of singularism and universalism, there is a third way of looking at the problem. Sorokin calls it Sociological *Mystic Integralism*, because it tries to find an harmonious synthesis between the two conflicting theories. It provides more subtle and difficult ideas than the sharp-cut alternatives of singularism and universalism at the cost of a somewhat mystical and metaphysical elaboration of the main issues involved. The individual is regarded as the incarnation of society; society is the universal reality permeating every individual as his generic essence. Society and the individual represent two different aspects of the same value. Neither can be given a secondary or derivative value or be made the mere means of the other. Sorokin's list of thinkers taking this developed philosophical position includes fewer names than can be cited under singularist and universalist thinkers. Among the better known are:

Cicero	8	*Macrobius*	4	*Milton*	6
Seneca	8	*St. John Chrysostom*	5	*Shaftesbury*	5
Plutarch	8	*Proclus*	8	*Rousseau*	8
Epictetus	6	*Maximus Confessor*	6	*Kant*	12
Marcus Aurelius	6	*St. Bernard of Clairvaux*	5	*Schiller*	8
Justin Martyr	5	*St. Francis of Assisi*	6	*Fourier*	5
Plotinus	12	*Hus*	3	*Emerson*	5
Origen	8	*Nicholas Cusa*	8	*Dostoevsky*	7
Porphyry	7	*Thomas More*	6		
Bruno	8	*Komensky*	7		

It will be noticed that some of these names, such as Milton, Kant, Schiller, Emerson, are also included among the less extreme forms of universalism, which is not surprising since, in some of their writings, they exerted a notable influence in favour of a universalist view of society, even though it did not always extend to a thorough-going mystical view. It is also evident that some writers on political theory were by no means consistent in their views in all their works. Rousseau is a notable example of a man whose opinions changed very considerably from those he first expressed in his *Discourse on Inequality* (1754). Sir Thomas More can be listed as a mystical integralist and also as a collectivist. Summarizing the broad development of human thought about the true nature of society in its relations to the individual, in so far as it is revealed by the number of writers in the various schools and their influence as they are assessed by relative weights on the scale of 1 to 12, quoted after their names, Sorokin arrives at the following composite estimate:

Table 3—CURRENTS IN SINGULARISM, UNIVERSALISM AND INTEGRALISM

Period	All Singularisms	All Universalisms	Mystic Integration
600 B.C.-A.D. 100	288	300	30
A.D. 100-600	37	253	166
600-1500	13	400	82
1500-1900	766	1002	97
1900-1920	228	184	0
Total	1332	2139	375

In the light of his findings, he concludes that the domination of the sensate culture favours the doctrine of sociological singularism which in such a period is alone considered to be truly scientific. Thus he points out that the text-books on sociology appearing between 1880 and 1920 almost invariably adopt the standpoint of moderate, even of extreme singularism. They reject as metaphysical and unscientific any attempt to look upon society as a primary reality. They will not regard any social organism as a mystical body impossible to explain, to express or to reduce to the individuals of which it is composed.

Quite otherwise were the thoughts of men during the greater part of their history, for they all regarded the body social, whether it be Church or State, as more real and more valuable than the individuals in it. All such universal views, characteristic of an ideational or idealistic culture, were discredited by the nineteenth-century insistence upon the supreme necessity of sticking to what were said to be 'the facts' and of avoiding theories and speculative generalizations. To believe that insight and explanation can be achieved merely by collecting and contemplating vast accumulations of facts is, as Sorokin asserts, quite unjustified. The delusion he attacks might perhaps be illustrated by saying that those who accept it seem to regard the process of acquiring knowledge as being rather like the method the Hungarians were said to use to make Tokay wine; namely, heaping up great piles of grapes and collecting the juice which runs from them without recourse to a wine press. Sorokin certainly does not ignore or despise facts, for all his theories have a most exacting and thorough factual bases. His view might be summarized by saying that facts are infinite, and that a fact is not a fact in any branch of knowledge unless it is a relevant fact. The operative word here being *relevant*. To decide what facts are relevant is to make a judgment about their value, and that is something which the facts themselves do not provide. Value in turn arises from the need to find some concept or theory by which the facts can be incorporated into an illuminating body of knowledge which should not only explain them adequately but which ought also to serve as a clue to further knowledge.

Sorokin has made a chart to summarize the results of weighting and counting the various contributions to the theory of society and social life which is reproduced here as Fig. 8.

Here is a new way of surveying the long record of speculation in the Western world about the all-important question of the true nature of human life in society, based upon the notion that all such views are the expression of one or other form of the philosophical ideas men have held about the reality and validity of their thoughts upon the true nature of general ideas.

Political theory is thus related directly and intelligibly to philosophical theory of which it can at once be seen to be a particular expression. Political theories themselves are shown to be capable of classification according to a comprehensive all-inclusive cultural scheme.

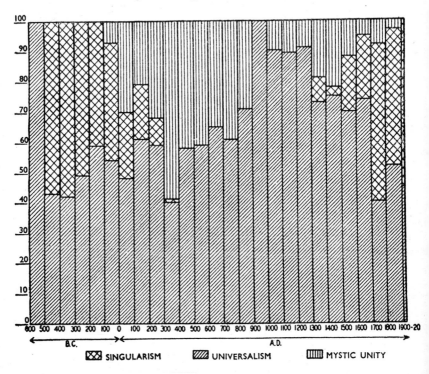

Fig. 8. *MOVEMENTS OF SINGULARISM, UNIVERSALISM, AND MYSTIC UNITY*

Armed with such a detailed analysis and description, students of political theories have a guide to the assessment of all notions on the subject and are correspondingly less likely to fall easy victims to the first theory presented to them with plausibility and force, as the unfortunate Germans succumbed in their millions to the half-baked crudities of Herr Hitler, and as millions of others have been deluded by ingenious speculations purporting to develop the teachings of Karl Marx and the ethical and economic doctrines of Communism.

Personality in Legal Thought

Sorokin reinforces his general attack upon the problem of society as a whole by a closer analysis of a more detailed aspect of it, that is

of the nature of associations or societies in the sense of limited group-
ings and collectivities active on a smaller scale and more restricted
in their scope and operations than is society or the state as a
whole.

The views that legislators and lawyers take of this question of the
reality of the juridical personality, of corporations and institutions,
may seem a highly technical and specialized matter. Yet, as Sorokin
points out, it is a very practical and pertinent matter, for the property,
liberty and very life of thousands of persons have depended and will
in future depend upon whether one or another view is taken of it. A
juridical personality in law means any body consisting of one or more
individuals regarded by the law as a unit and usually endowed with
the right to perpetual succession and to act as a single person. Relatively clear and simple as this idea may seem, it has been the subject
of every kind of contradictory theory and hypothesis. Using again as
his guide the broad philosophical concepts of realism and nominalism
which he employed in reviewing the history of metaphysical and political philosophy, Sorokin reduces the various conflicting theories about
the true nature of juridical personalities broadly to three main types,
recognizing however that each of the three has several sub-divisions.

These three classes are: first, the varieties of the realistic conception
of juridical personality among which he distinguishes:

Transcendental realism which puts the reality of the juridical personality in some supersensory essence or being. The best example is
the way in which the early Christian Church united and dissolved
everything in God.

The more mundane form of the realistic view is that which regards
the juridical personality as a real organism with a character of its own
over and above that of the individuals belonging to it, having its own
body and its own system, partly corporeal and partly psychological.
This view, labelled by Sorokin 'Empirico-organismic realism', was held
by some German theorists of law, such as Bluntschli and in part by
Gierke.

Another form of realism is the psychological realism which finds the
reality of the juridical personality mainly in some psychological essence
over and above the reality of individuals. Such are 'public opinion', 'the
group mind', 'common will', 'group aims' or 'group interest'.

The more naïve functional realism is content to see the reality of
the juridical personality in its functional unity which seems a reality
in its own right distinct and apart from that of its members. According
to such views, there can be a collective or individual responsibility or

collective and indivisible honour of the group different from the honour or the responsibility of its members. From this point of view, as of all the realist points of view, the group comes first and the individuals second. The feelings evinced towards a football team by its supporters or towards a regiment by those who have served in it might be examples. In contrast to all this stand the various nominalistic conceptions of the juridical personality which view it as a legal fiction and regard the individual members of groups as the only real elements in it apart from the various sensory objects (property, buildings, etc.) attached to it artificially. For the lawyer and statesman of this school of thought, a corporation is a legal fiction, an artificial device with no independent powers of action apart from those of its members or representatives. In a few interesting pages, Sorokin attempts to indicate the main periods in the trend of thought on this matter, concluding again that there has been no constant trend. The ups and downs of the realistic conception of the juridical person correspond, however, closely enough with those of general philosophical realism, with belief in sociological universalism and with the truth of faith.

Legal history does not unfortunately possess adequate sources relating to the legal thought of Greece on this subject, but such evidence as there is supports Sorokin's suggestion that, up to the fifth century B.C., the Greeks took a predominantly realist view according to which the individual then had no rights except by virtue of his membership of the state or of social bodies. He thinks that there is some evidence, admittedly not very much, that a more nominalistic view prevailed after the fifth century B.C.

The evidence is more abundant about the Roman view of the matter which began, like the archaic Greek, by being strictly realist. The distinctive character of life under the Roman Republic was the extent to which the Romans were at first enrolled into a large number of clans and tribes, in which they were closely bound together in kinships or family groups. Later in the history of the republic, the men of Rome are found associated in corporations or clubs. Each such grouping operated as a real unity and was regarded as such. The responsibility of the members and their property could not be distinguished from that of the corporation. At the end of the republic and under the Roman Empire there was a marked change. Many associations or unions of working men were abolished by the Senate in 64 B.C., and, although they were revived for political purposes by Clodius, a tool of Julius Cæsar, they did not recover their former status. Thereafter, and until the time of Justinian in the sixth century A.D., a definitely nominalist view was taken of corporations which, from the lawyer's standpoint, became legal fictions.

Meanwhile the rise of Christianity was powerfully promoting an extremely realist view of social organization, according to which all the values, rights, duties and property of the believers were merged into those of the Church. In the Middle Ages this movement was further strengthened by the naïve realistic mentality of the Germanic peoples. Roman law of the Imperial period survived, however, to influence thought on this subject, so that by the twelfth and thirteenth centuries a distinctly nominalistic note began to be heard. It developed, however, without entirely supplanting the earlier realism.

As late as the fifteenth and sixteenth centuries, realistic elements continued to be mixed with an increasingly nominalist outlook in Germany, England, Italy and France. Legal theories of the seventeenth and eighteenth centuries, with their development of the medieval doctrine of natural law, did not mark a complete swing-over towards nominalism, despite the pronounced form of nominalism evident in the characterization by writers such as Althusius and Hobbes of corporations and collectivities as mere collections of individuals. The tendency thereafter was all in favour of individualism, atomism and singularism, which became more evident in the nineteenth century when the influence of France spread Napoleonic legislation widely throughout Europe. Savigny, whose great work on Roman law was published in 1840, achieved a commanding authority by his renowned expression of the nominalistic theory of the 'legal fiction' doctrine which had its antecedents in Roman law of the Empire. Another interesting precursor was Innocent IV, the Pope who, in the middle of the thirteenth century, had developed a conceptualist view of the nature of corporations which served as a basis for the more thoroughgoing nominalism of his successors.

A realist reaction did not become manifest until the end of the nineteenth century, despite some mixed and not very clearly defined universalist and collectivist notions, such as those of Auguste Comte, Herbert Spencer, Durkheim and others. It was O. von Gierke who raised the standard of realist revolt against the strongly nominalist principles evident in the proposed revision of the German Civil Code. When the new code appeared in 1900, it was apparent that his objections had not been in vain. Political thought slowly began to turn against the full-blown nominalist conception to give greater emphasis to the power, prestige and right of collectivities at the expense of those of individuals. Communist, Fascist and Nazi doctrines depended for what shreds of respectability they could muster as thoroughgoing theoretical explanations of the true notion of society and of political parties and of the relation of the individual to them, upon a half-baked, twisted and distorted realism.

Sorokin compares the semi-developed pseudo-philosophies of Communism and Fascism to the cubist movement in art. Neither are satisfactory doctrines in their own right. Their significance lies solely in that they represent a fumbling revolt against the prevalent extreme nominalism of their time.

His conclusion is that just as the realist way of thinking about corporations and societies was prevalent in the ideational cultures, so nominalist doctrines in law become evident as sensate cultures rise and they weaken as such cultures decline. During their relatively short reign, idealistic cultural systems are characterized by mixed, eclectic and conceptualist theories of the juridical personality.

Unless these theories, and indeed the subject as a whole, are viewed within their wider cultural setting, Sorokin urges, they will never be intelligently understood, but every manner of fortuitous association with miscellaneous economic, religious, scientific, even geographical factors will be suggested as their proper explanation. This general defence of his main position as an historian and social philosopher is, of course, one he can use in support of all his summary surveys, but it appears specially forceful and apposite when applied to limited special problems such as that of legal philosophy in relation to collectivities.

Determinism and Indeterminism

The next 'First Principles' of social theory which Sorokin examines are those of the conflicting theories of determinism and indeterminism.

Again, with the co-operation of others, an independent review was made of the theories of the principal writers who, implicitly or explicitly, developed a theory illustrating these conflicting opinions which men have taken of their power to shape their own destiny.

Determinism denies that man has such power. Just as in the material world every effect or event has its cause, so in the human sphere, everything, including the minds as well as the actions of men, is regarded as the product of its cause. Indeterminism denies this necessary invariable relationship between phenomena and especially does it reject the idea that men lack free-will or the power of choice to modify their own fate.

Between these extreme and opposite views, there are several mixed theories. Some indeterminist theories allow freedom of the will, but believe, nevertheless, that many of man's actions are conditioned; some determinist theories are so qualified by special reservations, limitations and exemptions that they amount almost to indeterminism.

Other writers, such as Cicero and Plutarch, were not consistent, adopting determinism as a general principle yet refusing to believe in fatalism as a general creed. Cicero, following the writers of the New Academy, in speculative matters tended to regard probability as the only rule of life, but he did not carry over this view into his ethical writings, where he stuck much closer to the Stoic doctrines and the ethics of principle, which were, of course, more consonant with the old Roman ideational position. Other later writers deliberately combine both views, as Immanuel Kant tried to do with his theory of man's completely conditioned behaviour in this world of phenomena, but complete freedom in his real essence as a 'noumenal' being. Writers such as he and Malebranche used arguments which can be made to support both sides of the question. There are a large number of writers who cannot easily be classified under either of these two opposite schools of thought of determinism and indeterminism, and these Sorokin has necessarily omitted in constructing his estimates of the respective weight and opinion to be assigned to each class. As examples of the principal supporters of these contradictory points of view, the following names and their place in the scale of influence from 1 to 12 are selected from Sorokin's longer lists.

DETERMINISM

Pythagoras	8	*Heraclitus*	7	*Democritus*	8
Plato	12	*Zeno*	8	*Panaetius*	5
Cicero	8	*Nigidius Figulus*	4	*Varro*	5
Plutarch	8	*Marcus Aurelius*	6	*Epictetus*	6
Wycliffe	3	*Leonardo da Vinci*	8	*Luther*	8
Zwingli	6	*Melanchthon*	5	*Calvin*	6
G. Bruno	8	*Bacon*	7	*Kepler*	8
Galileo	8	*Jansen*	6	*Hobbes*	8
Guelincx	6	*Spinoza*	8	*Pascal*	7
Mandeville	4	*Hume*	8	*Malebranche*	7
Helvetius	6	*Holbach*	6	*Voltaire*	7
Diderot	7	*Kant*	12	*Priestley*	6
J. Mill	6	*A. Comte*	8	*Bentham*	6
K. Marx	8	*Engels*	6	*Spencer*	8
Bradley	7			*Tolstoy*	8

INDETERMINISM

Aristotle	12	Grosseteste	4	Glisson	3
Theophrastus	7	Albertus Magnus	8	Vico	7
Epicurus	8	St. Thomas Aquinas	12	Berkeley	8
Lucretius	8	R. Lully	5	Kant	12
Philo Judaeus	8	M. Eckhart	8	J. Edwards	6
Justin Martyr	5	Dante	8	Rousseau	8
Apuleius	6	Gerson	4	Condillac	6
Origen	8	Nicolas of Cusa	8	Fichte	8
Tertullian	6	Erasmus	5	Schiller	8
Plotinus	12	Loyola	8	Herder	6
Porphyry	7	Cardan	6	Goethe	8
St. Basil	6	Campanella	6	Whewell	6
St. Augustine	10	Gassendi	7	Schelling	8
Gregory I	4	Descartes	8	Carlyle	4
Maximus Confessor	6	Cudworth	5	Lotze	5
Alcuin	4	Leibniz	9	E. von Hartmann	8
St. Anselm	7	Malebranche	7	Dostoevsky	7
St. Bernard	5	R. Boyle	4	J. S. Mill	8
Abelard	4	Locke	8	Rickert	6
Peter Lombard	4	H. More	4	W. James	4
John of Salisbury	3	Bossuet	6	L. Stephen	7

It will be noted that, for the reason given above, Malebranche and Kant appear on both sides.

Summarizing the resulting balance of forces or influences, Sorokin arrives at the following table.

Table 4—INDICES FOR DETERMINISM AND INDETERMINISM

Period			Determinism	Indeterminism
580 B.C.-A.D. 100	..	..	678	212
A.D. 100-540	..	..	239	557
540-1500 ..	..	..	73	519
1500-1920	..	..	1302	1339
			2292	2627

In more detail he has constructed the following graph based upon the analyses of changing views by twenty-year periods over the same long stretch of time. His statistical tables, giving the detailed basis for this graph, are not reproduced here, but may be found in Volume II of Social and Cultural Dynamics.

Generally it is evident that determinism fluctuates with the fluctuations of other manifestations of sensate cultural forms, whereas indeterminism accompanies those of the ideational culture, the truth of faith, Realism and idealism. The mixed view indeterminism-determinism is characteristic of periods of idealistic culture.

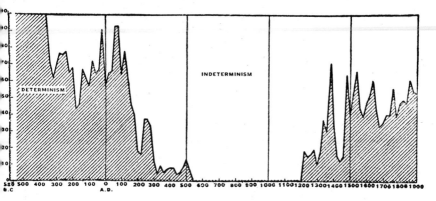

Fig. 9. FLUCTUATION OF DETERMINISM AND INDETERMINISM

Looking at the predominant opinion on the matter in our own times, Sorokin finds that the 'iron determinism' characteristic of most scientists and thinkers in the middle of the nineteenth century has softened considerably. No longer is mankind thought to be driven on by an inexorable, inevitable necessity. There is now a tendency to substitute the idea of probability for rugged determinism.

The Idea of Progress

Allied to the ideas of determinism and indeterminism, as fundamental explanations of the nature and destiny of human development, are other general notions on the subject of the progress and development of mankind. The idea of evolution stated by Charles Darwin in 1859 was a scientific statement which many took to be a complete proof of the reasonableness of that belief in progress which was then already widely shared and was being popularized by many writers, notably by Auguste Comte and Herbert Spencer. The doctrine of evolution has so completely coloured thought on the entire question of human development that the earlier theories it supplanted seem strangely remote, antiquated and obsolete.

As Sorokin's own theory of historical change is itself an attempt to explain the nature of the progress of history, it is not surprising to find that he is specially interested in the various notions on the subject which have influenced past ages. Apart from his largest work, *Social and Cultural Dynamics*, which presents the basic historical evidence from which his central ideas are developed, he has also returned to the subject in later books, such as his *Society, Culture and Personality* (1947), and more recently in *Social Philosophies of an Age of Crisis* (1950).

Attempts to account for the nature and direction of change in human cultural development have mostly proceeded either on the assumption that the change is always in one direction, whether for better or for worse, or on the assumption that the whole process follows a cyclical movement. Most people in the Victorian era believed that humanity was progressing steadily along the line of more freedom, democracy and increasing wealth. Such views are usually to be found in sensate cultural systems. In earlier classical antiquity, on the contrary, it was more general to believe the earlier traditional view that things were developing for the worse; that the Golden Age was in the past and that mankind was steadily departing from it.

In contrast to such linear theories are the cyclical theories. Sometimes they also characterize a sensate culture, particularly at a time when it is beginning to lose its hold on the loyalties of mankind. Oswald Spengler's vast work on *The Decline of the West*, which had great renown for a short while in Germany in the 1920's, attempted to popularize a somewhat imaginatively-drawn but essentially crude and subjectively conceived cyclical process. Efforts to explain cultural changes as purely mechanical uniformities are either the product of a sensate outlook or they arise at a time of mixed culture. Ideational theories of cyclical or endlessly recurring changes depict them as manifestations of inner transformations experienced by the ultimate or true spiritual reality, whether it be God, Brahma, Providence or Tao.

The ideational Hindu and Chinese cultures provide particularly striking cyclical theories. The Hindu theory of the cycle of world creation and dissolution regards it as occurring in four ages incessantly repeating themselves within the shortest time span in the pulsation of the world, 4,320,000 mortal years. These four ages are: the Krita Yuga (1,728,000 years), during which the creation of the world occurs; the Treta Yuga (1,296,000 years); the Dwapara Yuga (864,000 years); and the Kali Yuga (432,000 years), the age of decline and dissolution, which bears all the marks of Sorokin's sensate culture and which began, according to the *Vishnu Puráná*, in the fourteenth century. At the end of the Kali age, a Brahman with supernatural powers appears to destroy iniquity and re-establish the age of purity, or the Krita age, when the cycle recommences.

In China all the fluctuating processes of human affairs are regarded as but the special varieties of the eternal rhythm of the Yin, or negative essence, and Yang, or positive essence, each of which has its root in the other, and both make up the alternating rhythm to be observed, as the Chinese thought, in the fate of dynasties and of mankind. Sorokin characterizes this predominant Chinese view as being in the main that of a mixed culture. The ancient Chinese and Taoist cultures were, however, mainly ideational, while the later Confucianism was a more sensate culture with a doctrine of progress in three stages, beginning with the anarchy of a primitive epoch, the Disorderly Stage, to which a small capitalist society succeeded; the Stage of Small Tranquillity; that in turn giving way to the Stage of Great Similarity, marked by social order, mutual benevolence and reverence.

In Western European civilization, Sorokin draws attention to the uniformly cyclical theories of the sixth and first part of the fifth centuries B.C. in Greece, and their prominence in the fifth and fourth centuries, also with a more complicated period succeeding from the third century B.C. In the fourth century B.C., some ideas of progress began to appear along with a revival of older ideas of retrogression, which can be detected in early writers such as Homer and Hesiod before the sixth century B.C. Before Christianity had won any real influence, a new version of the cyclical conception was favoured by Stoics and Neo-Platonists. In all these confused streams of thought, Sorokin detects one expressing the still-lingering optimism of the decaying sensate culture, especially from the third century B.C. to the first century A.D.; another more pessimistic stream portending its decline, and a third, a definitely cyclical view, foreshadowing the generation and growth of the succeeding ideational culture, which was to last almost unbroken up to the thirteenth century A.D. From then up to the sixteenth century, a newer note can be discerned. The ideational inheritance, shot through with more sensate impulses, produced the idealistic colour of the Age of the Renaissance.

The general belief in astrology maintained the vogue of cyclical theories which endured with or without such support through the fifteenth and sixteenth centuries, although writers like Bodin, G. Bruno and Campanella contributed notably to a change in favour of the progressively linear conception of human history. The modern 'idea of progress' had its origin unmistakably in the seventeenth century. From then onwards it suffused men's thinking in literature, science, philosophy, political and social theory. Those like G. B. Vico, who continued to advocate cyclical conceptions, were little heeded.

I

Fontenelle, Montesquieu, Voltaire, Adam Smith, Priestley, Herder, Kant and others, helped to establish ways of thought which prepared the path for the application by Herbert Spencer, Lamarck and Darwin of the idea of linear evolution in biology and in the social sciences.

It was not until the twentieth century that mankind awoke to the realization that belief in the idea of progress itself was a very recent faith and that it has had historical antecedents of a very different character. In the nineteenth century, as Sorokin points out, the prevalent opinion took some linear, and usually a progressively linear, conception of change as the chief topic or main ordering principle in the social and humanitarian sciences. Anthropologists, sociologists, historians, economists, political and social philosophers and theologians have all popularized some type of the theory of progress, whether it be progress from ignorance to science, from instinct to reason, from despotism to liberty, from inequality to equality and so forth; sometimes regarding the development as progress in a straight line, sometimes as progress by stages, such as Comte's three stages, the theological, metaphysical and positivist. Now, however, such views are no longer blandly accepted as the unquestionable pronouncement of scientific discovery. In biology, in which the doctrine of evolution received its classic statement, it is still the dominant philosophy. Nevertheless a new interest is being given to cyclical and undulating pulsations in the phenomena of life. The social sciences have thrown overboard the notion that all human societies pass through a uniform sequence of stages in their course of development. Economic theory is no longer concerned so much with the economic stages of development to which German economists especially devoted attention in the last half of the nineteenth century, but it now concentrates more upon cyclical, recurrent and fluctuating aspects of economic phenomena. Nothing more strikingly illustrates this reversion to interest in cyclical theories than the great vogue of Spengler's *Decline of the West*. There has been no work of comparable influence supporting the older linear view of social development since 1914.

From such considerations, Sorokin concludes that it is probably correct to hold that the idea of a progressive linear evolution in the development of mankind and society is associated with a rising sensate form of culture, and that it is not found in the predominantly ideational culture, where cyclical theories are more generally favoured.

It is impossible to leave this topic without pointing to the obvious fact that Sorokin's own work is a resolute effort to demonstrate and to justify a pronouncedly cyclical view of historical development. He is, of course, very well aware of the fact, and in the fourth volume of his great work, on *Social and Cultural Dynamics*, he analyses, more thoroughly than any other writer has so far attempted to do, the broad philosophical and sociological ideas and concepts involved in a thoroughgoing cyclical theory of history. There he faces the question how cultures change; examining in turn such problems as the extent to which cultural systems change as a whole or in parts, the rise and diffusion of sociocultural phenomena, the ways in which changes in cultural forms synchronize and the extent to which it is possible to detect rhythm and phases in such movements, resolutely attempting to identify two-three-five-phase and still more complex rhythms.

Not content with his demonstration of the nature of cultural change, Sorokin goes on to seek for reasons to explain why changes occur, and to found his own views upon the self-generated internal origin of such changes, which he describes as the principle of immanence of cultural change. These views will be described more fully in Chapter Eleven. It is first necessary to grasp in broad outline the general view Sorokin takes of history. It is not possible to focus within one volume the whole tremendous panorama of historical development which he presents and at the same time to deal in any detail with the more theoretical problems of sociology arising from his conclusions.

CHAPTER SIX

Science

Sorokin's review of the historical development of the guiding principles of human thought and philosophy extends to include a survey of some fundamental principles of modern science and therefore of other more specialized general principles analogous to those of determinism and indeterminism already examined above. Such are the basic elements or categories of human thought concerned with time, space, number and causality and the general scientific theories to which they make an essential contribution.

While it is true, as Kant pointed out, that knowledge cannot be had unless the mind is able to think in terms of cause and effect, or of space, or of time; nevertheless, Sorokin observes it is equally clear that different minds at different times have used these inescapable notions, these fundamental *a priori* categories, as Kant called them, in very different ways.

Theories of Causation

Both the ideational and the sensate mentality make use of the indispensable category of causation, because both believe that everything in the world results from some cause or may be explained by some reason. But whereas the sensate mentality regards the relationship between cause and effect as constant and invariable, such an idea is by no means characteristic of the notion or category of causation in an ideational cultural system. The prevalence of indeterminism in ideational epochs has already been described, and the ideational notions of causality not surprisingly are those of indeterminism. The explanation lies in the fact that the ideational mentality seeks in the world beyond the senses—in God, Brahma, Tao, Providence or the devil—for the true cause of all happenings and events. The sensate mentality will not look beyond the world of sense perceptions or the sensate world for such explanations. Idealistic and mixed mentalities will look for them both, to the supersensory as well as in the domain

of the senses. These logical expectations derived from a bare consideration of the nature of each dominant cultural system are confirmed, Sorokin holds, by a survey of the various views expressed on
the question by writers in various epochs.

In India, for example, the Hindu's conception of causality in the
Vedas and in the Upanishads was predominantly ideational. The
course of nature and of the world were regarded in these works as
manifestations of the supersensory Brahma or other powers. In China,
however, Sorokin considers that a more mixed view of causality prevailed. Nevertheless, as he points out, all changes were accounted for
by Chinese sages not by causality or special causes but in the first
place by Tao, the Principle of Order that rules the world, and then
by the derivative principles of Yin and Yang. Such notions seem just
as wildly remote from the scientific atmosphere of modern Europe as
do those of the Hindus, since they also seek explanations of things and
events in a world beyond the senses, in an imaginary framework com-
pounded of fantasy or of dreams. To dispense with the notion that
every effect must have a cause and to look for all explanations of
happenings in the world to such notions as order and harmony as
the Chinese and Japanese are said to have done, is to live in a
different universe from that of Western European culture. Yet the
nature of Chinese civilization makes it clear that, whatever may have
been their underlying philosophy, the Chinese were capable of close
attention to concrete things in medicine, in chemistry and in
agriculture.

In Western European thought, the ideational and sensate views of
causality fit neatly enough into the broad trends of development for
which cumulatively impressive evidence has already been produced.
Before the fifth century B.C., as the writings of Homer and Hesiod and
as Greek religion and mythology make clear, the Greeks considered
happenings in the sensate world to be caused and controlled by supersensory agents. Beginning with the second half of the sixth century
B.C., and lasting throughout the fifth and well into the fourth centuries, these earlier supernatural notions were mixed with more sensate
views in the idealistic conception of causality best illustrated by the
philosophy of Plato and of Aristotle. In the *Phaedo* and *Timaeus*, Plato
develops his view of the supersensory idea as the real cause of observed
facts. Aristotle gives a more developed theory in his doctrine of the
four classes of causes: formal, efficient, material and final. Of these,
the material cause or matter, and often the efficient cause, belong to
the sensate world, but the formal cause and especially the supreme final

and first cause, or God, belong to the ideational world. Aristotle clearly seeks to relate in one system of thought the mundane with the transcendental, mechanism with finalism, and the sensate world with the ideational world. His influence, like that of Plato, endures to this day. After the fourth century B.C., his views were soon reduced by the Stoics and Epicureans to a sensate dead level, in which the efficient cause alone was considered to provide all that a theory of causation required. From the beginning of the Christian era until the fourth century A.D., the most diverse views—ideational, sensate and mixed— are all found, but the trend was towards a rise of ideational theories of causation, not only with Christianity but in the Neo-Platonic thought of writers such as Plotinus. This trend ended in the fifth century A.D., in a complete victory for Christian ideational views of causality. They endured almost to the end of the twelfth century A.D. During these long ages, the will of God was generally accepted as a sufficient ground or explanation of all forms of change. From the end of the twelfth to the fourteenth century, a change is noticeable which resulted in the replacement of the ideational conception of causality by the mixed and particularly the idealistic idea. The time was at hand for a revival of the mixed Aristotelian doctrine of fourfold causality, to some extent accompanied also by the simpler Platonic idea.

These revivals of Greek idealistic thought are evident in the works of such men as Thierry de Chartres, Gilbert de la Porré, Alexander of Hales, Robert Grosseteste, Roger Bacon and others, ending with Albertus Magnus and St. Thomas Aquinas. After the fifteenth century the ideational conception of causality steadily lost ground before the rising sensate views. It was a tendency powerfully aided by the works of Copernicus, Galileo, Gassendi, Pascal, Kepler, Newton and above all by Descartes and the Cartesian philosophers from whom indeed the origin of modern philosophy is commonly dated. A generation later it culminated in the radical denial of the validity of any non-experimental inferences in the doctrine of Hume, whose view of causation eliminated the whole theory of cause by maintaining that we could know nothing more than the contiguity and succession of phenomena, and that the idea of any necessary connexion in their sequence was a purely human artificial product added by our mind. From this view, Kant's theory that causality is an *a priori* form or category of the human mind was a logical development, as was also the modern scientific habit of regarding causality as a mere routine of perception, best expressed perhaps mathematically as a purely functional relationship, without further enquiry into its nature or fruitless speculation as to what might lie behind the observed purely quantitative uniform relationships.

The idea of a necessary connection between a cause and its effect, which survived in the philosophy of Hume, has since been given up by many thinkers and in its place nothing remains except the idea of probability. A causal bond is considered to exist when it is possible to establish the existence of a high degree of probability in the uniformities observed to occur. The teachings of such well-known men as H. Poincaré, Mach, K. Pearson, Cournot, Clerk-Maxwell, Pareto, Planck and Einstein have powerfully aided this purely mathematical approach.

The result, Sorokin holds, has been a plunge into chaos. The attempt to base all knowledge upon a theory of probability, to reduce the notion of causation to a routine of perception, is to destroy the boundary line between science and non-science, truth and falsehood, the causal and the incidental. When there is nothing to choose between one causal law and another except expediency or the purely pragmatic test which finds that one proposition is more convenient than another, the world and reality become something liquid, frameless, uncertain and fantastic.

In scientific theory, as in other fields, the sensate cultural system has worked itself out by developing a scepticism about science and empiricism itself, thus sapping the very foundations of its own knowledge.

Sorokin goes on to illustrate this development by referring briefly to the variations in other fundamenal concepts of scientific knowledge, especially the notions of time, space and number.

Time

There are the ideational theories of time looking for absolute time in another world than ours, and there are the sensate theories for which time is a phenomenon relative to the movements of the world of the senses. Writers such as Poincaré and Mach reject absolute time and space as metaphysical and useless because they cannot be measured. For them, as for thousands of scientists, that alone is real which is measurable. The properties of time, therefore, are nothing but those of the clocks, and the properties of space are but those of the instruments of measurement. Number also plays an entirely different role in an ideational cultural system from that which it occupies in a sensate system. The use of numbers as symbols, the belief in magic numbers, is characteristic of the 'numerology' of ideational thinkers and is entirely foreign to the scientific mathematics of our sensate age for which quantitative knowledge alone is real knowledge. Sorokin does not deal in any detail with the history of mathematics, but he refers in a footnote to the fourth volume of his *Social and Cultural Dynamics* (page 752) to the somewhat discouraging results of the anti-intuitional mathematicians and symbolic logicians to prove anything and everything in mathematics without any recourse to intuition, as Whitehead and Russell sought to do in *Principia Mathematica*, for instance.

Atomic Theories

When these first principles and categories of human thought show such marked fluctuations, it is also to be expected that general scientific theories to which they contribute and in which they are somehow held together, should also change. Sorokin illustrates the argument by briefly tracing the history of the atomistic theory, the theory of light and the mechanistic and vitalistic interpretation of the phenomena of life.

In doing so he corroborates the expectation that atomism, as a form of materialism, should develop in association with the empirical system of truth, with mechanistic materialism and in general in a sensate cultural system. In Greek tradition the atomic philosophy was traced back to a Phœnician, but its sudden vogue at the hands of Leucippus and Democritus in Greece at the end of the fifth century B.C. was shortlived. The idealist movement under Socrates, Plato and Aristotle had no use for atoms. Epicurus almost a century later attempted to revive the outcast theory, but had no noticeable success. Asclepiades in the first century B.C., from whom Lucretius learned, was almost alone in following atomic philosophy, and Lucretius himself (99-55 B.C.), who first brought the doctrine prominently before the Romans, did not succeed in popularizing it. After the death of Galen in 200 A.D., atomism disappeared from Western Europe for a thousand years, although some acquaintance with it survived, through Byzantium, among the Arabs. In the twelfth century, however, atomic ideas made a hesitant reappearance, as the writings of Adelard of Bath and William of Conches testify. These few and faltering beginnings found little echo. In the thirteenth century, Roger Bacon took the prevailing view against atomism. Despite the partial recovery of the Greek and Roman classics, particularly of Lucretius (in 1418), it was not until the seventeenth century that atomic theories began to come into their own, particularly through the works of Francis Bacon and Gassendi.

Without attempting to follow in detail the various views of the ultimate nature of reality expounded by Descartes, Boyle and Newton, to whom Sorokin refers, or by Francis Glisson and Leibniz, whom he omits, it is clear that the seventeenth century launched scientific thought upon an atomic conception of matter which was notably developed a hundred years later by Lavoisier, Dalton and Gay-Lussac. In the twentieth century, however, the firmly held belief that atoms are physical realities came under attack. The sequel may perhaps be best indicated by Eddington's statement in 1928 that 'the physical atom . . . is a schedule of pointer readings'.

Sorokin's brief and compressed historical review, necessarily much further abridged here, indicates clearly enough that atomism is positively associated with the empirical system of truth and with sensate culture, and that it owes its vogue and popularity to the type of mentality supporting them.

Biological Theory

Similar assertions can be made about the development of biological theories, particularly the association of vitalistic theories with ideational culture and of mechanism with materialism and sensate culture. Sorokin illustrates these matters by a brief reference to doctrines about the origin of life itself, showing that in an ideational culture epoch, such as the Middle Ages, most people believed in the spontaneous generation of life (abiogenesis), whereas in our modern sensate culture such a view is completely rejected in favour of biogenesis on the ground that it alone can be experimentally justified, regardless of its logical inability to contribute anything to the baffling problem of the origin of life.

Theories of Light

Theories about the nature of light may not seem explicable by Sorokin's theories, yet he points out the interesting fact that the three main theories about the nature of light are associated with the main cultural epochs. They were first, that light emanates from the eyes, the visual-ray theory; second, that particles are detached from the surfaces of all bodies which are impressed on the eyes, the corpuscular theory; and lastly, the wave theory that light is an impulse propagated through a pellucid or diaphonous medium such as the modern luminiferous ether.

That the corpuscular theory should be associated with atomic theories is plausible enough. In ideational periods very few people bothered themselves about the nature of light, but the general tendency was to believe the emission or visual ray theory.

In idealistic periods there were mixed views, with the visual ray theory and the undulatory or wave theory predominating. From the sixteenth to the twentieth centuries, the visual ray theory gave way to the more sensate undulatory theory and still more to the corpuscular theories. The twentieth century again shows a reaction against the nineteenth century views, Sir William Bragg going so far as to say in 1921 that 'on Mondays, Wednesdays and Fridays we use the wave theory, on Tuesdays, Thursdays and Saturdays we think in streams of flying energy *quanta* or corpuscles'.

Sorokin's investigations into scientific theories do not extend as deeply as those into the history and forms of art and philosophy and he does not contend that all scientific theories and the oscillations in their prestige and credibility can be demonstrated to have a tangible connexion with the changes in ideational, idealistic and sensate forms of culture. Nevertheless the critical and fundamental concepts he has selected and studied seem to establish adequate grounds for believing that, in the field of science as in that of art and philosophy, his main cultural systems may afford a frame of reference and interpretation capable of holding together and illuminating not merely the rise and fall of various activities, fashions and theories but of emphasizing, in a manner never before realized, their essential interconnection and fundamental unity. Their utility in this respect will stand out all the more clearly if they are compared for example with other efforts to discover plausible cultural and sociological correlations of scientific thought, notably the extraordinary contortions and verbal jugglery to which those unfortunate folk are committed who decide to rest satisfied with Marxist-Leninist interpretations of the world and of man.

CHAPTER SEVEN

Ethics Law

From scientific and philosophical thought and speculation, Sorokin turns next to human endeavour and conduct and to the theories men have elaborated about them. Between the theory and the practice of morality there is often a great gulf. Men often see and approve the good, but follow evil to the extent that they are not restrained by law and the police. Sorokin accordingly distinguishes the lower level or the 'moral minimum' which society demands of all its members, expressed in its purely juridical norms and values; and the moral and ethical values which in a developed, integrated ethical system represent the developed human conscience, the peak of the moral mentality of the society.

Ethical systems can readily be classified as ideational, sensate or idealistic. The commands of an ideational ethical system are absolute, as is to be expected from its nature and purpose. Its nature is usually determined by its origin in the will of God or of some supersensory power. Its purpose is to bring its followers into unity with that supreme and absolute source of value. There can be no question of its principles being used as a means for anything and anybody. An ideational ethical system cannot be intended merely to increase the sum of sensate happiness, comfort, pleasure and utility. Consequently any notion of expediency or relativity is quite foreign to it.

A sensate ethical system, on the contrary, is a series of man-made rules, justified and deserving of respect only to the extent that they increase the total amount of happiness, comfort, utility and pleasure enjoyed by man, either individually or as a group. Such a system is essentially relativistic, since the rules change if conditions change and they lose all their force if they cease to produce the happiness, pleasure and other tangible practical ends for which they were designed.

An idealistic ethical system occupies a position midway between the ideational and sensate systems. It derives its main principles, which are absolute, from the command of God or of some other supersensory, supreme authority, but it acknowledges secondary principles such as the commands of reason. These are relative and therefore changeable. So also its aims are service to the absolute ethical value, or God, and are therefore transcendental, and at the same time they are related to conditions of the everyday world, since it holds that happiness in this life is the reward of those who serve God.

Sorokin accordingly reviews the long history of men's thoughts and speculations upon the grand questions of right and wrong and on the ground and source of all value. His aim, once again, is to arrive at some reasonably precise estimate of the principal types of ethical theory and of the relative influence and importance of the writers and thinkers in the two main schools of thought: the sensate and the ideational.

Sensate theories of happiness range from the more inclusive and philosophical class which regards the aim of human conduct to be the attainment not merely of the total sum of sensual pleasures, but of the more noble, lasting and more refined non-sensual pleasures as well. This is the philosophical doctrine usually referred to as eudæmonism. There is a second less inclusive branch of the ethics of happiness which is content to regard the desirable and the good in life as the sum of separate, singular, sensual pleasures. This type of ethical theory is more carnal than eudæmonism and is satisfied with short-term results. It is the doctrine of Hedonism. Utilitarianism, the third form of the ethics of happiness, emphasizes in Sorokin's opinion, the means of obtaining happiness rather than explaining what happiness itself is.

Ideational ethical systems typify the ethics of absolute principles. The ethics of love, as in the purer Christian tradition of St. Francis, for example, is a well-known form of the ideational system. The ethical principles of some ideational societies seem to have been of a very different order, involving human sacrifices and similar harsh and inhuman practices and beliefs.

Idealistic ethics merges the nobler forms of eudæmonism with the ethics of principles.

In illustrating fluctuations in the influence of the various schools of thought, Sorokin concentrates upon distinguishing the ideational school advocating the ethics of principles including the ethics of love, and the sensate school advocating the ethics of happiness, utilitarianism or eudæmonism.

Supporters of the idealistic theories do not form a third separate class, but are placed in the one or in the other of these two main classses which they seem chiefly to favour. Without reproducing here the statistical tables summarizing the results of his analysis of ethical theory, or the detailed list of thinkers contributing to the two main forms of ethical theory, it will suffice to present the charts based upon that data.

From these diagrams it is apparent that the ethics of happiness was of small account up to the second part of the fifth century B.C. Moral values were held sacred. They were regarded as the commands of the immortal gods, not to be called in question or doubted by mortal man. In the second half of the fifth century B.C., and in the fourth century, there is a great and sudden change. The ethics of happiness in a noble

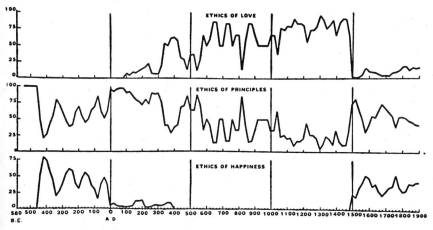

Fig. 10.   FLUCTUATION OF ETHICAL CURRENTS

and eudæmonistic form then appears, and before long the more sensate ethics of the Sophists. Both Plato and Aristotle are placed by Sorokin in the idealistic class as men who believed in the ethics of principles. Both are, therefore, included as examples of the ideational form of ethical philosophy, although Sorokin holds that Aristotle is nearer to the sensate school as Plato is to the ideational school.

Throughout the fourth, third, second and first centuries B.C., the ethics of happiness was in the ascendant, declining in the first century of our era and going underground in the fourth century A.D. Then, from the fifth century A.D. to the end of the fifteenth century, ideational values seem to have dominated men's thoughts. To learn the will of God and to obey His commandments was then the supreme rule of conduct. All sensate considerations, such as individual happiness or enjoyment, were held to be of no account in comparison with holiness and devotion of the whole life to God. Thousands of men and women sought to accomplish their vows of poverty, obedience and chastity as monks or nuns in seclusion from the world.

Although no writer before the end of the fifteenth century can be found to expound a sensate system of ethics in opposition to this otherworldly philosophy, a considerable change in the climate of opinion begins to be observable from the end of the twelfth century onwards. A place begins to be found in the works of such writers as Peter Abelard, St. Thomas Aquinas, Roger Bacon, Dante and Petrarch, for a note of sublime eudæmonism allowed always only in so far that it does not contradict the commands of God. All such writers had an ideational training and a religious outlook. Nevertheless the same idealistic tendency noticeable in the literature of the period (see Chapter Four) can be detected in their works.

The sixteenth century, the time of the Renaissance and Reformation, saw a sudden enormous increase in sensate systems of ethics. The seventeenth and eighteenth centuries witnessed a slight reaction, but in the nineteenth and twentieth centuries sensate ethics in a frankly utilitarian and hedonistic form dominated, not merely progressively to subordinate the ethics of principles or of love, but also to weaken the eudæmonistic ethical doctrines. It is worth while to compare Fig. 10 with the chart illustrating the fluctuations in the view taken about the nature of universals (Fig. 7 on page 112), for it is evident that single-minded devotion to universal or general concepts, such as duty, honour, love, is not likely to be so general among nominalists as among realists, a fact which the two diagrams help to show.

In a few interesting paragraphs, Sorokin again relates his views of ethical development to those developed in Germany by Max Weber and Ernst Troeltsch and in England by R. H. Tawney on the subject of religion and the rise of capitalism. Sorokin agrees with these writers in their views about the ways in which the reforming theories of Luther and Calvin, and of the other dissenting creeds, undermined ideational ethics by justifying, glorifying and sanctifying a utilitarian sensate mode of life. He completely rejects, however, their theory that Protestantism was in any real sense the cause of modern capitalism. Both the rise of Protestantism and the rise of capitalism and of modern economic practices were really manifestations of the great underlying movement of cultural life away from ideational and otherworldly values towards a sensate, mundane, carnal system. The same essential transformation, although in a different form and degree, took place within the Catholic doctrines and moral teachings of these centuries. To regard, therefore, the Protestant Reformation as the cause of capitalism is about as logical as to regard the growth of whiskers on a man's face as the cause of his growing from boyhood to manhood. This short reference indicates how Sorokin's theory of cultural development is able to set in a new and illuminating perspective an exceedingly plausible and well-established sociological theory of economic development which, however, must now be given up in the terms in which it has hitherto been stated.

As the high periods of the ethics of happiness, Sorokin notes 1560-1620, 1760-1780, and finally from 1880 to our own day. He also advances the more hazardous view that most of the sensate systems have become more sensual, more relative, more earthly and more carnal than they were during the greater part of the history of Greece and Rome. Certainly he finds little difficulty in illustrating this view by reference to certain aspects of contemporary American life with its elevation of utility and hedonism into the guiding principles and dominant traits of life and behaviour. He points to the way in which almost anything is now turned, if possible, into a source of monetary gain, whether it be titles, religious preaching, the birth of quintuplets, quadruplets, or fame in sport, politics or crime. Money-makers tend to be accepted as the natural leaders of society. Socialists and communists who make a violent denunciation of this state of affairs part of their stock-in-trade, have, on a final analysis, no better principles to offer. Their aim also is money and material satisfaction, but they want it for larger social groups and for the masses, not forgetting themselves.

The vague notion that modern Communism may offer a deeper, more satisfying faith, almost fit to be dignified with the title of a new religion, can therefore conclusively be shown to be a delusion. The Marxian thesis, for which millions of converts are actively being sought, has been summarized as one purporting to be able to show 'that all constitutions, laws, religion and other so-called spiritual results of man's historical activity are in the long run determined by the material forces of production—tools and machines—together with, of course, natural resources and the skill to operate them.' After abolishing such so-called spiritual results, the Marxists usually attempt to bring them in again by a back door. Stalin's *Dialectical and Historical Materialism*, for instance, has a passage to the effect that 'far from denying the significance and role in history of social ideas, theories, views and political institutions, Historical Materialism emphasizes the role and importance of such factors in the life of society, in its history. . . . Their significance lies in the fact that they facilitate the progress of society and is the greater, the more accurately they reflect the needs of development of the *material* life of society. New social ideas and theories indeed arise only after the development of its *material* life has set new tasks before society. But once they have arisen, they become a most potent force which furthers the *material* progress of society. It is precisely here that the tremendous organizing, mobilizing and transforming value of new ideas, new theories, new political institutions becomes manifest.' The keyword in the above quotation has been put here in italics to indicate how its whole doctrine illustrates Sorokin's theories of the sensate cultural development of our times. Judged by that standard, the High Priest of the new creed has no new insight to offer. Indeed, like Aaron of old, he sets up a Golden Calf because that is what the people demand, or what he thinks they will demand. The appeal such a doctrine may be expected to make to the crushed, depressed, dragooned and poverty-stricken masses of Russia would not be difficult to understand. Had it gone no further there would be less cause for complaint. What is historically and scientifically untenable is the attempt to put forward so crude and limited a doctrine as a basis for a pretended new social theory, as a general principle of ethical validity.

Russia, and those who in their hearts give allegiance to the ideas circulated in Russia by the authority of the Communist Party, for no other ideas are allowed, is clearly some centuries behind the times. It seems that a purely sensate philosophy, already becoming obsolete in the West, is being proclaimed as a new gospel in the East. That it is new there is one secret of its strength. Another is the extent to which the Communist doctrine has been able to stimulate the loyalties, the sense of fellow-feeling and partnership which comes when groups of men work together in a common enterprise. There is probably no greater force, short of religion, making for social cohesion and national unity than this inspiration arising from joint activity for common end that everybody wants. Cleverly realizing this human characteristic the totalitarians have apparently gone far to exploit it successfully by a combination of propaganda and compulsion. So much so that many of their victims and not a few spectators are for a time deceived.

The essential hollowness of a pseudo-religion, openly and for long very violently anti-religious, that has no other principle than the pursuit of material welfare is, however, becoming generally evident. Moral atomism, relativism and nihilism are its inevitable outcome, for it has no absolute principle. To that result add the rule of force and coercion in the relations of individuals and groups. Sorokin published this verdict two years before the outbreak of the world war in 1939 with its long record of almost unbelievable horror and barbarity and it aftermath of crime and unrest.

In the light of Sorokin's principles, it is not difficult to see the moral bankruptcy of the Fascist, Nazi or Communist police states. For such systems serve no moral values transcending individual or national self-interest narrowly conceived as an increase of wealth or of power. Ask to what good ends the wealth and the power are to be devoted and there is no answer—except more wealth and more power. What is yet more damning is that objective values are regarded as of no account in the pursuit of such ends. The police state owns no loyalty to the principles of true culture, to the beautiful, the true and the good. These words mean merely what the gang leaders want them to mean at any one moment. As a result it has been sufficient to label any nonsense as the latest Marxist-Leninist interpretation for the tame and docile masses to accept it, a situation reminiscent of a circus in which well-trained animals respond to accustomed noises from a bell, a whistle, or a whip. The value and dignity of human life has no meaning in such a system, which spurns the sacred rule that human beings are never to be used for purely selfish ends as tools or instruments for another's satisfaction as they notoriously are so used in vast numbers not only in the slave gangs and concentration camps of modern police states.

The outcome of the ethical section of Sorokin's work is to establish once again that throughout human history, the ideational cultural systems had greater comparative strength than the sensate cultural systems. Summarizing his statistical conclusions on this aspect of his survey, Sorokin presents the following totals:

Table 5—TOTALS OF THE INDICES OF RELATIVE INFLUENCE OF ETHICAL DOCTRINES

Period	Ethics of Happiness	Ethics of Principles	Ethics of Love
540 B.C.-A.D. 100 ..	239	356	—
100 B.C.-A.D. 600 ..	28	305	120
A.D. 600-1500	3	71	307
1500-1900	799	1061	228
Total	1069	1793	655

It is, as he points out, not very strange that social life should require mankind to put happiness below principles. He is not therefore inclined to think that there is much hope in the future for a scientifically calculated moral engineering of a purely utilitarian, hedonistic or eudæmonistic kind.

K

Criminal Law

After a fairly comprehensive investigation of the changes which have occurred in men's theories about right and wrong, Sorokin proceeds to a yet more detailed examination of the practical action men have taken in their criminal codes to give effect to their views. For these codes indicate not merely what forms of conduct are considered wrong in a given society, but *how* wrong they are thought to be.

Never before has any historian of comparative law undertaken so laborious a study and analysis of the content and its change in time of the main criminal codes of France, Italy, Austria, Germany and Russia. It was not possible to include Anglo-Saxon criminal law in the survey because it has not been codified.

After the period of early Feudal Law up to the twelfth century, Sorokin analyses codes of law to discover how ideas have changed about crime and punishment from the twelfth to the fourteenth century, from the fourteenth to the eighteenth century, in the eighteenth century, in the nineteenth century, and in the twentieth century. Just over one hundred criminal acts typical for all time and all societies are classified in nine groups:

They are crimes against

Physical person.
Moral person.
Property.
Religion and religious values.
The family.
Sex crimes.
The certainty of the evidential means and documents (*e.g.*, forgery, perjury).
Social economic customs and habits.
The state and political order.

Sorokin's summary review of the history of the criminal codes of the five countries establishes how the types of punishable actions fluctuate from one period to another. He shows that it is not true, as it is commonly believed to be, that in the course of time the number of the types of action punishable by criminal law increases. They change and the changes are similar to those followed by all compartments of culture, a reminder, if one were needed, that criminal law also is an inseparable part of an integrated culture.

When a culture passes from the sensate to the ideational form, a series of actions not regarded as criminal in the sensate period are included in the criminal class. They are mostly crimes violating ideational values, particularly religious values, and action is taken against them with little or no regard for mere individual or social utilitarianism, hedonism or eudæmonism. New forms of punishment are also introduced of an ideational nature, such as interdiction and excommunication. The punishments tend to be more severe than those provided by normal sensate criminal law, probably because the ideational period succeeds one in which sensate impulses have run riot, with the result that the human personality is deeply demoralized and disorderly. Ideational values, moreover, have the task of restraining the natural inclinations of sensate man, and that naturally requires greater pressure than sensate law would apply. It is hardly necessary to point out that this is not to affirm that severe punishment is necessarily a sign of an ideational culture.

The contrary change from the ideational to the sensate form of culture eliminates almost all ideational crimes from the class of criminal actions. Other crimes are revalued from the standpoint of minimising penalties upon such ideational actions as remain punishable and of penalizing especially actions endangering the hedonistic, utilitarian values of the society, and especially those of its commanding and controlling groups. This is a result which might be expected on philosophical grounds also, because in a sensate age, a nominalist philosophical outlook is unlikely to believe in the reality of the general principles or universals which an ideational realist age wishes to foster.

In so far as it is possible to generalize upon the comparative severity and amount of punishment in codes of either ideational or sensate inspiration, it seems that the governing factor is the extent to which the predominant type of culture is deeply rooted and established. If it is firmly planted, then punishment tends to be mild and moderate. When, however, cultural forms are changing, then penalties tend to become more severe. It is a tendency seen in the cruelty of settlers conquering new lands from native populations whose ethical ideas and practices are widely different from their own. It appears with astounding force in times of social revolution. Sorokin cites in evidence the cruelties in the Roman Republic in the first century B.C.; in the Dutch Revolution of 1566 and in Cromwellian England. The cruelties of the Roman Catholic Inquisition, with its fierce persecution of heretics, are another example. But never have cruel penal laws or pseudolaws exerted a more disastrous influence than during the French Revolution after 1789, or in the Russian Revolution after 1917, which eclipsed all previous records of butchery and oppression not merely in magnitude but in duration also.

Sorokin sums up these tendencies by quoting one of his earlier generalizations to the effect that whenever differences and conflicts arise within groups about standards of conduct and their observance or, as he describes it, whenever the ethico-juridical heterogeneity and antagonism increases, then the amount as well as the severity of punishment imposed by one part of a group on the other tends to increase. Other things being equal, the greater the differences and the antagonisms, the greater such increase will be. As they diminish, so the quantity and severity of the punishment tends to diminish also.

So brief a summary is necessarily inadequate upon a theme so vast that Sorokin himself was forced to omit from his volumes the extensive and detailed analysis of the mass of data upon which his conclusions repose.

CHAPTER EIGHT

Social Relationships
Politics and Economics

It remains to be seen how far Sorokin's theories can illustrate and illuminate those aspects of mankind's past which have usually been regarded as the special province of history, namely, the story of wars, revolutions and social relationships generally. From the title of Sorokin's largest work, *Social and Cultural Dynamics*, it might be assumed that he is interested in history as a sociologist rather than as an historian in the ordinary sense of the word. It should be clear from the previous chapters that, on his principles, the study of social forces and of society, which is the subject-matter of sociology, is but another aspect of the study of the forms and types of culture in history. There is, therefore, but one reality for the sociologist and historian alike and that is what he describes as the socio-cultural world, one and indivisible. Nothing but the inherent complexity of so vast a world and difficulties of presentation are responsible for the separate treatment of cultural and social movements. That is neither new nor surprising. What is new in Sorokin's work is his determined attempt to deal as exhaustively as possible with each and to attack with the utmost resolution the task of demonstrating the nature of the mutual interrelatedness of each. In the third volume of his *Dynamics*, therefore, Sorokin turns to the problems of society, selecting three main themes for detailed analysis: social relationships, including the family, village, guilds, church and state, and economic conditions; war between states, and finally internal disturbances within states.

Social Relationships

The first of these themes, social relationships, does not lend itself to statistical illustration, and, while this is not true of the second or third, it is unfortunately the case that adequate statistics are not to be had relating to wars and revolutions, particularly in earlier times. From a review of literature illustrating the history of social relationships, Sorokin draws a series of conclusions about their nature and development, of which merely a bare outline can be given here. For a fuller description and analysis, together with a list of the sources on which his studies were based, the reader must be referred to Sorokin's own works. The third volume of *Social and Cultural Dynamics* is, of course, the chief, but his earlier joint works with Zimmerman and Galpin, *A Systematic Source Book in Rural Sociology* (Minneapolis, 1930), and with Zimmerman, *Principles of Rural Urban Sociology* (New York, 1929), are also relevant.

Sorokin selects for historical study the Franco-German human universe in the Carlovingian and feudal periods, reviewing in turn the nature of relationships in the feudal state, the Church, the family, guilds, *Bünde*, corporations and other associations, village communities and urban communities. These were the main groups of which medieval society consisted. Their predominant characteristic in the early Middle Ages, up to the ninth century A.D., was that they were each held together by familistic bonds of various degrees of purity and intensity. *Fidelitas*, loyalty, is the keyword, for it supplied the most general bond, the common and universal form of social relationship in the Middle Ages. The subjects of the king were his *fideles*. It is true that *fidelitas* was established by a solemn ceremony which might be regarded as being in the nature of a contract, but it would be wrong to hold that the relationship once established was contractual in essence. It was much more akin to relationships within a family.

Compulsory relationships likewise were not absent from medieval societies. They were inevitable in the military organization. Apart from that, their main role was to link the serfs, the unfree and the semi-free classes to the free upper strata of society. Such are the broad characteristics of social relationship in an ideational society. Sorokin dates the first initial weakening of this early, predominantly familistic relationship at the end of the eleventh and at the beginning of the twelfth centuries. The change then foreshadowed was in the direction of increasing contractual relationships at the expense of the familistic relationship and to some extent of the compulsory relationship also.

Thereafter the trend was to become more pronounced, although, from the thirteenth down into the sixteenth centuries, the picture is very complex and somewhat contradictory. It was a period in which an ideational society was weakening under the impact of sensate ideas. The transition began to show itself in a disorganised system of social relationships which was provocative of unrest and disturbances. It is clear that contractual relationships and compulsory relationships in particular both grew at the expense of familistic relationships, and that this trend continued through the seventeenth and eighteenth centuries with the marked ascendancy of absolute monarchies typified by Louis XIV and by Frederick the Great. They did not survive unchallenged. In the nineteenth century and up to 1914, contractual relationships triumphed at the expense of compulsory relationships and, to a lesser degree, of the already weakened familistic relationships.

Now, however, there are signs of a change. Compulsory relationships are replacing contractual relationships and pseudo-familistic relationships are being developed. Of them Sorokin gives a pessimistic account. The new dictatorial police states cannot establish a real familistic relationship, even if their rulers and sycophantic entourage wished to do so. They are able to arouse some temporary emotion in the masses by attacking and villifying those whom, rightly or wrongly, the masses have regarded or have been induced to regard as their enemies. This is no way to create a family spirit, and indeed it was not long before the new rulers began to treat the masses as though they had conquered them. The bosses of the police states are described by Sorokin as 'dictatorial wrecking companies', who are not builders of the future but mere wreckers of the past. Sorokin reaches this conclusion after following the story of the developments in social relationships in some detail as they are manifest in the history of the state, the church, the family, village and urban communities, corporations, guilds and confraternities, in the bonds between the free strata of society and those between the free and unfree strata. Sorokin's own sketch is necessarily much shorter than he would wish it to be on a theme so vast that volumes would be needed to do it justice. To present its bare outlines in so summary a fashion is to do it less than justice, but sufficient will have been indicated to prepare the way for the first broad conclusion Sorokin draws, namely, that there has been no uniform trend in the processes analysed. It is only necessary for him to tabulate the broad main pattern of relationships for this fact to stand out clearly.

Eighth to twelfth centuries—Familistic, compulsory, contractual.
Thirteenth to sixteenth centuries—Weakened familistic, contractual, compulsory.
Sixteenth to eighteenth centuries—Compulsory, familistic, contractual.
Nineteenth century to 1914—Contractual, familistic, compulsory.
1914 onwards—Compulsory, familistic, contractual.

Whatever may be thought of Sorokin's analysis, it at least has the merit of going deeper into the question than any previous theories have done.

For example, Sir Henry Maine's well-known generalization that, in Western society, social relationships have developed from status to contract seems merely a rough approximation when contrasted with Sorokin's more precise statement of the matter. Similarly, it is impossible to agree with those who consider that there has been a trend or progress towards increasing sociality, solidarity, altruism (familism) or the reverse. Nor is it true that history shows ever-increasing compulsions and antagonisms between men and their fellows.

To state the course of development in human social relationships aright is but the first part of Sorokin's aim. He next wants to know what are the reasons for the fluctuations, to what extent are the sequences he describes likely to be found in the history of societies other than those of one part of Western Europe and, finally, how do they relate to his concept of ideational, idealistic and sensate societies.

Why then, in the first place, does one form of social relationship weaken and give way to another? Sorokin answers this question by invoking his principles of limits, according to which there are relatively few possibilities of innovation in basic social forms and processes, and by invoking also his theory of immanent changeability. If it is asked whether he means anything more by these impressive words than that things change because they do change, the answer is that he is able to give a deeper, richer content to his theory than such a reduction to tautological nullity implies. This is a claim to be more fully vindicated in the sequel (see page 236 to 240). The essential aspect of the matter is that forms of social relationship, like all sensory phenomena, belong to the world of becoming. Change is the law of life, biologically, psychologically, culturally. Not merely life but the material environment in which men live, act and feel is constantly changing also. Friendship may, therefore, give way to aversion or hatred, devotion to contempt, and familism into contractualism or compulsory exploitation. That such an explanation does indeed exhaust the matter may be seen more clearly when it is put into concrete terms. A leader, warrior, lord or priest, may by his inherent qualities sustain and inspire genuine familistic relations with lesser folk who depend and are willing to depend upon him. But it is not likely that all his successors will exhibit the same qualities, neither is it probable that his subject peoples will continue for ever to perpetuate a form of relationship when its ground or essence no longer exists. The formal relationship between the leader and his followers may no doubt survive for some generations, but it is then probably no more than a shell of its previous reality. The shell will easily become brittle and break in such circumstances. The search for a more secure and satisfactory relationship becomes inevitable.

Contractual relationships, which seem to promise to make good the deficiencies of the familistic system, before long reveal inadequacies that are felt to be intolerable. Sorokin illustrates the situation by referring to the replacement of the serfdom and villeinage of the Middle Ages by free and relatively free labour contracts. It was, he said, a great and noble achievement. In time, however, conditions changed. Suppose, he says, that hungry but free workers, with hungry families depending upon them, confront employers who are in no such economic difficulties. Then the freedom of one party is nominal and the contractual relationships he may be forced to make are in reality of a compulsory nature.

In the nineteenth century a crisis overtook the contractual wage relationship which could not be continued, or was not continued, except by driving hard bargains at the expense of the weaker party, which were inevitably felt to be inhuman and unjust. Here conditions again had changed. Sorokin does not pursue his analysis. It would, however, seem necessary to enquire how far that crisis in contractual relationships was in reality a direct outcome of vast and unprecedented increases in human population, which we have now learned to attribute less to a sudden and reckless increase in the size of families than to improvements in health and sanitation which enabled children to survive who would inevitably have died in the inferior conditions of previous centuries. The result was that the labour market was flooded with the offspring of parents who were quite powerless to bring about the necessary expansion in the national economy which would alone have provided them all with a living. To contemporaries it may have seemed that the fault lay with the parents, who, through ignorance or improvidence or both, were unable to rear their children and to launch them into the world as their parents and grandparents had on the whole contrived to do. Many employers, large numbers of whom had risen by fierce energy and determination to survive from the ranks of this huge surplus population, so used the contractual system that it became in effect a form of compulsion. On the whole, they made the system work by securing the necessary expansion of national wealth, although at an enormous cost. But what was the alternative at such a time? In later days also, new forms of economic compulsion arose, when millions became unemployed, not because they were faced with harsh contractual terms but because they could obtain no contract of any kind and were forced to rely upon public or state aid for survival. Juridically, says Sorokin, men were still free to accept the contract or not; but factually, in such overwhelming economic crises, there is no contractualism any more. It had to be replaced by something even worse; compulsorily imposed work with a small compulsory remuneration. The shell stays, the content is changed.

What happened in the former freely-operating contractual wage relationship has also occurred in other fields where, through changing conditions, contractualism has completely changed in character. Earlier liberties of speech, press, meetings, unions and political suffrage continued to exist in law. In fact, says Sorokin, in some countries they became monopolized by various private and public agencies. Before long the masses ceased to believe in their fictional freedoms and fell a ready prey to demagogues who openly slandered and vilified their liberties and the whole social system in which those liberties were supposed to exist. Hence the ascendancy of Communism, Fascism and Hitlerism.

In the relationships between nations, there has also been a breakdown. The old doctrine, held as sacred in Roman law, that contracts should be fulfilled, *pacta sunt servanda*, has given way to expediency. The Germans, who broke their promise to respect the neutrality of Belgium in 1914, not surprisingly had no intention of observing the Treaty of Versailles. Since 1919, the lack of honour among nations unhappily has all too many tragic illustrations and new examples continually occur. When expediency replaces strict regard for the sanctity of contractual obligations, the road to cynicism and nihilism becomes short and it will inevitably be taken. A thorough-going nominalist can take a short way with notions such as honour when self-interest drives him to do so. The compulsory relationships which the police states are imposing can provide no remedy for the consequences of refusing to honour contractual obligations and, in Sorokin's view, they are inevitably doomed. To withhold freedom, as they do, before long kills the chained and exhausts the chainers.

In this way, Sorokin expounds his apparently self-evident tautology that the causes of change in social relationships, so unmistakably recorded in history, are self-generated or immanent in the social process itself. At the same time, he makes it clear that there are strict limits to the forms of social relationships, so that, when one form is exhausted or worked out, there are no more than two other forms by which it may be replaced.

From the nature of the change, at which the very few examples quoted above can merely hint, it is not difficult to see the answer to the second major question that Sorokin poses, namely, whether there is anything inevitable in the sequence of such changes as can be observed in the history of Western European society. From the nature of the case, there is clearly no reason why the observed sequences should be universal and not merely one among others that are possible. How do the observed changes fit Sorokin's ideational-idealistic-sensate classification of social and cultural phenomena?

It seems that the more ideational any culture is, the more conspicuous are its familistic social relationships. The more sensate it is, the more those relationships are likely to be compulsory and especially contractual. Sorokin does not state the connection more positively, for he realizes that a definite answer is hardly possible to the question whether the apparent association of familistic and ideational culture is merely a coincidence or whether it has a deeper significance and is of a logical and functional character.

There are indeed, he thinks, good grounds for supposing that the association is more than merely coincidental. Ideational values, being those of absolute and religious principles, inhibit the sensual and carnal desires of those who are loyal to them. Consequently the urge to drive hard bargains is swamped by a fraternal spirit towards fellow brothers in God or in Spirit. A more fundamental reason is that in an ideational society it is the group, or the ideational principle of brotherhood in God, the *corpus mysticum*, which it is supposed to enshrine, that alone is real. The individual does not count, except in so far as he makes up the collective oneness of the society in which all are dedicated to a higher purpose. Such a view of the matter conforms to the findings in Chapter Five on sociological theories of universalism and singularism and on the philosophical theories of realism and nominalism.

Abstract considerations of this sort are, of course, proposed by Sorokin as no more than a general guide in interpreting the actual events of the Middle Ages in Europe. The social and cultural world of that time was not *purely* ideational, a caution stressed at the beginning of this study. There was, for example, the institution of slavery which the leaders of the Christian society inherited from the age-long tradition of the pagan world and which, despite their aversion to it, they could not quickly liquidate, although they proved to be the main agency first to mitigate it and later to abolish it. In this way, Sorokin attempts to account for the considerable development of compulsory relationships at this time in the shape of slavery and its medieval form as serfdom. He also draws attention to the fact that the familistic relationships were sharply limited by the extent of the ideational society supporting them. Outsiders were unable to participate in its benefits and were indeed often treated with the utmost cruelty. Sorokin's thesis can be illustrated by the strife between the patricians and plebeians in the early Roman republic; by the ferocity of the Christian crusaders and by the medieval treatment of the Jews and others regarded as heretics.

It is easy to see why a sensate society with its nominalist philosophy, not believing that groups or collectivities have any supersensory or transcendental reality, substitutes contractual or compulsory relationships for those of a familistic type. Not merely does a sensate culture put all the emphasis upon the independent existence and the desires and values of the individual, but those values themselves are thought of in sensory terms as denoting material commodities, objects and wealth. Consequently all men free to pursue their own way are almost certain to seek the same things. Competition and the struggle for existence cannot be much softened by appealing to the competitors to respect human brotherhood, the *corpus mysticum*, because it is of the essence of the sensate mentality to deny that such mystical entities are real. An idealistic society is required to soften and to control these extreme self-seeking drives and appetites. In the thirteenth, fourteenth and fifteenth centuries, Sorokin considers that social relationships showed that mixture of the familistic, contractual and compulsory forms which is one of the distinguishing marks of an idealistic culture.

The appearance of sensate man in the sixteenth century caused a tremendous explosion which rent the older fabric of social relationships. Violent, emotional and greedy, he was not to be restrained by the word of God or by his own bond. Physical compulsions alone could control him, and hence it was that the sixteenth, seventeenth and eighteenth centuries saw a new growth in compulsory relations and a notable increase in the real powers of central governments. The lesson was learned, and by the nineteenth century, after the French Revolution, sensate man was becoming more balanced and reasonable and more ready to settle down. He developed, says Sorokin, into a solid contractual citizen who wanted to bargain instead of to fight, to live and let others live. Hence the recent age of contractualism, the mature form of the crystallized and balanced sensate culture.

How this apparently stable state of affairs gave way in the twentieth century, and was followed by a greater amount of compulsory relationships than the world has ever before seen, is a matter of contemporary experience. Sorokin has alluded to what he regards as some of its causes. He characterizes recent efforts to devise some alternative to the contractualism that has broken down as being analogous to the efforts of the cubists to find new art forms. The result, which has taken the form of Hitlerism, Communism, Fascism and Socialism, is not familism or altruism but the collectivism of the hard labour prison, with its hatred and its coercion. It is a regime fundamentally opposed to familism and anything like it. The dictators successfully destroyed contractualism, but replaced it mainly by compulsory and mechanical slavery: soulless, mirthless, companionless, largely devoid of real altruism, real familism, real solidarity. It has created so far only the pseudo-solidarity of the executioners among themselves and the forced and pathetic alliance of their victims. During the years which have elapsed since this apt description appeared, the most fearful events have confirmed its deadly accuracy, not merely in Germany and the countries overrun by the Nazis, but in Russia also and in Eastern European nations overrun by Communists.

The results have been clearly destructive of human relationships as they have been developed in the course of Western civilization. How to build anew among the wreckage left by the hordes of modern spiritual huns, vandals and mongols, who have devastated the human heritage, bringing disasters far worse than those caused by their earlier prototypes, remains the problem to which Sorokin could merely point in 1937. Such, however, is his dynamic energy and concern for human values that he has by no means left this vital question at the point of merely stating our apparently insoluble current problems. Academic eyebrows in many centres of learning may perhaps have been raised upon hearing of the foundation in Cambridge, Massachusetts, in February, 1949, through the inspiration and under the leadership of Professor Sorokin, of the Harvard Research Center in Altruistic Integration and Creativity. Its immediate relevance to our current human situation should, however, be clear in the context of these pages. Sorokin has already issued the first of its publications, his own book, *Altruistic Love: A Study of American 'Good Neighbours' and Christian Saints* (Boston, 1950), and has edited and contributed to its second volume, *Explorations in Altruistic Love and Behaviour* (Boston, 1950). Other volumes are in course of publication.

Political Theory

Forms of government and leadership have obvious links with the question of social relationships in general, but they are usually discussed independently of the broader social and cultural environment in which they arise. It is one of Sorokin's many merits that he refuses to regard the two problems apart from each other, and that, before dealing with the political, juridical and ethical questions of the forms of government, he first considers the broad sociological background against which governments and leaders of governments are operating.

His thesis is simply stated. Ideational cultures breed theocracies; sensate cultures give supreme power to the rich, to the military, or to groups which physically dominate society, whether they be the organizers of economic or other empires, inventors and scientists or various manipulators and bosses down to powerful leaders of criminal gangs.

Idealist societies have a political regime and leadership, partly theocratic and partly secular, of the type of sensate societies. Stated as a logical deduction from his general principles this thesis is illustrated by supporting examples. The Brahmanic Buddhist, Tibetan and Taoist parts of Chinese culture have been essentially ideational, and their aristocratic and sociopolitical regimes have been theocratic in their essentials. The two thousand year ascendancy of the caste of Brahmans of India was such that although, formally, they did not rule, they were able, through their prestige and superiority, to make India in effect a decentralized theocracy. In Tibet there has been an age-old centralized theocracy under the Dalai Lama.

Western civilization shows similar characteristics. Before the sixth century B.C., Greece, then with a predominantly ideational culture, was governed by a king-priest. Already, before the time of Solon (*c.* 639-559 B.C.), Athens had, however, come under the domination of the rich and physically powerful. Ideational motives continued to exercies their influence, as may be seen in the poetry ascribed to Solon. Later, in the theories of Plato, with his advocacy in *The Republic* of the rule of philosopher-kings, a pronounced idealistic doctrine was developed, but it is clear that fully sensate views were then already current in the doctrines of Gorgias or of the sophist Thrasymachus whom Plato combats. Aristotle also took an idealistic stand in opposing the sensate forms of government: tyranny, oligarchy and mob rule; and in praising instead the three good forms of government: monarchy, aristocracy and polity instead. His warning that, above all, every state should be so administered and so regulated by law that its magistrates cannot make money was certainly not much heeded by the later sensate societies.

Rome shows a very similar development. The traditional account of the kings of the sixth century B.C. shows them to have been regarded as religious leaders. Their sacred duties survived the creation of the Republic in 510 B.C. A chief priest, *pontifex maximus*, then inherited part of the kingly religious powers, but the chief secular magistrates, the two consuls, were also invested with sacred powers and they performed sacred duties. All three, however, were elected by the people. It is well known how these awe-inspiring functions gradually paled into the light of common day. At the beginning of the first century A.D., a *pontifex maximus* was brutally assassinated by a political gangster, the butcher Marius, and a generation later that same exalted office was secured purely for personal political ends by a free-living, free-thinking, dashing political adventurer Caius Julius Cæsar, then only thirty-seven years old. The later Empire, despite the foundations so carefully laid by Augustus, failed to restore any ideational character to Rome's supreme leader, and at most succeeded in conferring upon him some pseudo-idealistic prestige which it soon became extra-ordinarily difficult to sustain because of the notoriously despicable characters of many of the succeeding emperors.

A very different state of affairs resulted from the increased power of Christian ideationalism towards the end of the fourth century A.D. Before long, Christian leaders, such as St. Ambrose, spoke and wrote as though the emperors were under their tutelage, a position which the emperors themselves seemed content to accept. From the fifth to the thirteenth centuries, Europe had a predominantly theocratic regime precisely at the time that its culture was ideational.

Signs of a changed outlook begin to be discernible at the end of the twelfth century, when the first efforts begin to be made, by Marsilio of Padua and others, to claim some greater weight for the secular arm, reconciling, after the manner of idealistic theories, in one system both the spiritual and the secular power. As though conscious of the impending danger, Pope Boniface VIII, in 1302, issued his Papal Bull *Unam Sanctam*, declaring, 'I am Cæsar, I am Emperor.' The subsequent arrest of the Pope and the removal of the Papal See to Avignon were sufficient answers to such a boast, providing conclusive signs that the days of theocratic government were over. The Babylonish captivity lasted from 1309 to 1377, and it was followed by the Great Schism in which two Popes, one in Avignon and another in Rome, disputed the heritage of St. Peter until the middle of the fifteenth century. It is unnecessary to pursue the story in detail. The collapse of theocratic government before the end of the Middle Ages in Western Europe is a matter of common knowledge. It may, however, be permissible to add to Sorokin's account a brief reference to the survival into the nineteenth century of the States of the Church in Italy with their antiquated, inefficient and corrupt administration, contrasting so unfavourably with a reformed state system such as that achieved in England. All who have read Sir George Trevelyan's *Life of Lord Macaulay* will recall the pungent language in which that doughty liberal idealist castigated the effete theocracy which he encountered during his first visit to Rome. Bad as that regime clearly was, the results of contemporary decay in the leadership of sensate societies in Italy, Germany and Russia are yet more horrible.

Sorokin catalogues the major activities, up to about 1936, of the minority parties who within living memory seized power in those countries; how they tore up the law of the land, stifled criticism, prohibited religious, moral or scientific beliefs deemed unfavourable to themselves, developed the most gigantic propaganda agencies in the effort to make themselves respectable and to manufacture that public support they knew themselves to lack. Along with all their crimes against the freedom of the human spirit went strict control and perversion of the educational system, monopoly of all the means of communication and the beastly terrorism and brutality of a secret police. He might have added that little better demonstration is needed of the consequences of complete lack of principle among large numbers of the population of a sensate society than the evident fact that the gangsters were able to recruit all and more of the thugs and bullies they needed to staff their censorships, their secret police, their concentration camps and their firing squads. That men can be so easily found for such inhuman brutal work is the clearest proof of the most shocking depravity. Their refusal to recognize any personal responsibility for the maintenance of moral values surely spells the death of civilization. The numbers of those with a sufficiently robust faith in liberal principles and in the absolute values of the human spirit, in the right and good, who accepted exile or death sooner than submit to the gangsters, armed as these were with the most formidable powers most brutally executed, were indeed large. Far larger were the masses whose loyalty to principle was too weak to ensure that the subversive movements might be brought to nought.

Lest it should be thought that the word 'gangster' is used here and elsewhere in this work (e.g., on pages 83 and 113) as a mere expletive, hate-word or animal growl in the same way that Communists shout 'Fascist beast' or 'enemy of democracy' or 'enemy of the people' at those they wish to attack, it may be as well to amplify Sorokin's arguments a little. A gangster is one whose dominant motive is a hatred, which he is prepared to back with the utmost violence, terrorism and brute force, of anything limiting his arbitrary power to use for his own personal satisfaction, in complete disregard for the principles of natural law and the rule of law, the possessions, the persons and the lives of other men and women, obviously without their consent. Political gangsters often try by some lying pronouncement uttered in the name of 'the people', the Reich, the Party, or 'the people's democracy', or by the trickery of fake elections, to simulate the willing assent of their victims to the swindle by which they are robbed, despoiled, starved or murdered. A gangster, therefore, is not merely uncivilized. He is the active enemy and wrecker of civilization.

Edmund Burke, who witnessed the first outbreak of gangster-rule to occur in modern times on a scale carrying a threat of mortal danger to European civilization, recorded his astonishment that the mobs of the French Revolution were able so easily to loot, rob, murder and to exult in murder. Contrasting this triumph of what he called 'the swinish multitude', with his own no doubt over-idealized picture of the way of life they sought to destroy, he provided in imperishable language an obituary of a ruined culture. 'Antient opinions and rules of life,' he said, were being taken away 'to be replaced by a barbarous philosophy which is the offspring of cold hearts and muddy understandings.' 'The age of chivalry,' he lamented, 'is gone. That of sophisters, economists and calculators has succeeded; and the glory of Europe is extinguished for ever.'

The melancholy future for Europe proved infinitely worse than he dared to imagine or that Sorokin dared to forecast in 1936. Bad as the violence and brutality of the French Revolution undoubtedly was, yet never in its most lurid moments could it have been believed that, after another hundred and fifty years, careful plans would be made, buildings and equipment would be provided, and a personnel recruited and trained to operate slaughter-houses for the extermination of men, women and children by the hundred thousand. Would Edmund Burke or any of his contemporaries, including those who professed such indignation at his contemptuous reference to 'the swinish multitude,' have dreamed that among the fruits of another century and a half of civilization would be the concentration camps and mass-murder installations of the German Nazis and the vast slave-labour camps of Russia and Central Europe in which hundreds of thousands would be condemned to toil, to starve and to die, beaten and tortured more brutally, more consistently and more persistently for far longer than the worst sadist could continue to ill-treat animals? When merely to be able to

L

flee home and country destitute, to escape such a fate, would be regarded as a boon? Those who attempted to answer Burke by saying that he pitied the plumage but forgot the dying bird certainly could not now repeat their question-begging sophistry.

The decay of a sensate political system, horrible as its results have proved, is upon Sorokin's theory only to be expected as the full consequences of sensate political theory and the sensate way of life are worked out in practice. Like all deep cultural movements, the course of politics and government follows its own immanent development. The destruction of Fascist and Nazi governments which has occurred since Sorokin described them in their heyday as evidence of the decay of sensate political life, could only be regarded as an inexorable immanent consequence of their own inevitable road to ruin if it is believed that it was their own immanent development which brought about the war in which they were overthrown. *Deus quos vult perdere dementat prius*: those God wants to ruin he first drives mad. The total result is therefore intelligible from the standpoint of Sorokin's claim that his theories provide keys to a better understanding of the past.

Once understood, they help to make comprehensible and even predictable scores of details about any given political system. A single quotation from the Code of Hammurabi or from a speech by Moses would, for example, be likely to indicate that it relates to an ideational society from which it is permissible to expect a theocratic government; the statement of laws as absolute commandments or taboos of supersensory powers; supernatural sanctions against offenders (*sacer esto*, excommunication, expiation of sins or crimes, etc.); a legal system employing supernatural techniques (ordeals); laws protecting ideational values of no direct interest or concern from a utilitarian, hedonistic point of view; education strongly influenced by theology; the inclusion of oracles, saints and seers in the political structure in which its leaders themselves undertake sacred duties; little development of contractual relationships and no great position of influence or authority reserved for the rich or physically powerful.

Such are some of the clues to historical understanding which Sorokin's theory provides relating to one limited aspect alone of the subject-matter of the present work. Amplified as they might easily be by references to earlier chapters stating the characteristics of ideational art, literature and philosophy, they are of cumulatively impressive significance. There will be scholars here and there to whom they may bring little that is new, especially in relation to specific areas of history in which, indeed, they may need considerable modification and restatement. But for the great majority of those with a general interest in the course of broad, sweeping social and cultural developments in past ages, Sorokin claims that his scheme delivers keys that open a multitude of doors and hidden passages in history.

Such claims should be judged not alone by the extent to which Sorokin's own scheme provides a reliable clue to the past, but also by the extent to which it shows up the inadequacies of earlier efforts, a study best pursued in the light of his recent work *Social Philosophies of an Age of Crisis*.

Liberty

The degree of freedom enjoyed by any individual in society is clearly an aspect of his social relationships and of the nature of the political authority to which he is subjected. It is also an aspect of that individual's own character or nature. Sorokin insists particularly upon this subjective aspect of the matter, since he argues that the only meaning human liberty can have arises from the relationship between human wishes and the means of satisfying them. Anyone who has many more aims, ambitions or wishes than he can attain with the resources at his command, inevitably feels limited, frustrated and not fully at liberty. Another person possessing the same resources, but with very much weaker desires and ambitions, will not be conscious of any lack of freedom. This last type of freedom is the inner type of freedom characterizing ideational societies. In the familistic social relationships described above, the apparent restraints imposed on its members is not felt by them as a restraint at all, because it provides them with a free realization of their wishes and desires.

Sensate freedom is not regarded in the same way as being capable of attainment through a limitation of desire. All the emphasis is put upon the external means of satisfying desire and upon the possession of those means by the individual. Sorokin points to the fact that sensate man cannot understand ideational liberty which for him appears to be at best self-illusion and at its worst a self-seeking doctrine making use of high-sounding phrases and ideas in order to exploit and enslave other people. Similarly, men devoted to an ideational culture look upon sensate freedom as a miserable subjection to external material conditions, and they consequently regard those exposed to it as playthings of blind material forces. A multi-millionaire will not feel free if his vast wealth does not enable him to gratify every whim or fancy. A stern ascetic, whose aspirations for union with God are satisfied, will not regard his sparse diet of bread and water as a deprivation.

The mixed form of freedom, blending wishes with desires in even measure, is characteristic of the well-balanced man who is not insensitive to material gratifications but, by self-discipline and control, does not allow his wishes for them to outrun his means.

Thus Sorokin is able to take one of the time-honoured topics of prudential morality and to relate it easily and intelligibly to a broad general historical philosophy. It is easy to see, for example, why the demand for political and civil rights does not develop in an ideational society whose kingdom is not of this world. It throws a new light upon the story of the struggle for human rights and fundamental freedoms when the effort to achieve them is seen to occur in sensate societies. The first theories about them in the field of political freedom appeared in Western Europe in the twelfth and thirteenth centuries. Not all classes of society were directly and equally involved at first in the social disturbances which led to the production of documents such as Magna Carta (A.D. 1215). The movement then begun in England has since steadily extended to encompass all classes, both sexes and all ages, as the long history of English constitutional law and the feminist and youth movements and nursery schools of modern times attest. The French Revolution in 1789, inaugurated by the Declaration of the Rights of Man, showed how deeply the sensate trend had affected all classes in France. The widespread unrest throughout Europe in 1848 was yet another symptom. Now, however, as in other cultural and social developments, marked changes have occurred in the attitudes of several countries towards personal liberties and political freedoms.

The Communist regime in Russia dismissed them as bourgeois prejudices. The Fascists of Italy and Hitler's Nazis, for ostensibly different reasons, followed the Communists' example. Other dictatorial regimes have done the same.

In countries still on the whole faithful to the doctrine of liberty and individual freedom, there have been, since Sorokin wrote, the most tremendous increase, although still under constitutional forms, in the powers of central governments. Brought into being under the stern necessities of a war for survival against the avowed enemies of liberty, these constitutional restrictions on free enterprise nevertheless have not lacked support, especially from the advocates of national planning or social engineering. In England, where Lord Keynes was perhaps more influential than any other man in disturbing traditional views, there has been a striking clash between the views of political and economic planners and those who mistrust them. Attacks on state control, such as those by Professor von Hayek in *The Road to Serfdom* or by Professor Jewkes in *Ordeal by Planning* and others, succeeded in capturing public attention, while more balanced and factual studies of the real nature of the process of social organization, such as those provided by the works of Professor C. E. Merriam, by Professor Herman Finer and by Richard Warner's *Principles of Public Administration*, have been very little heeded.

In seeking an explanation of the change from ideational to sensate ideas of liberty and freedom, Sorokin again neglects the influence of external forces, and puts all the emphasis upon his doctrine of immanent change. Each system breeds its own decay. There is a limit to the extent to which the most ascetically-minded ideational man can suppress the satisfaction of his bodily needs. The great masses of mankind put this limit very much higher than would a saint. When they are denied physiological, psychological or social satisfactions, they will try to get them. If they cannot obtain them peacefully, they will resort to violent means. Disorders, riots and revolts thereupon arise gravely to undermine society. If the process is not stopped, there will be a serious loss of vitality, followed by emigration, suicide or death.

That sudden and relentlessly-imposed frustrations can cause the decline and death of whole tribes and communities is, Sorokin considers, proved by the fate of many primitive peoples, Melanesians, Polynesians and Fijians, for example. The conventional explanation that exposure to unaccustomed infections brought by white races and that their consequent proneness to disease accounts for their decline, is, he holds, disproved by the fact that other primitive tribes, similarly exposed, have not died off as long as their ways of life were not interfered with seriously. The contrasting fate of the aboriginal Indian tribes in North and South America, and of the Maoris in New Zealand in the last hundred years illustrates the point.

Sensate liberty is possibly more rapidly self-destructive than ideational liberty because of the well-known rapidity with which repeated sensations pall. The need to satisfy any particular sense, that of hunger, for example, can be fairly easily met. But as long as sensory needs rule, the satisfaction of one of them merely tends to increase the demands of others. The more sensate men have, the more they want, while it becomes impossible to find the means to satisfy them all, because economic resources cannot be expanded fast enough. When it has been possible for a limited number of very wealthy people to command everything they need, the result not only for them but also upon the society in which they live, has often been demoralizing, devitalizing and disintegrating. Such was the fate of the Roman aristocracy in the decline of the Republic. Driven by desire they exhaust themselves in the search for new sensations until they may become, like Dorian Gray of Oscar Wilde's story, the oversensual seekers for perverse pleasures, which soon debilitate body and mind, spreading a trail of corruption wherever they go. They will not stop at scandals, indecencies, but by robbery and murder they ruin themselves and the society of which they are a part. No wonder, therefore, that it becomes necessary to restrain them. On the firm ground that 'the boon of liberty is a boon only when the privilege of its use is accompanied by a sense of responsibility', Sorokin is quite prepared to approve restrictions upon the liberty of speech and of the Press, great boons as he recognizes them to be. But when such liberty begins to be used for the printing and circulation of all kinds of valueless and indecent stories, purely sexual novels or artistically rotten and otherwise sensational plays, or for calumny, the discrediting and undermining of all values, or for most irresponsible and socially dangerous fiery propaganda—then, says Sorokin, such liberty becomes a social liability rather than an asset. Society must control such disintegrating forces or perish. There must be self-control and the limitation of desires if society is to survive, but this leads necessarily to ideationalism. In this way Sorokin demonstrates the immanent nature of the breakdown of sensate forms of liberty and of the rise of ideational liberty.

Government and Administration

The discussion about the various kinds of social relationships, political systems and liberty has been up to now in predominantly general terms. Seeking to penetrate more thoroughly into the subject, Sorokin goes on to look at them from the quantitative standpoint. He distinguishes between various systems on the basis of the number of social relationships involved in each. From that point of view social systems can vary almost infinitely.

The simplest system contains only one social relationship, a society whose members have but one link, that, for example, of collecting Nicaraguan postage stamps. An 'Association of the Collectors of Nicaraguan Stamps' is a social system or group that regulates only one relationship out of hundreds of others which its members possess. If that were really the only link between people in society it would be an example of a perfect *laissez-faire* system. The complete opposite to so simple a system would be a fully totalitarian system in which there were no free individual activities but all behaviour was controlled and regulated. Instead of one link between individuals, a dense series of links would then characterize the social network. In practice it is virtually impossible to point to absolute totalitarianism or to an absolute *laissez-faire* system. Some social groups multiply the fibres of the network of relationship and therefore tend more towards totalitarianism; in others, or at other periods, regulatory and regimenting rules are given up so that many fibres drop out of the network which thus moves towards *laissez-faire*. Such fluctuations are a constant feature of social and political processes.

History can be looked at again, in order to detect these periods of the decrease or of the intensification of social relationships or of the contraction and expansion of governmental control. Such a study not merely simplifies an otherwise confused and tangled story, but it shows up at the same time the meaningless verbiage, the thoughtlessness and superficiality of an enormous literature on socialism, communism, capitalism and liberalism and political organization generally. Instead of presenting the study of human societies as a clash of warring 'isms', it reveals the common basis of all of them, at the same time as it explains their variations on the basis of the varying number and complexity of their internal network of links; the number of fibres in each social network making up the relations of rulers and ruled; of authority towards its subjects. The reality of sharp differences and the fierce opposition between extreme types of the unorganized and the highly organized community are certainly easier to understand in the light of such an attempt to describe their true nature scientifically and dispassionately.

From this standpoint of the degree of government control, it is possible to understand the similarity which makes recent Communist, Fascist and Nazi systems species or classes of the same genus or large class of totalitarian states among which are to be found the state systems of ancient Egypt, Peru, Mexico and of China, especially in the eleventh century; of Rome under Diocletian, of Byzantium and of other systems of government in East and West. In all such states, the government controlled almost all economic life, much of family relationships as well as religious, educational, military and other activities. Like a spider's web, the network of the state system was so closely woven that the individual was hardly able to take a single step without touching it and bringing it into action. These early forms of totalitarianism were, Sorokin considers, more totalitarian than the Western state systems of the nineteenth century. Without attempting any statistical presentation of the rise and fall of totalitarianism, Sorokin briefly notes some of the more prominent fluctuations,

The Roman Empire, beginning at the end of the third century A.D. and especially under Diocletian, became very markedly totalitarian, and so it remained until it fell in the fifth century. Merovingian and Carlovingian Empires had a far less totalitarian form, while the feudal states, which followed, dropped an enormous number of relationships from the state network. Sorokin adds that the dropped functions were taken over by other organizations. Although his remarks are true of the central government, they should not, therefore, imply that the individual was liberated from external controls. With the decline of feudalism and the rise of national state systems, under rulers such as Louis XIV or Frederick the Great, the network of governmental control once again became denser.

By the end of the eighteenth century, *laissez-faire* liberalism had swept away many of the mercantilist controls and ushered in an era of private enterprise in which individuals were very largely left to manage their own affairs, usually on a contractual basis. Their freedom, although large in relation to what had been attainable hitherto, was by no means complete. The first encroachments upon it, admittedly in a very modest form, occurred before 1850. The first signs of the growth of the welfare state of modern times may be seen in Bismarck's policy of state insurances in Germany. It is unnecessary to list all the forms of state interference, beginning with the protection of women and children in industry, the creation of a police force, the inspection of factories, mines, workshops and ships, the enforcement of public health and sanitary rules, compulsory education and many other extensions of state activity, all of which began in England and in some other countries before the year 1900. They point to a trend which, as Sorokin says, made a tremendous jump with the World War of 1914-1918 and another jump, since he wrote, with the World War of 1939-1945. His conclusion, in 1937, that the present is an age of sharp rise in totalitarianism and of an increasing interference of the state government in all affairs has been shown to have been inescapably correct.

At the same time it is permissible to point out that, in our own times, far more conscious attention is being given to the administrative problems implicit in these developments. The rise of the administrative welfare state under responsible parliamentary government surely makes the close network of relationships encompassing the individual to-day a very different affair from that in which he was enmeshed in earlier times. It has, for example, been argued (by Richard Warner, *Principles of Public Administration*, London, 1948) that the modern welfare state system can be regarded as the logical way of giving fuller effect to the grand principle of the division of labour upon which the efficiency of all social life must clearly depend. Sorokin adopts a similar standpoint when he points to the fact that social organization is not a mere matter of State organization, but that it includes also the organization of churches, voluntary societies and other bodies. The striking thing about the development of the modern welfare state has been the transfer to the central or local government of many social activities undertaken by these non-governmental agencies. The Church has historically been the chief victim in many countries of such revolutions in modern times, after which it has ceased, for example, to be the sole social means of providing educational facilities or to be the sole registrar of births, death and marriages. However, qualitative distinctions of this sort, vitally important as they are from the standpoint of individual freedom, in no way weaken the very evident truth of Sorokin's contention that the sheer number and complexity of the relationships between governments and peoples have most notably increased during the first half of the twentieth century.

Turning to the question whether ideational or sensate cultures are more likely to strengthen than to weaken the links between government and peoples, Sorokin finds that *logically* there is no direct or very close relationship except in the following respects.

Ascetically ideational cultures care little for State or government, so that no strongly marked totalitarian system is likely to be found when they prevail. Their lack of organization leaves them particularly vulnerable to foreign invasion. This logical expectation is verified by the history of the predominantly ideational Hindu culture in India.

Actively ideational cultures tend to create strong governments, usually directed by the paramount religious organization, so that they should lead to totalitarian theocracies. This, in fact, occurred to some extent in the Middle Ages. The theocratic rule of the Calvinists in Geneva, and especially in Scotland, affords another example.

Sorokin finds rather more difficulty in explaining the fluctuations in totalitarian systems in the sensate societies of the last four centuries. Why, after the powerful central controls developed by the early national States, was there so pronounced a swing away from their totalitarian tendencies in the eighteenth and early nineteenth centuries? Sorokin puts it down to the 'overripeness' of sensate society occurring in a time of relative peace and security, a state of affairs abruptly shattered by wars which have stimulated, as they always do, a new totalitarianism in the twentieth century.

War is not the only disturbance which, in ideational as in sensate cultures alike, sternly compels societies to organize and discipline themselves if they are to survive. Economic calamity, whether caused as in earlier times by famine, flood or other natural disasters, or, as in our own time, by catastrophic economic depressions, such as that in the United States after 1929, can have similar results. Illustrations abound in the measures taken by authorities to save the lives of peoples threatened by such calamities. In ancient Egypt, the great power of the Pharaohs rested on such a basis. In China also, at a very early period, government control of production, distribution and consumption had to be accepted as the only means of fighting famine.

In ancient Greece and in Rome, the story was much the same. As the needs of the growing population outstripped local resources, the state was forced to organize relief measures. In Rome the trend is remarkable, particularly around the time of Tiberius and Gaius Gracchus, whose Corn Laws of 123 B.C. represented a most thoroughgoing effort to apply for the first time in Rome on a large scale, the rational spirit of the Greeks in the interest of organization and material efficiency. These were but slender and unsuccessful beginnings. Centuries later, the failure of the Romans in the later Empire to achieve a successful economic and social organization culminated to produce, under Diocletian, a most thoroughgoing state-socialist organization of industry and labour which Sorokin considers was little different from that which he witnessed himself during the calamitous times in Russia between 1917 and 1922.

For the Middle Ages, he lists the famine years in France and in England, all of which provoked increased governmental interference in economic relations. It should perhaps be added that the interference was not always very effective, since the absence of an adequate administrative service made the actual achievements of government intervention of much smaller practical effect than was intended. To the list of famines might also be added that of plagues—notably the Black Death of 1348-9.

There is probably little need to add to Sorokin's long list of examples to prove that sudden catastrophes tend to provoke governments to devise remedies. His theory of the basis of social organization may, however, be a little further developed. If, he says, all human beings were wise, moral, exceedingly social and altruistic, government of a compulsory nature would be unnecessary. They would themselves, of their own will, do all that was needed. As this happy state of affairs is notoriously not realized in practice, the necessity for government arises, as the sages of all ages have proclaimed, from the iniquity of mankind. Social life is, therefore, in a state of permanent emergency. To this doctrine, that there must be compulsory direction if the energies of lazy and unworthy men are to be directed to socially desirable ends, among which is the need to rescue mankind from famine, may it not be added that leadership and direction might equally well be required by a society of angels? Administration, in short, is a branch of human activity with which no society can dispense. A group of angels faced with sudden calamity or natural catastrophe would be forced to organize. They might be presumed to organize voluntarily, so that the execution of each individual's task would not be felt as a threat to their freedom or liberty. What would be true of the society of angels could equally well be true of societies of sinful imperfect men. If they overwhelmingly desire an increased measure of common effort, then they should be willing to put up with the administrative means, the government regulation, the thick network of planned and ordered relationships without which that common effort cannot be achieved. They would not then feel conscious of the loss of liberty as an evil. Totalitarianism as such would have no terrors for them. Such, it may be added, was the state of mind of the overwhelming majority of the British people when, in 1940, they alone stood undefeated against the victorious Nazi aggressors. No love for totalitarianism as such inspired their resolve to accept the most thoroughgoing restrictions and controls upon what food they should eat, what clothes they might wear, or what work they should undertake. It was because they loved liberty more than life that they were willing to accept any sacrifice. They did not interpret liberty according to a narrow nominalistic standard or by any cool economic calculus of cost and advantage. It was not merely that they had to save their lives. This they could have done by surrender. They were inspired by devotion to a purpose transcending their own immediate security; by devotion to the idea of a free society and a free world and a hatred of bullies and aggressors who were destroying freedom. Here surely was the secret of their strength and a reason for their survival. The same spirit will inspire the stand all free peoples are ready to make against current communist or any other forms of totalitarianism. Writing before 1937, Sorokin declared that the harshness and brutality of those totalitarian regimes marked them in his opinion for inevitable decay. They will, he said, either be killed by the peoples subject to them or they will vanish by enfeebling and destroying the peoples they oppress.

Economic Fluctuations

Sorokin concludes his review of peaceful change in society as distinct from changes caused by war and internal disturbances, by a review, made in co-operation with five other scholars, of economic fluctuations. He is easily able to show that the majority of writers on this subject, however sharply they disagree on many points, all accept the idea that there must be close links between the cultural and the economic aspect of life. Some, like Marx, regard economic conditions as determining the forms of cultural life, others take a contrary view and subordinate economic activities to the broader cultural conditions, including the religious outlook, of any given period of history.

What then is the true relationship, if any, between the fluctuation of economic conditions and cultural life, and particularly of the ideational and sensate forms of culture?

Factual studies of this great problem are beset by enormous difficulties. The bare facts about the realities of economic life over vast stretches of history are either woefully inadequate or altogether missing. When some few facts exist, it is almost impossible to extract much from them. What, for example, was a good, poor or average standard of living at the beginning of each of the last twenty centuries, and how did one compare with another? It is obviously impossible to answer such a puzzle with any pretension to scientific accuracy. To do so would involve some reasonably secure estimate of a whole series of factors: money income; quantity and quality of goods consumed per head of the population; the more elusive gratification derived from power, prestige, freedom, contentedness, health, morality, and the outlets for directive and creative abilities.

The evident objection that it is impossible to derive a clear-cut definition of economic well-being from so nebulous general notions as these does not deter Sorokin from the search for the best estimates he can make of his own criterion or from criticisms of much contemporary social science, which he regards as fundamentally fallacious, because it attempts to proceed as though in possession of clear-cut ideas of such concepts as economic welfare or well-being, which, by their nature, cannot be clear-cut or definite. Tested by his own notion of economic well-being, the inadequacy of many attempted definitions based on income-and-expense accounts is clearly evident.

Many contemporary business barometers, made up of such factors as steel production, building construction, power consumption and so on, are of no greater utility. They cannot be projected backwards into the past. Instead of attempting to proceed by means of such inadequate notions, Sorokin and his colleagues have tried to use a ten-point scale of values in assessing past economic conditions. It is as follows:

10 excellent economic situation of the highest prosperity.
9 very good.
8 good.
7 very satisfactory.
6 satisfactory.
5 fair.
4 almost fair.
3 rather bad.
2 bad.
1 very bad.

Many who study and write about the past are probably able to form some such judgments about the state of economic activity at the various periods of history in which they are interested, although not all formulate their standards of appraisal in such methodical detail. Still less do they consciously analyse the long list of symptoms of prosperity and depression, eighteen of the most important of which were listed by Sorokin and used as guides in the studies undertaken by his collaborators. They are:

1. Mention by contemporary chroniclers of the existence and increase of economic enterprises.

2. Contemporary testimony about poverty and prosperity.

3. Appearance and growth of comparatively large individual fortunes.

4. Evidence of the growth or decline of agricultural enterprises and agricultural populations.

5. Evidences of the foundation, growth and increase of cities and city buildings.

6. Opening and development of new trade routes by land, water and air.

7. Evidence of the rise of labour movements.

8. Expansion or shrinkage of colonizing activities.

9. Population movements, growth or decline in size or density, the increase or the decrease in mortality-rates.

10. Epidemics and deaths from disease.

11. Direct evidence about the standard of living, prices, wages, employment, unemployment, and the accumulation of wealth.

12. War and peace.

13. Flourishing or decay of the arts, philosophy and science, the creation or importation of art objects.

14. The building of temples, monasteries, cathedrals and other religious centres, their adornment and enrichment or decay and dissolution.

15. The growth or decline of schools and other institutions of learning.

16. Political unification or disintegration.

17. Internal peace or disturbance.

18. Political expansion or decline.

Such being the main criteria and standard of evaluation, it remains to consider how they are to be applied both in breadth (that is to say, over how wide an area of any country or empire) and in depth (that is to say, to how many of the various classes of society the evidences of economic conditions may be regarded as applicable). Sorokin and his colleagues have made a gallant attempt on the basis of this comprehensive series of ideas to survey the economic history of the ancient world. As a result they present a series of charts which are reproduced here.

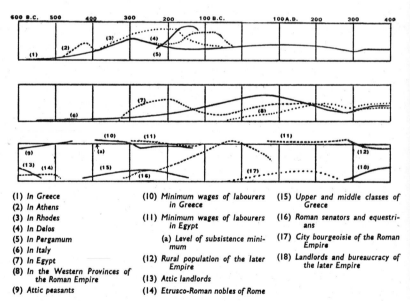

(1) In Greece
(2) In Athens
(3) In Rhodes
(4) In Delos
(5) In Pergamum
(6) In Italy
(7) In Egypt
(8) In the Western Provinces of the Roman Empire
(9) Attic peasants

(10) Minimum wages of labourers in Greece
(11) Minimum wages of labourers in Egypt
(a) Level of subsistence minimum
(12) Rural population of the later Empire
(13) Attic landlords
(14) Etrusco-Roman nobles of Rome

(15) Upper and middle classes of Greece
(16) Roman senators and equestrians
(17) City bourgeoisie of the Roman Empire
(18) Landlords and bureaucracy of the later Empire

Fig. 11. GENERAL ECONOMIC SITUATION IN THE ANCIENT WORLD, 600 B.C. TO A.D. 400

The broad general conclusions drawn from this analysis, which, it must be emphasized, is no more than the best provisional estimate that can be made in the lack of adequate data, may be stated in summary form. Economic prosperity characteristic of sensate cultures, making happiness and well-being their aim (eudæmonism), is not found in periods of ideational culture, but occurs in association with sensate cultures at the period of their ascendancy and before their decline. Such, for example, seems to have been the situation in Greece. Economic prosperity was not very high in the ideational sixth century, but it rose considerably with the rise of the sensate culture in the fifth and fourth centuries. It was more pronounced in Athens than in the rest of Greece, and still more marked in centres of Hellenistic culture, such as Rhodes, Pergamum and Alexandria.

These improvements were not equally enjoyed by all classes of the population. In the earlier periods the predominantly familistic form of social relationships ensured that economic benefits were more generally shared by all classes. The development of a more sensate culture, by giving full rein to the greed and egotism of its leaders, replaced those familistic bonds by contractual and compulsory relationships, which were no longer protected by religious and moral checks. The exploitation of the poor by the rich in turn provoked revolt and rebellion and caused a general decline in economic prosperity of the society as a whole.

In Rome, the labouring classes also failed to enjoy the same sudden rise in economic well-being as the senators and business classes (equestrians); but in the first, second and third centuries A.D., they seem to have benefited by a considerable improvement which put them in a much better position than, say, the labouring classes in Egypt at the same time. Sorokin also notes the interesting fact that the economic position of the Etrusco-Roman landlords suffered a decline as the ideational culture of earlier times began to give way to the more sensate culture of the sixth and fifth centuries B.C. Later, however, the landlords, together with the bureaucracy, began to improve their position when the sensate culture declined and the ideational culture rose in the third and fourth centuries A.D. Sorokin explains this state of affairs by saying that the landlords with the priests were the main organizers of the social, moral and economic order in the ideational society before the sixth century B.C. As a rule, any class charged with this task of organizing a social system of values, including economic values and activities, almost inevitably improves its own economic status at the same time.

Additional support for such a theory is forthcoming from a study of the situation in France and in Germany, the main results of which are also summarized in two charts. Looking first at the chart of general economic conditions in France from 800 A.D. to 1926 (Fig. 12), it is at once apparent that, in the ideational Middle Ages, the situation was 'very bad' or 'rather bad', and at its best no better than 'almost fair'.

After the eleventh century and up to the second quarter of the fourteenth century, a period of predominantly idealistic culture is associated with very marked improvements. The subsequent decline was in large measure due to the devastating results of the Black Death in the middle of the century. But, despite this disaster and the Hundred Years' War which France was fighting with England, sensate culture and society soon begin to recover, quickly reaching a relatively high level of economic prosperity. A temporary decline occurred at the end of the sixteenth century, mainly as a result of the wars of religion. These religious wars were, like the Reformation by which they were provoked, themselves an immanent consequence of the developing sensate culture and mentality. Recovery was fairly rapid, and after some fluctuations, of which the chief were caused by the economic disasters and unsuccessful wars at the close of the reign of Louis XIV, the Revolution and the Napoleonic Wars, the curve of prosperity steadily rose until the war of 1914 again brought down the standard of living.

A specially interesting feature of the chart is the separate particulars provided for the chief classes of French society. The clergy, aristocracy and landowners, as the chief bearers of the medieval ideational culture, enjoyed relatively their best position in the Middle Ages. The popular notion is that they continued to improve their position by grinding the faces of the poor, until the poor, unable any longer to endure their miserable condition, were forced to revolt. The facts are rather the opposite. Contrary to commonly accepted ideas, the aristocratic classes declined relatively to the general economic levels, indeed Sorokin considers that the aristocracy never fully recovered from the Crusades and the medieval communal movements. The Revolution of 1789 finally almost destroyed them, and their place was taken by the new types of great landowners, not, however, before they had loaded the fair land of France with their magnificent chateaux in the seventeenth and eighteenth century.

The bourgeoisie and the intelligentsia rather than the nobles and the clergy were the main bearers of the sensate culture, and the manner in which they improved their position relatively to the other classes of French society is sufficiently evident from the chart.

The labouring classes, the peasants and craftsmen, reached what was relatively the highest point in their economic fortunes during the

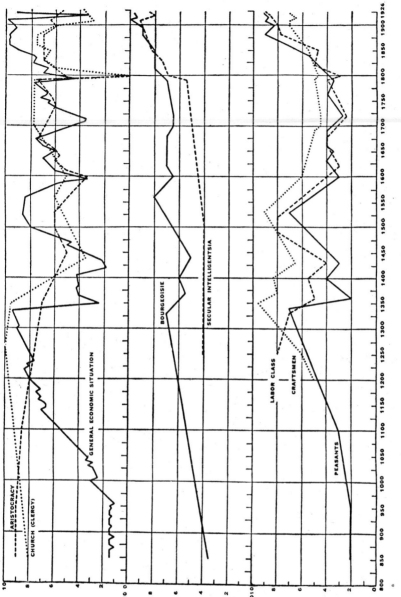

Fig. 12. GENERAL ECONOMIC SITUATION IN FRANCE, A.D. 800-1926

M

idealistic culture of the the thirteenth and early fourteenth centuries. Social and moral principles were then held sufficiently in reverence to ensure that these classes then shared in the increasing national wealth and income. The succeeding sensate centuries deprived them of this moral protection, and it was not until the great scientific and technological discoveries of the nineteenth and twentieth centuries had so markedly increased national prosperity that the relative economic welfare of the labouring and artisan classes again registered a notable improvement.

In Germany, a somewhat similar general development occurred with, however, not quite the same marked contrast as that observable in France between ideational poverty and sensate prosperity. The charts, which are self-explanatory, emphasize the calamitous effects of the Thirty Years' War on German economic life. Central Europe and Austria are included as part of Germany up to A.D. 1500

The German landed aristocracy and clergy, as the main bearers of the ideational culture, enjoyed relatively their best economic situation in the period dominated by ideational culture. The lay intelligentsia, the bureaucracy and the capitalistic bourgeoisie rose relatively to the other classes with the rise of sensate culture. Sorokin has not estimated the economic consequences of the introduction of the welfare state which, on his principles, may plausibly be regarded as an effort to recover some of the virtues of a familistic order of society described on page 150.

Owing to the longer survival of the aristocratic tradition in England and in Scotland, where it is reinforced by the solidarity of the Clans, hopes may be brighter for the success of such a task than they might be in other countries which have either violently broken with such tradition or indeed have never known it. Nevertheless the effort to re-create familistic altruism in contemporary industrial society by a compulsory redistribution of the national income has given rise to many doubts. One of the chief is the fear that the policy of depriving people through taxation of many benefits they could otherwise secure for themselves may end by greatly weakening the initiative springing from self-interest, yet fail to generate a true altruism of a familistic society, if indeed it was ever hoped to produce it. The more usual view no doubt is that the fuller material life which the welfare state should secure for each individual member of it will endow them with abilities and resources able to lift the national income and everybody's share in it to new levels high enough to overcome any adverse effect upon individual enterprise which otherwise would prove a serious

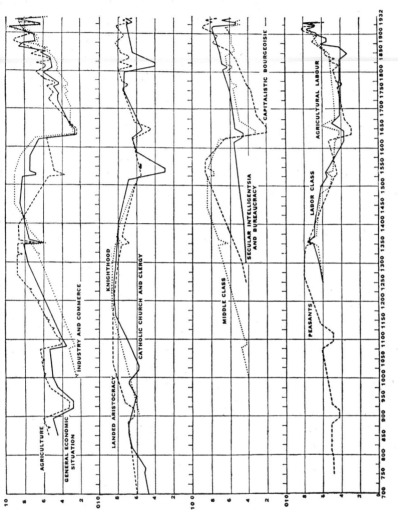

Fig. 13. GENERAL ECONOMIC SITUATION IN GERMANY, A.D. 700-1932

menace both internally and in relation to the competitive position of the country in international trade.

Sorokin's view of general economic history, based upon his review of trends revealed in the records of the past, is a more thoroughgoing attempt to get to grips with the problem as a whole than anything produced by his predecessors. It has affinities with the findings of some of them, Max Weber's, for example, but it is broader and deeper.

Summarizing his own main conclusions, the guiding lines of his general philosophy of economic history are as follows:

1. The economic situation of a country or nation, or of any other large or small social system, does not remain constant, neither does it show any uniform trend but it rises and declines.

2. There are short-term and long-term fluctuations.

3. The economic level of ideational societies tends to be at a lower level than that of sensate cultures.

4. Idealistic or mixed cultures which arise as ideational cultures decline and sensate cultures advance, normally show a relatively high economic level in relation to that of ideational culture.

5. Sensate cultures provide relatively the highest levels of economic welfare, but a peak is reached after which the culture breeds conditions unfavourable to its continued existence. These immanent consequences of the full development of sensate culture adversely affect all its values, including its economic values.

6. The above relationships between economic conditions and predominant cultural types may be obscured or destroyed by external forces, such as plagues, famines and wars, but, apart from such calamities, they conform to and are explicable by the basic differences in behaviour and mentality of ideational and sensate man and by the relatively greater harmony and balance of idealistic man.

7. Where there is no integration of a culture as a whole, or where a culture and economic life are not sufficiently well related and brought together, it is not possible to discern or to predict relationships of the type indicated in the preceding paragraphs.

8. The economic well-being of the various classes of people in the same economic or cultural system does not vary uniformly for them all.

9. In each of the main cultural systems, one or more classes are its main bearers, agencies and integrators.

10. The main bearers of ideational cultural values are the sacerdotal class (priests, clergy, Brahmans, Lamas, etc.) and the religious landed aristocracy.

11. The main bearers of sensate cultural values are the capitalist-commercial bourgeoisie, the secular bureaucracy and the independent, free-thinking, scientific, artistic *intelligentsia* and professional classes.

12. Peasants and agricultural labourers are very rarely the main bearers of any type of culture, because it would seem that they rarely attain the relatively high degree of mental development and integration needed for such a role.

13. The classes which integrate a culture are immanently destined to rise socially and economically as it rises, and to decline as it declines. Self-evident in relation to the leaders of sensate culture (No. 11 above), it may be less obvious why leaders of ideational culture (No. 10 above) should ever become wealthy. The fact is, however, that such men cannot escape the responsibility of exercising political, economic and social power and authority nor the privileges by which such responsibility has traditionally been accompanied and rewarded.

14. The growth in the wealth of ideational leaders undermines the ideational regime.

15. Sensate culture is also undermined by its own immanent developments. One example is the conflict between the secular intelligentsia and the moneyed bourgeoisie. Both are children of the same sensate culture, and their fate and their destiny are inevitably bound up with its fate. Such conflicts occur as the sensate culture begins to decline and they are suicidal. The capitalist class, attacked as it were from within by a relatively leisured class of intellectuals who could not exist without it, seems to lose its energy, virility, determination and self-confidence and especially its self-respect. Sorokin might have illustrated this point by a reference to the career of George Bernard Shaw among others, who, after undermining the foundations of capitalist society, left a large personal fortune, despite his vigorous protests at a scale of taxation he had done his best to recommend.

16. The economic fortunes of the labouring classes do not fluctuate so widely as those of the classes who lead, direct, or integrate cultures. In an ideational culture, the incomes of the working classes are usually low because the general economic level of such a culture is itself low.

In idealistic cultures, the general level tends to rise, because, in the dawning sensate culture, a greater attention to the good things of this world stimulates desires and improves economic efficiency. At the same time, however, ideational cultural forces remain vigorous and able to restrain and control the increase of greed and to delay the decrease in the familistic feelings and the decline in the sense of justice of the leading classes.

As a result the growing wealth tends to be more fairly shared and the labouring classes benefit to a relatively greater degree than they do later on, when sensate forces are fully released and victorious sensate man puts his own gain first and cares much less for social justice than did his idealistic or ideational predecessors.

Nevertheless, technological progress in a fully efficient sensate culture is such that it raises the general level of economic welfare to so high a pitch that all classes benefit, including the labouring classes, who are very much better off than their forefathers, despite, it must be added, huge increases in their numbers.

17. When a sensate culture declines, the general economic level declines, and the position of the labouring classes also worsens. Such a decline may be hastened by war, revolts, revolutions and a sharpening of the class struggle, as is happening in our own time, despite appearances to the contrary, due it would seem in part to monetary inflation.

18. There is a definite, although not close, association between the rise and fall of economic well-being and the dominant type of culture. Economic processes and activities are more subject to the influences of the external world and of nature than are cultural processes, and they may therefore be subject to considerable changes which are unrelated to the immanent development of the cultural life in which they occur. However, it is not true, as the extremist adherents of the materialist or economic interpretation of history assert, that the association between economic conditions and cultural activities is such that any change in these economic conditions is immediately reflected in cultural life also.

What is said above relates to the levels of prosperity and economic well-being of societies, that is to say to the quantitative aspects of economic life. Equally marked differences are observable in the qualitative aspects of economic activities in the contrasting cultural forms. Theories of production, distribution and consumption; the forms of social relationship in the various cultural systems; theories of capital, property, profit, usury, price, almsgiving—all show the most marked differences in ideational, idealistic and sensate societies. So much so that Sorokin affirms that contemporary economic theory, arising as it does in a purely sensate society and frame of reference, cannot be applied in any intelligible way to the economic life of an ideational society. This is an aspect of the history of economic life and theories which, says Sorokin, is badly in need of study.

CHAPTER NINE

Wars and Revolutions

The Fluctuation of War

U p to this point the theories of historical change studied by Sorokin have related in the main to ideas in the minds of men, their nature, sequence and fluctuations. They are ideas which have governed or influenced the actions of individual artists, poets and philosophers, of large groups of men and women, or of whole societies and peoples. With the study of economic change, the social aspects and applications of Sorokin's theories became increasingly prominent. From theories of economic relationships and activities he proceeds to investigate human behaviour in the raw as it is exhibited in wars and revolutions.

With justification, he claimed in 1937 to be among the very few pioneers in the methodical study of war. It may sound a strange, presumptious claim to make when, for several generations, there has been continual complaint that too much attention has traditionally been give in historical works to wars and the records of wars. The trouble is that it has not been methodical attention. Much of the literature on the subject has been inspirational rather than accurate, consisting of the prejudices and interests of the authors rather than an accurate history of the wars they describe. National campaigns and small skirmishes receive a great deal of attention in the county or district in which they occur, so that scales of magnitude of wars in the minds of children between, say, the Napoleonic Wars and the Battle of Bunker Hill get all awry and men and women consequently grow up with as false a set of ideas upon the relative magnitude of wars as they would get upon the comparative sizes of the moon and of Jupiter by looking at the stars at night.

To correct such false perspectives completely is an impossible task. However great may be the desire for true, objective, scientific knowledge about the exact incidence of war upon the social life of past ages, the amount of trustworthy information upon the subject is too fragmentary to allow reliable conclusions to be drawn from it. Such is the poverty of our resources that, until the second half of the seventeenth century, it is exceptional to find even roughly accurate reports upon essential aspects of wars: the size of the fighting forces, the number of lives lost in fighting and among the civilian population, and the economic cost. Those reports which survive are frequently grossly inaccurate, such as the estimate of Herodotus that the Persian army contained a million men. The true duration of wars is also often in doubt. A state of war may have existed without much fighting having occurred; or there may have been many skirmishes and local clashes of which no record survives. The Hundred Years' War between England and France in the fourteenth and fifteenth centuries, if measured in actual fighting time, would prove to be of much shorter duration than the World War of 1914 to 1918.

When an effort is made to extend the study of warfare by relating it to the broader social groups or countries from which the armies were drawn, further complications arise, because there is no accurate knowledge of the size of their populations. If the study is carried over several centuries, there is the additional complication that the size and extent of the territory of those countries does not remain constant any more than do their populations. These difficulties are further aggravated when wars are waged by coalitions of several countries together, or when, as in the Middle Ages, wars were fought with the aid of mercenary foreign troops.

Having faced this formidable list of difficulties, Sorokin cannot be accused of undertaking lightheartedly the tremendous task of attempting to weigh and measure the incidence of warfare in Western civilization since the dawn of recorded history. He confines himself to three obvious and outstanding quantitative elements in war and he presents his conclusions as no more than a study of the variations in those three quantities. They are the strength of the army, the number of casualties, both killed and wounded, and the duration of the wars in which they were involved. All other aspects, such as economic costs, or the diseases and deaths caused to civilian populations, are ignored.

Almost all the important wars, about nine hundred and sixty-seven in all, were studied on this basis, as they occurred in the history of Greece (24 wars), Rome (81), Austria (131), Germany (24), England (176), France (185), Netherlands (23), Spain (75), Italy (32), Russia (151), Poland and Lithuania (65).

The wars of Germany, Spain, The Netherlands and Italy are fewer, because they are studied from the sixteenth or seventeenth centuries and not from the tenth or eleventh centuries, as are the others, except of course Greece and Rome, whose wars all occurred in the epoch of ancient history. Sorokin is content to claim no more for such an analysis, based as it is upon an exhaustive study of the best authorities, than that it very probably more nearly approaches reality than the mere guesses, incidental and fragmentary statements and *ad hoc* theories which have generally done duty in this field in the past.

Without entering further into questions about the statistical techniques used, the sources and their conflict and agreement, all of which can be studied in detail in Sorokin's work, the results of his enquiries may be reproduced in graphic form (see Fig. 14).

Such is the broad picture based upon as exhaustive a study as the facts of history allow. It stands in marked contrast to the many partial, conflicting and imaginative theories set forth from time to time by astrologers, numerologists, astro-physicists, sunspot theorists, climatologists, geographers and others. Many other illusions dissolve and disappear when confronted with this record. Elaborate notions about the cyclical appearance and disappearance of wars, ideas about a constant trend leading to the reduction and elimination of wars or their constant and steady increase are alike shown to have no basis in history. All that can be said is that the curve of war in history fluctuates. Consequently all attempts to predict the inevitable recurrence of wars are made in vain. Wars are not the main or general cause of scientific progress, neither are they necessarily manifestations of exuberance or of the vital and cultural effervescence of any society. Wars are likely to occur in periods of prosperity or of depression; under autocratic and under democratic regimes; in literate or illiterate societies; in agricultural or in industrial societies; in communities of every variety of political and religious belief.

Sorokin holds that it is a waste of time to pursue an enquiry into the causes of wars on the basis of such conditions as those noted above. He suggests instead that, because war involves essentially a breakdown of the organized relationship between states, the investigation should concentrate upon searching for reasons for the breakdown. This is, of course, often undertaken, but the investigators frequently make the mistake of seeking to explain the breakdown by one principal factor or operative variable. It may be that the principle or variable proposed is the size, density or growth of the population; or changes in the means and techniques of production; or variations in prosperity and depression; or changes in political regimes. Whatever the main factor may be, it can never account for more than some local and secondary traits of war, because it can always be shown that the variables supposed to

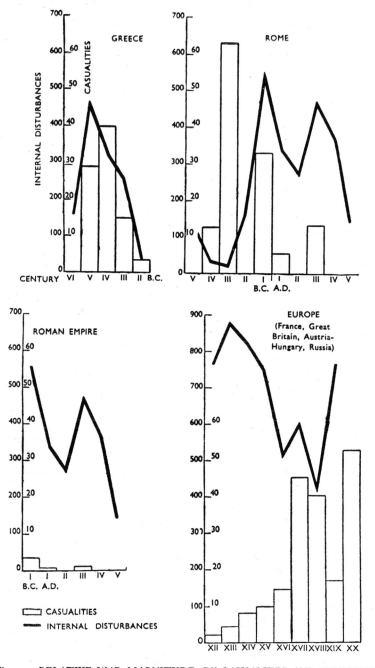

Fig. 14. *RELATIVE WAR MAGNITUDE, BY CASUALTIES AND INTERNAL DISTURBANCES*

cause wars are also to be found in peaceful societies as well. Neither does Sorokin consider that trends of wars or peace can be accounted for directly by his own main factors of historical change, the alternation of ideational and sensate cultures. The most that he would claim is that these factors account satisfactorily for some aspects of the nature and trends of war and peace. Among them he selects the following for special mention.

Sensate wars rarely have religious or ideational colour. They are fought for economic, imperialistic, utilitarian ends, although they are presented to the world in much more high-sounding language.

In a dominant ideational culture or period, wars are more generally fought for religious or other ideals. In the Middle Ages, for instance, most wars were religious in nature, and the religious motive endured, still strong, until the eighteenth century. Partisans of the economic interpretation of history, who uniformly fail to understand that sensate economic motives have little relevance as an explanation of conduct in an ideational culture, are reduced to extraordinary expedients in their efforts to prove that their theories can account for the causes of ideational wars, such as the Crusades, for example.

Whatever may be thought of Sorokin's general philosophy of history, it is evident that his demonstration of the essential relativity of the various factors or canons of interpretation, such as this economic factor, is of fundamental and far-reaching importance, not merely for history but for the social sciences generally. It completely demolishes, for example, the Marxist materialist interpretation of history, which it shows to be practically irrelevant throughout vast stretches of time involving more than half the recorded history of mankind.

Sorokin next observes that neither in logic nor in experience are there any grounds for believing that ideational culture is more peaceful or more belligerent than sensate culture. The militant forces making for war and inhibitory forces making for peace in each may be very different but they can be equally strong. Thus predominently ideational Europe of the twelfth century and predominantly sensate Europe of the nineteenth century had comparatively few wars.

Sorokin's own theory is that wars notably increase in periods of transition from one main cultural phase to another. This may be because crystallized and settled cultures tend to be comparatively peaceful if no strong external factors intervene. A transition from ideational to sensate cultural values, or from sensate to ideational values involves severe disruptions which weaken or remove many of the factors within a society making for order and stability. In the first place, the whole cultural system of values—religious, scientific, philosophical, artistic, juridical and moral—loses much if not all of its force. Next the main types of social relationship associated with either system, whether familistic, compulsory or contractual, also begin to crumble. Then also many other relationships are changed, including forms of government, ideas about freedom and about government regulation, all of which further upset and unsettle established ways of life. Of course, changes of this description do not necessarily occur at the same time in all states and societies. It is therefore necessary to take into account the possibility that only one of the states involved in war may be in transition, or that two or all may be involved, or that parts only of states may be changing. Similarly, one state may be changing from an ideational to a sensate form, while the other or others may be changing from sensate to ideational forms or not subject to change at all, as when a stable society is invaded by another in a transitional state.

There seems, moreover, to be a time lag between the rate of internal change and disturbances and the outbreak of wars between states, a fact brought out by the diagrams on pages 186 and 195-200. Attempting to interpret the findings recorded in his diagrams, Sorokin looked at the chart of war and disturbance in Rome. In the fourth century B.C., the Roman Republic had, he considers, a firm, strong and crystallized predominantly ideational culture. The third century B.C. was the most militant century in Roman history. The reason cannot be found in internal disintegration or transition. It must, therefore, be the result of external attack by the Carthaginians. Sorokin says that he does not know what the internal state of Carthage was at that time. Such hints that we have, however, are not inconsistent with the view that Carthaginian culture, with its highly developed trading and agricultural enterprises, was predominantly sensate. There is, however, no doubt that, in the second and first centuries B.C., society in the Roman Republic was undergoing a radical change. The old, stern ways of life were giving place to a sensate concentration upon the good things of this world. Wars against Rome's neighbours in the Mediterranean became also vast booty hunts. Internal disturbances became more acute. The Gracchan efforts at reform were shortly followed by the devastating social wars, and these in turn were succeeded by the civil wars. Then followed an era of comparative peace at home and abroad. The new sensate culture had crystallized and a period of stability ensued, until it also waned and was replaced by a new and vital ideational culture. Again wars and internal disturbances increased, although the lack of reliable data makes it impossible to indicate their magnitude with any precision.

Whatever may be thought of Sorokin's reading of the history of ancient Rome, it at least has the great merit, which so many popular manuals on that subject lack, of pointing to the profoundly different character, culture and outlook of the Romans of the early Republic from those of the early Empire. By drawing attention to the correspondingly great cultural changes in the fourth century A.D., Sorokin's emphasis upon the self-generated immanent changes in social life in Rome throws new light upon customary notions about the causes and the nature of the decline and fall of the Roman Empire, and indeed of that Græco-Roman civilization of which the Empire and its culture were the latest manifestation.

Throughout almost the whole of the ideational period of European history after the fall of the Roman Empire, and until the period of change which began to become apparent in the twelfth century, there are no sufficiently reliable records upon which any valid calculation of the extent of war during those centuries could be based. On the basis of such information that exists, Sorokin supposes that these centuries with their crystallized ideational culture were, comparatively, not very belligerent.

The transition to the very different sensate culture was, however, marked by steadily increasing outbreaks of warfare until that sensate culture itself became dominant and crystallized in the eighteenth and nineteenth centuries. Wars by no means came to an end, but their toll upon human society became somewhat less deadly than before. As in turn the sensate culture began to weaken and decay at the end of the nineteenth and in the twentieth centuries, the curve reflecting the scale and intensity of war again soars.

Whether or not Sorokin has found the right way to explain the incidence of wars, it should at least be clear that he is not wrong in asserting that most of the popular theories about the causes of wars are fallacious. He regards the many political groups which have advocated one policy after another to prevent wars as little better than quack doctors or medicine men. Referring to some of the remedies suggested, he mentions preaching birth control to reduce the density of the population; advocating a certain political regime whether communism, fascism or democracy as a panacea against war; clamouring for limitless prosperity as the surest means to eliminate war; staging big demonstrations with energetic red-flag waving as an organization of peace; transferring the manufacture of munitions from private enterprise to state bureaucrats. None of these devices touch the main cause and all have been and will remain essentially impotent. Writing, as he did before 1937, that the endless efforts to promote these panaceas have not prevented wars but have resulted in the development of intensive war-psychology and sinister preparation for future wars on an appalling scale in all countries, he clearly showed a degree of insight into the subject which was not so evident amongst the holders of the views he criticized.

Sorokin's conclusion is that the main weapon against war is the crystallization of the system of cultural values and of social relationships.

Riots and Revolutions

Internal disturbances in the relations between social groups are another social and cultural phenomena studied by Sorokin, and again his historical, statistical method of approach reveals the inadequacy of many currently-held notions on the subject.

Accurate scientific ideas about social disturbances should, he considers, provide some general measure to determine at least four or five essential aspects of any social disturbance. In the first place, the proportionate extent of the area of the disturbance must be known. By this Sorokin does not merely mean the number of square miles of territory involved but the number and kinds of cities, villages and other settlements in which the disturbance occurred.

Secondly, the proportion of the population taking an active part in the disturbance, for or against it, must be known; thirdly, the duration of the disturbance; fourthly, its relative intensity or the amount and sharpness of violence; and lastly, the importance of the effects of the disturbance must all be assessed. Unless the study of social disturbances is reduced to some kind of order on these lines, it is impossible to get any coherent idea of the true nature and effect of social unrest.

Sorokin's five factors also enable comparisons to be made between the extent of social disturbances between nations differing widely in size and population. As he points out, a disturbance created by 10,000 people is a very different matter in a population of 10,000,000 from what it would be in a population of 100,000,000. His five factors make it possible to register the fact clearly, for they would only show as disturbances of equal significance those involving the same *proportion* of populations, social areas, degree of violence and duration.

In attempting to measure disturbances in various countries by these four scales, Sorokin again encounters the difficulties met with in at-

tempting to measure wars. The recorded facts are lamentably fewer
and less adequate than scientific precision demands. Moreover, the
assessment of internal disturbances involves a greater exercise of judgment, since there is less measurement of numbers killed and wounded
and more guesswork in determining the violence and effects of disturbances. That is to say, the subjective element is a greater source of
probable error.

Once again Sorokin does not claim more for the results he presents
than that they are based upon as complete a survey of the whole subject as he found it possible to make. He has investigated some seventeen
hundred major social disturbances, a far larger number than any other
student of unrest and revolutions has yet surveyed. After experiment
with various scales and procedures, he and his collaborators adopted
one which he claims reflects this aspect of social relations in history in
all essentials without serious distortion.

The manner in which he constructed his scales of measurement is as
follows: the scales adopted are based upon the following different
assessments of the factor involved. It is important to remember that
Sorokin neglects minor disturbances in order to concentrate upon the
important upheavals. The social areas of the disturbances are weighted
from 1 to 100 according to the following scale and as the disturbances
occur in:

1   A rural county or similar limited area.
3   Several rural counties or a small town.
5   A larger town.
10 Several towns of medium size or in one important city or in a
    small feudal region, or a small province.
20 A larger feudal region or province or in a small part of a capital
    city.
40 Several large provinces or in the whole capital city.
60 The capital city and several provinces.
80 Almost the whole country.
100 The entire country.

Clearly these are strictly proportional gradings. A town or province
may vary very much in size at different periods but proportionately
their relation to the social area as a whole will probably be much
about the same.

The duration of disturbances is measured on the following scale:

1   Momentary or short-term shock.
3   Longer disturbance.

5   Lasting several months.
10 About a year.

For every additional year up to 5 years, add 5 to 10. Thus a disturbance of 5 years gets a value of 30. From 6 to 15 years, add 4 to every year above the 5 years with their value of 30. Thus a disturbance of 15 years gets a value of 70. Over 15 years, add 3 for every year above 15. A disturbance of 25 years gets a value of 100. Add 3 for every year above 25.

The intensity of the disturbance is assessed in five classes. The weight assigned to each is given in parenthesis after each.

1   Without violence (1).
2   Slight violence (3).
3   Violence on a considerable scale, fights, murders, arson, looting (5).
4   Still greater violence and overthrow of the government in various centres, but without serious and lasting social and political effects (7).
5   Still greater violence with the irrevocable overthrow of the central government and with deep and lasting consequences (10).

The masses involved in each disturbance are assessed in five classes also, according to whether they involve:

1   A few individuals, in plots and murders (1).
2   A small group (3).
3   A large social class (5).
4   Larger masses of the population, including several extensive social classes (7).
5   Practically all the active and adult population (10).

These last two classes are combined in one scale by Sorokin, resulting in a composite weight for every combination of each of the two sets of five grades as follows:

Table 6—VALUES GIVEN TO INTERNAL DISTURBANCES

By the Masses Involved	By the Amount of Violence and Effects				
	I.	II.	III.	IV.	V.
I.	1	3	5	7	10
II.	3	10	15	20	30
III.	5	15	25	35	50
IV.	7	20	35	50	70
V.	10	30	50	70	100

There are thus three numerical values assigned to each disturbance: social area, duration, and a combined figure to include the masses involved, together with the amount of violence and its effects. The geometric average for each of these three values is then calculated as the indicator of the disturbance to which they relate. The sum of the geometric averages of all the disturbances in twenty-five-year and hundred-year periods is then calculated, and the movement of disturbances in the history of the country from period to period can be shown. It remains to allow for the varying sizes of different countries when the disturbances in all of them are grouped together, as, for example, when it is desired to show one curve of disturbances for all the European countries. Sorokin allows the following weight values to different countries at different periods of their history:

Byzantium: up to the middle of the seventh century (the period of the loss of most Asiatic possessions and of Egypt), 5; up to the end of the twelfth century (the conquest by the Crusaders in 1204), 3; thereafter, 1.

England: up to the middle of the eleventh century (the Norman Conquest), 3; thereafter, 5.

France: 5 throughout.

Germany: up to the end of the eighth century, 3; thereafter, 5.

Italy: 5 throughout (a relatively high figure, due largely to location of the Roman Catholic See in Rome).

The Netherlands: up to the end of the sixteenth century, 1; for the seventeenth century, 3; thereafter, 1.

Poland and Lithuania: up to the end of the fourteenth century (time of unification), 3; up to middle of seventeenth century (period of great power), 5; thereafter (until partition of Poland), 3.

Russia: up to the middle of the thirteenth century, 3; thereafter 5.

Notwithstanding the shortcomings and imperfections of his results, Sorokin claims, with apparent justification, that they are likely to have far greater precision and accuracy than the merely verbal attempts to convey some idea of the magnitude of social disturbances which they render obsolete and replace. Most languages have but six words for comparison: small, smaller, smallest; and great, greater, greatest. Unattracted, as Sorokin professes himself to be, by the effort to reduce everything to numerical terms, he has been forced in the interests of clarity and distinctness of ideas, to adopt his system of numerical indicators in preference to a verbal scale of merely six quantities, all of them imprecise.

Whatever doubts he might have had about the reliability of his

N

methods and results, they were removed, he records, after he had arranged, through a prominent scholar, for two anonymous critics to read and comment upon a preliminary draft of his work. One tried to tear it all to pieces, describing it as an absurdity and nonsense, the other thought it a complex and cumbersome procedure for proving what every qualitative historian already knows and accepts. Sorokin's conclusion, after two such contradictory verdicts, is that there is no hope of progress except by retaining his own method of quantitative measurement and by using it as far as possible more accurately than he has succeeded in doing. The facts upon which his curve of disturbances is based may be found listed chronologically in an appendix to his third volume on *Social and Cultural Dynamics*, where they occupy over forty pages of small print, where the authority describing the disturbances is given and where each disturbance is classified as falling under one of five classes:

Political disturbances mainly directed towards changing the existing political regime.

Social and economic disturbances.

National and separatist disturbances.

Religious disturbances.

Disturbances with specific objectives, such as some personal change in government, resistance to a specific law or tax and disturbances without any single dominant objective but with two or more equally strong objectives. This latter class includes the many disturbances which lack any marked predominant specific objective.

After these preliminary explanations, Sorokin's various charts will repay study.

The curve of internal disturbance in Greece is given in Figs. 14 and 15.

The most turbulent centuries in Ancient Greece were, like the periods of maximum war activities, not those of decline but when Greek culture reached its peak in the fifth and fourth centuries. The most common and frequent disturbances were predominantly political, then came the nationalistic, social and economic disturbances. The latter were most frequent in the fifth century B.C.

The curve for the Roman Republic and Empire, unlike that of Greece, shows that there is no uniformity in the movement of the curves of social disturbances and of war. Figs. 14 and 16.

During the desperate Punic Wars, internal dissensions almost disappeared, but in the first century B.C., when internal disturbances reached unpredecented heights, war also was at a high level. At first

the disturbances in Rome had predominantly political and socio-
economic causes. After the second century B.C., Rome was already
an Empire, so a number of separatist nationalist and regional movements appeared and these persisted until the fourth century A.D., when
their place was taken by religious struggles.

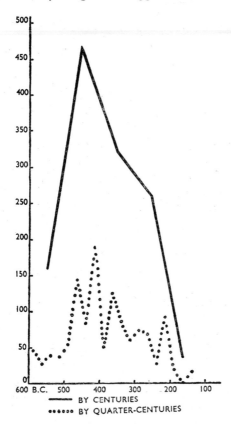

Fig. 15. *MOVEMENT OF INTERNAL DISTURBANCES
IN ANCIENT GREECE*

Byzantium again shows a curve distinct from those of Greece or
Rome (Fig. 17). Less a naturally evolving cultural system than a
mature system transplanted from Greece and Rome, it is not surprising that its earlier evolution should differ from that of a spontaneously and gradually growing culture. The brilliant sixth century,
which includes the reign of Justinian (A.D. 527-565), had few disturbances; the periods of decline in the seventh and eighth centuries
had a high rate of disturbances, whereas the twelfth and thirteenth
centuries, which were also periods of decline, had a low rate. The
ninth, tenth and eleventh centuries, when Byzantium was on the

whole prosperous and flourishing, had a mixed record of internal peace and considerable unrest. The great majority of the disturbances in Byzantium fall into Sorokin's fifth class of those due either to mixed

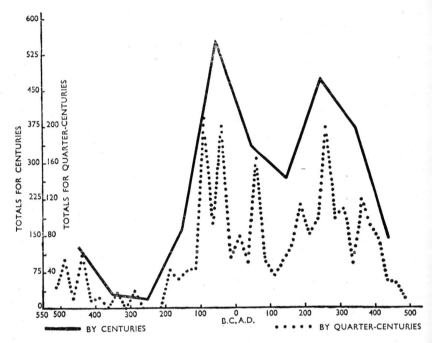

Fig. 16.   MOVEMENT OF INTERNAL DISTURBANCES IN ANCIENT ROME

motives or to the pursuit of some single specific objective. They were not predominantly of a marked political, economic or religious type. Once again no immediately obvious causal connexions are apparent.

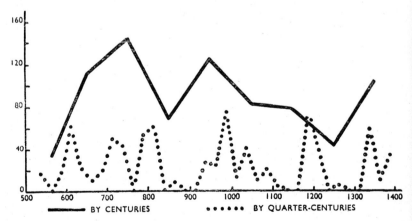

Fig. 17.   MOVEMENT OF INTERNAL DISTURBANCES IN BYZANTIUM

In France also the record gives no possibility of connecting internal
disturbances with periods of prosperity or of decline. Neither does it
support any notions of a universal persistent social trend (Fig. 18).

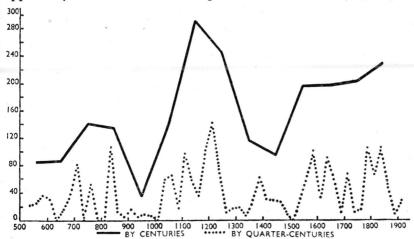

Fig. 18. MOVEMENT OF INTERNAL DISTURBANCES IN FRANCE

France also shows many disturbances of the mixed type. These and
political and socio-economic disturbances predominate with, however,
conspicuous religious disturbances in the sixteenth and seventeenth
centuries and to some extent in the thirteenth century also.

In Germany and Austria there is a similar lack of correlation between
internal disturbances, war, social, economic or cultural blooming or
decay (Fig. 19).

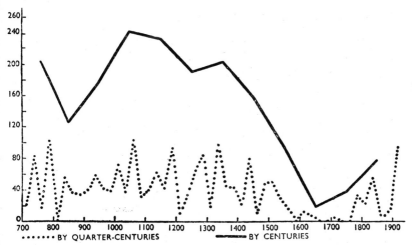

*Fig. 19. MOVEMENT OF INTERNAL DISTURBANCES IN GERMANY
AND AUSTRIA*

Most of the recorded disturbances were of the 'mixed' type, although religious disturbances dominated during the fifteenth, sixteenth and seventeenth centuries. Nationalistic and separatist movements were of some importance in the tenth and eleventh, and for a short time at the end of the eighteenth and beginning of the nineteenth centuries. The curve of disturbances in England again shows no continuous trend and no periodicity (Fig. 20).

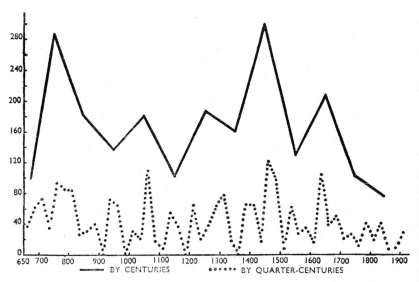

Fig. 20. MOVEMENT OF INTERNAL DISTURBANCES IN ENGLAND

It will be of interest to quote, in addition to reproducing Sorokin's chart, the indicators of the relative magnitude of social disturbances, in order that readers familiar with English history may consider how far their own estimate of the relative magnitude and importance of the various upheavals in English national life is reflected in Sorokin's arithmetical assessment.

The most turbulent quarter centuries in English history were:

A.D. 751-775 (94.50), A.D. 776-800 (85.78), A.D. 801-825 (83.47), A.D. 1051-1075 (110.03), A.D. 1451-1475 (122.24), A.D. 1476-1500 (97.81), A.D. 1626-1650 (104.88).

The largest single disturbances are:

692-694 (27.16), 1066-1070 (55.22), 1138-1153 (49.20), 1215-1217 (41,21), 1265-1267 (22.91), 1297-1300 (25.94), 1381 (24.10), 1455-1483 (34.74, 43.75, 43.75, 38.28), 1641-1649 (77.27), 1650-1562 (27.16), 1688 (25.59).

Sorokin characterizes the disturbances from the fifteenth to the eighteenth centuries in England as markedly religious; he notes that nationalistic, separatist disturbances have played a tangible role, but that the majority of other disturbances were of the 'mixed' type.

The Italian peninsula, judged by Sorokin's indicators, seems to have been one of the most turbulent regions in Europe, an experience which Sorokin suggests may have some relation to the location there of the Roman Catholic See, the focal point where all the antagonistic interests of most of the European countries converged and clashed (Fig. 21).

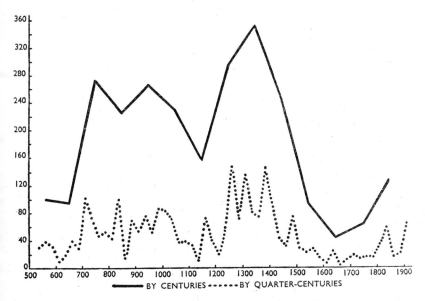

Fig. 21. MOVEMENT OF INTERNAL DISTURBANCES IN ITALY

The majority of Italy's upheavals were of the mixed type, purely religious disturbances playing no marked part.

Sorokin's interesting charts relating to the internal disturbances of Spain, the Netherlands, Russia, Poland and Lithuania are not reproduced here, but they may be seen in the third volume of his *Social and Cultural Dynamics*.

The composite chart for the internal disturbances in Europe as a whole appears as Fig. 22 on the next page.

Summarizing the results of his long and exhaustive studies, Sorokin draws attention to some of the more important conclusions and deductions to be drawn from them. In the first place, the occurrence of important social disturbances in the life of social bodies is so frequent that these recurrent outbreaks, like tensions and sickness in individual

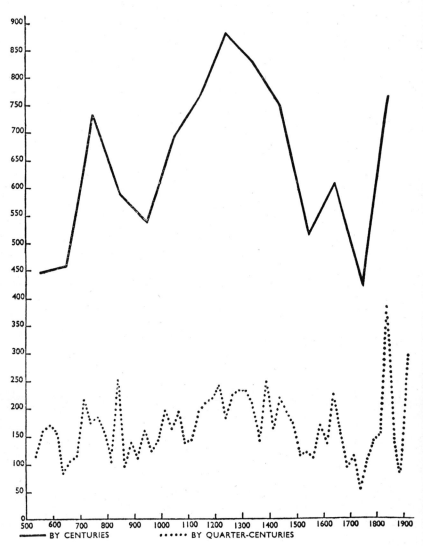

BY CENTURIES   •••••• BY QUARTER-CENTURIES

Fig. 22.   MOVEMENT OF INTERNAL DISTURBANCES IN EUROPE

human organisms, or storms in nature, must be regarded as a normal occurrence in the life of any social group. On an average, for all the countries studied, there has been one significant disturbance for every five years of peace.

Sorokin has worked out the average ratio of years without disturbances to those with disturbances with the following summarized results:

Table 7—FREQUENCY OF IMPORTANT SOCIAL DISTURBANCES

Country	Number of Years Studied	Number of Disturbances in Period	Average Occurrences of Disturbances in Years	Number of Years with Disturbances	Average Ratio of Years without to Years with Disturbances
Ancient Greece, 600 B.C.-146 B.C.	454	84	5.4	122	2.7
Rome, 509 B.C.-A.D. 476 ..	985	170	5.8	219	3.5
Byzantium, 532-1390	858	49	17.5	89	8.6
France, 531-1933	1402	173	8.1	246	4.7
Germany and Austria, 709-1933	1124	150	7.5	204	4.5
England, 656-1933	1277	162	7.9	247	4.2
Italy, 526-1933	1407	251	5.6	365	2.9
Spain, 467-1933	1466	242	6.1	424	2.4
The Netherlands, 678-1933	1255	103	12.1	263	3.8
Russia, 946-1933	987	167	5.9	280	2.6
Poland and Lithuania, 1031-1794	763	78	9.8	146	4.3

Such a record disproves the fairly commonly-held opinion that some nations are inherently orderly and free from social convulsions, whereas others are by nature disorderly.

Are some nations more prone to violence in their upheavals than others? Sorokin has worked over his materials to show the intensity of revolutions in five classes from pure and bloodless disturbances down to the most violent, cruel and blood-stained outbreaks. There is little to choose between the nations studied in this respect. Practically all of them have shown a tendency towards bestiality. He gives no comfort to those who plan or hope for bloodless revolutions, the chances of which, on the basis of the existing record, are about five to one hundred. Neither does he agree, therefore, with the naïve folk whom he has heard declare, 'If Communism would come to our country, it would certainly be free from its Russian excesses and terror and bloodshed and other barbarisms'. He disbelieved this naïve optimism many years before the advance of Communism in Eastern Europe added yet more ghastly evidence of the diabolical inhumanity and depravity of its dupes, tools and supporters.

Another calculation enables Sorokin to show that as far as the average duration of major social disturbances are concerned, the majority of them, like sicknesses in the lives of individuals, come and pass their acute stage within a period of a few weeks. Disturbances with a duration of more than a year have accounted for about 15 per cent. of the total. About 80 per cent. of all disturbances lasted less than a year. It is also remarkable that the magnitude of the disturbances fluctuates from century to century much less than is commonly supposed. Some compensating reaction seems to be released to damp down the growth of disturbances or to prevent their complete elimination. At the same time, and perhaps for the same inherent immanent reasons, it is not possible to point to any continuous trend either towards orderly peaceful progress or towards ever-increasing disorderliness.

The ups and downs of major internal disturbances do not occur in wave-like regularity. Despite some ingenious theories to the contrary, among which Sorokin selects those of the Italian thinker Guiseppe Ferrari, there is no recurrent definite periodicity. Ferrari's theory was that four successive generations completed a cycle. The first generation are the 'predecessors', the men of thought who analyse, describe and criticise the existing order of things without attempting to overthrow it. Building on their knowledge and ideas come the next generation of 'revolutionaries', the men of action, who destroy the existing order in favour of a new and improved state of affairs at which the predecessors merely hinted. Extreme and fanatical, they succeed on the whole in making things worse. New problems arise, as the old ones remain unsolved, so that the excesses of the revolutionaries provoke the rise of the 'reactionaries', who prove just as unsuccessful in the attempt to put the clock back and to repair what the revolutionaries had destroyed. They also fail and the unsoundness of their plans, matching the failure of the revolutionaries, provokes a middle way which the fourth generation of 'accomplishers' promote. Free from fanaticism and coming on the scene when many problems are ripe for solution, this lucky generation succeeds in restoring order, prosperity and social well-being. The cycle is complete, but the relative good fortune of the new age allows a fresh set of theorizers and academic critics to arise who again provoke a new generation of revolutionaries to be succeeded again by reactionaries until the cycle is closed once more by a new generation of accomplishers. Ferrari accompanies his ingenious theory by a series of historical data substantiating it in the experience of several European and some Asiatic countries. His material, however, is arbitrarily selected and arranged according to his own subjective principles. When the facts about revolutions and disturbances are comprehensively collected and weighed objectively, they are not found to support the notion that outbursts and disturbances recur every 115 to 120 years as Ferrari supposed. This is but one of many theories of historical change, none of which have yet produced a satisfactory explanatory scheme able to fit the facts.

Such being the state of affairs in accounting for the past, Sorokin concludes that attempts to predict the future are equally unreliable. All the ingenious folk who busy themselves with forecasting, planning, social engineering or controlling the course of socio-cultural processes, are victims of delusions, mistaking their own wishes for reality. For the pleasing notion that nature does not make leaps is a delusion. There are indeed gradual changes, but accompanying them are many abrupt, sharp and sudden turns which make nonsense of any attempts to prolong the curve of change and revolution beyond the point it has so far reached.

The theory of orderly progress was a typical product of the capitalist regime at its height in the last quarter of the nineteenth century. Two generations of English students of economics trained on the well-known *Principles of Economics* of Alfred Marshall, will recall that he put on the title page of his book, first published in 1890, the words *Natura non facit saltum*. And with reason, for it is more evident now than when Sorokin wrote in 1937 that the capitalist regime Marshall described was one of the most orderly of social systems, giving the greatest assurance of internal and external peace, of sensate liberty and of individual freedom. A not dissimilar impression of that period was given, after it had collapsed, by another Cambridge economist, J. M. Keynes, in the opening pages of *The Economic Consequences of the Peace* (1919).

We can now see how correct were Sorokin's doubts whether the destruction of capitalism to put socialism, fascism, communism and Hitlerism in its place would have any other result than the increase of war and disturbances and a radical limitation and final elimination of sensate individual liberty. On the basis of his statistics up to the year 1925, Sorokin reported that the twentieth century was on a rising tide of internal disturbances and that so far it had been the bloodiest period, one of the cruellest and least humanitarian, in the history of Western civilization and perhaps in the chronicles of all mankind. Those optimists who in 1937 did not perhaps take this judgment very seriously may now be less likely to question its substantial truth.

Another deduction from Sorokin's results is that the movement of internal disturbances in the countries studied does not coincide with the outbreak of international wars. The two movements do not synchronize, neither does there seem to be any positive or negative association between them. Sorokin worked over his results several times before arriving at this conclusion, since in the history of Greece, Rome and Russia there seemed to be some slight indication that disturbances tended to occur most frequently during and around years of war. He was, however, forced to conclude that the relationship was neither simple, uniform nor close. He tried again by investigating the plausible notion that there is a positive association between unsuccessful wars and big disturbances, and again between successful wars and the absence of such disturbances. Despite some impressive examples of just such connections, the weight of all the evidence does not confirm that they are the general rule. The connection in fact is not a necessary one, but it arises because both the onset of wars and of internal disturbances are each related to a more general factor, that of the transition from one cultural system to another.

It is here that Sorokin states his own explanation of the origins of great social disturbances. Other conditions being equal, they occur during the periods when the existing culture or the system of social relations, or both, undergo a rapid transformation. When that culture or system is strong and crystallized, the internal disturbances tend to decrease and stay at a low level. The record he produces (Fig. 22, page 200) show that there have been three main peaks in the fluctuating occurrence of major internal disturbances, the eighth, the thirteenth and fourteenth centuries, and the nineteenth and twentieth centuries. All three were periods of transition, either in the system of social relations of Europe or of its entire cultural system. These were the greatest turning-points of European history.

The eighth century, the period of the Carlovingian Renaissance, did not, it is true, involve the replacement of the predominant ideational culture by a sensate culture, but it did usher in some great changes in the system of social relationships and in the forms of social, economic and political organization or reorganization.

The thirteenth and fourteenth centuries were those of the greatest transition, for then it was that European culture began its radical change from an ideational to a sensate culture; from the feudal to the modern system of social relationships, that is to say, from predominantly familistic to coercive and contractual relationships; from theocracy to secular government; from ideational freedom to sensate liberty.

The nineteenth century was preceded by the final liquidation begun by the French Revolution of the post-medieval relationships in social organization in Europe, the sweeping away of coercive relationships, and the establishment of predominantly contractual relationships. By the middle of the nineteenth century, this process was virtually completed and Europe settled down to its new contractual, free-market system.

The main and indispensable condition for an eruption of internal disturbances, therefore, is that the social system or the cultural system or both shall be unsettled. Other popular theories attributing internal disturbances either to growing poverty and hard material conditions or, on the contrary, to increasing material progress, are sharply contradicted by the facts. The economic, materialist interpretation of history is again proved inadequate, limited and quite unable to yield the scientific, intellectually satisfying explanation of the trend of human affairs which its devotees, particularly the Marxists, so stridently claim it has provided. Sorokin notes in passing that an explanation of the conditions provoking men to commit suicide markedly similar to his own, has been conclusively demonstrated by Emile Durkheim, who pointed out that they are to be found in any destruction of social and cultural networks (*anomie*) which has the effect of demoralizing and isolating an individual.

It is quite unrealistic to ascribe increases in criminality to illiteracy, mental deficiency, poverty, and low standards of living. Many countries suffering from such conditions have relatively fewer criminals in their midst than has the United States, whose steadily rising standards of life have not banished or reduced the toll which criminals annually levy upon American society. The circumstances provoking suicide and crime are precisely those which produce riots and revolutions: the difference between them being merely one of scale, between single individuals and social groups.

Sorokin does not claim to be able to explain all the ups and downs in the record of disturbances by assigning them to periods of profound cultural change but he regards it as one of the most important reasons, perhaps even the most important reason, always present and inherent in all disturbances, their presence or absence, increase or decrease. His explanation of the conditions in which internal disturbances occur is therefore the same as that which he offers for the increase of war (see page 187).

On the same grounds, he would expect that the forces generating disturbances rarely, if ever, work in one country alone. In fact they seem to work in many countries simultaneously, for the direction of the curves of the indicators of social disturbances between the countries studied is identical, although in no two countries were the curves parallel, neither did they have the same direction in all centuries. The significance of this common experience is that acute revolutionary disturbances can rarely be isolated and confined to one country; they are, and should be, of general concern.

They are, in fact, social and cultural phenomena and they cannot be satisfactorily explained on any other basis.

CHAPTER TEN

Personality and Behaviour

The conclusion from the preceding chapters is plain. The dominant type of culture moulds the type of mentality of the human beings who are born and live in it. Other conditions being equal, a person's mentality will be ideational if he has had no contacts except with those of a pure ideational culture. If his contacts are with the sensate culture, he will have a sensate mentality. A person in contact with different types of culture will have a mixed cultural mentality. Close association with nothing but an unintegrated culture, or with a multitude of cultures of contradictory character, will produce unintegrated personalities, unless by happy, although unlikely chance, the perfect balance between an ideational and sensate culture is struck to produce the integrated unity of the mixed idealistic culture. Such exceptions are rare and they are hardly ever perfect.

Cultural mentality is one thing. Actual concrete behaviour by no means corresponds closely to it. It is a common every-day experience to find that prosaic, selfish, ugly, inhuman acts are justified by their perpetrators to the world, often quite sincerely, by high-sounding language as deeds of the utmost nobility and grandeur. It is not, therefore, true that ideas rule the world in the literal meaning of those words.

The differences between the thoroughgoing sensate and ideational mentalities, themselves rarely if ever found in their pure forms, are considerably reduced when the actual behaviour rather than the beliefs of their exponents is studied. Elementary biological needs ensure a common minimum of similarity between both types. Members of ideational societies, such as ascetic monasteries, have not always mortified the flesh to the same extent as their founders and conspicuously holy brethren have succeeded in doing. Failure to live up to high ideational standards is then apt to be excused, justified, or glorified by specious pretexts of one sort or another. Murder and savagery have notoriously been permitted or encouraged in ideational cultural societies as long as unbelievers or infidels are the victims. Various forms of sexual license and the accumulation of riches have also found indulgence in manifest contradition with the essential principles of the ideational way of life. In these and other ways, Sorokin allows for the influence of external circumstances of life upon cultural change. Such aberrations are exceptions and however persistent or impressive they may seem, they should not be allowed to obscure the essential quality and the reality of the ideational mentality and of the ideational way of life. Differences between the bearers of the ideational and sensate cultures are less great in their respective conduct and personality than in their mentality, nevertheless they are real differences and they may readily be perceived.

To the very great, although not very clearly definable, extent that mentality or cultural outlook finds outward manifestation or expression in behaviour, it is inevitable that there should be striking contrasts between the acts of the predominantly ideational and the basically sensate cultural types. If the present book has not succeeded in indicating the reality of this difference, Sorokin's own works accumulate ample evidence, adequate to establish the truth of the fact that strongly contrasting productions in the arts, in science, philosophy, religion in moral systems, systems of law, in forms of political, social and economic organization, result from general patterns of culture not only divergent but themselves forming coherent systematic wholes; cultural super-systems, as Sorokin calls them.

These artistic and cultural manifestations are themselves a form of behaviour. To build the Parthenon or the Cathedral at Chartres, a modern laboratory, hospital, cinema, theatre or law-court, involves the capital and labour, in other words, the activity of hundreds of men over a very long period. By their fruits they are known. They are also known by what they leave undone. It may be concluded, therefore, that the dominant type of culture conditions the forms, the stimulation and inhibition of certain actions and reactions, and it conditions also the activities closely related to the satisfaction of elementary biological needs. The key-word clearly is *conditions*, for it is not claimed that the relationship between the type of culture and type of conduct is everywhere as complete or as close as is the relationship between the type of culture and its related mentality.

In an effort to test these conclusions by another statistical survey of history, Sorokin presents the results of an investigation made by an independent research worker.

The accounts given of individuals mentioned in the ninth edition (1875) of the *Encyclopaedia Britannica* were analysed and classified as belonging to the sensate, ideational or mixed cultural classes. The number of lines given to each in the *Encyclopaedia* was regarded as a rough indication of each person's relative influence. Then geometric averages for the total number of persons and of lines in each 50-year period from 950 B.C. to 1849 A.D. were computed. The sum of the geometric averages for all the personalities in each of the three classes in every fifty-year period was regarded a 100, and the percentage of each of the three types in every period was established.

The results are given in Table 8.

These figures show, Sorokin concludes, that within every fifty-year period except five, for which data will probably always be lacking, all three types, ideational, mixed and sensate, are to be found coexisting. The ideational type is less frequent than the sensate and mixed, as would be expected for the reasons just explained. Despite erratic movements, there are definite long-term waves in the relative rise and decline of each type, and these agree broadly with the conclusions reached on other grounds relating to the prevalence of each cultural system. For instance, the period 950 B.C. to 851 B.C. appears dominated by the sensate type of personality, which is consistent with what is known as Creto-Mycenæan culture.

850-801 B.C. is a transitional period.

800-501 B.C. shows a notable increase in the percentage of ideational types, as would be expected from what is known of the early history of Greece.

500-451 B.C. seems well balanced, with a slight domination of ideational types, which tallies with the idealistic culture of Greece at that time.

450 B.C.-A.D. 1 shows a decisive change, sensate and mixed types. grow at the expense of the ideational.

A.D. 1-249 indicates a sudden but unstable spurt of the ideational type, characterising a period of violent transition.

A.D. 250-899, notwithstanding erratic fluctuations for a few fifty-year periods, the record shows a perceptible trend towards an increase in the ideational types.

900-1199 and 1200-1399, a decline in ideational types followed by their rise in the next period.

1400 onwards shows a steady trend in favour of either the mixed or sensate types.

This empirical study was made independently by a student unaware of the main conclusions to which Sorokin's other work was pointing.

*Table 8.   GEOMETRIC AVERAGES FOR TYPES OF HISTORICAL PERSONS, 950
B.C.   TO   A.D.   1849, INCLUDED IN THE ENCYCLOPAEDIA BRITANNICA (1875)*

PERIOD	Ideational		Mixed		Sensate	
	Number	*Per Cent*	*Number*	*Per Cent*	*Number*	*Per Cent*
950–901 B.C.	0	0	0	0	17.9	100
900–851	13.7	12	0	0	102.7	88
850–801	0	0	18.0	100	0	0
800–751	21.6	53	0	0	19.2	47
750–701	53.4	76	11.8	17	5.2	7
700–651	9.8	34	11.1	38	7.9	28
650–601	21.5	22	35.6	37	38.6	41
600–551	69.6	38	61.0	34	50.7	28
550–501	120.4	40	67.5	22	114.2	38
500–451	124.6	37	107.6	33	100.9	30
450–401	68.6	11	228.9	38	306.2	51
400–351	79.6	13	326.0	56	180.7	31
350–301	43.2	7	279.9	45	290.1	48
300–251	33.1	12	192.1	70	59.7	18
250–201	12.6	5	85.3	35	148.1	60
200–151	12.5	5	96.3	39	145.1	56
150–101	0	0	43.6	45	51.8	55
100–51	16.9	4	112.4	24	333.8	72
50–1	69.4	11	224.2	35	339.1	54
0–49 A.D.	179.9	31	119.3	21	272.9	48
50–99	46.0	9	219.2	43	240.7	48
100–149	100.0	26	208.4	55	72.0	19
150–199	23.7	7	238.4	76	54.7	17
200–249	121.5	43	133.5	47	29.8	10
250–299	102.7	56	32.8	18	46.9	26
300–349	78.0	23	126.2	37	139.0	40
350–399	204.7	40	190.2	38	111.7	32
400–449	80.4	22	165.2	45	123.7	33
450–499	22.8	11	113.4	52	80.4	37
500–549	77.9	28	84.6	30	115.9	42
550–599	45.6	30	58.6	39	48.0	31
600–649	58.5	40	45.2	31	42.2	29
650–699	29.6	45	19.0	29	17.2	26
700–749	43.1	44	15.3	16	38.7	40
750–799	33.8	48	12.6	18	23.6	34
800–849	57.0	36	74.1	47	26.3	17
850–899	91.0	37	76.6	31	76.8	32
900–949	16.8	14	51.7	42	54.5	44
950–999	18.1	10	75.6	42	87.2	48
1000–1049	38.2	15	75.0	29	148.5	56
1050–1099	24.4	6	145.6	37	218.7	57
1100–1149	72.5	17	176.6	41	177.3	42
1150–1199	74.8	15	210.9	41	228.0	44
1200–1249	66.1	15	166.9	36	231.3	49
1250–1299	172.0	33	185.9	35	167.0	32
1300–1349	91.4	26	181.7	51	81.2	23
1350–1399	144.6	23	152.5	24	330.4	53
1400–1449	141.4	18	322.7	42	302.1	40
1450–1499	240.9	15	602.1	38	730.9	47
1500–1549	543.4	17	1037.5	33	1543.1	50
1550–1599	485.9	14	1429.7	41	1528.1	45
1600–1649	537.0	12	1861.5	42	2023.5	46
1650–1699	949.4	19	1641.8	34	2179.0	47
1700–1749	724.0	17	2014.4	44	1534.0	39
1750–1799	901.6	10	3566.6	41	4329.9	49
1800–1849	1460.0	9	7301.1	50	5870.5	41

It provides historical evidence that there is an association between the type of dominant culture and the frequency of the type of conduct and personality. Sorokin supplements it by a survey of the types of Roman Catholic Popes and of the monarchs of France, Russia, Austria and England. The Roman hierarchy would not be expected to yield many sensate characters, but Sorokin's statistics show that conspicuously ideational types disappear after about A.D. 942, except for the century 1045-1144. From 942 to 1044, and especially from 1342-1549, a slightly sensate type of Pope dominated. Kings, on the other hand, can hardly be expected to be ideational types. Apart from the English kings, they were indeed of increasingly sensate types as Western culture expanded. Nevertheless from 1250-1399 the ideational type of monarch increased. In England this period was longer, from 1216 to 1413.

A final calculation is based upon the number of men active in the field of business, on the one hand, and of religion on the other. These contrasting types probably reflect well the contrast between sensate and ideational behaviour. Again, as would no doubt be expected, business did not become an avenue through which historical importance could be achieved until the period 350-101 B.C. Thereafter it again fell away, but reappeared between A.D. 1100-1149, and began, after minor fluctuations, to grow and maintain itself. Sorokin considers that this evidence establishes that there are indeed ideational, sensate, idealistic and mixed, including the unintegrated, forms of behaviour and types of personality, and that each type occurs most often in respectively the ideational, sensate, idealistic or mixed society.

CHAPTER ELEVEN

The Nature of
Cultural and Social Change

The survey of history undertaken by Sorokin leads, as all wide-ranging historical surveys inevitably must, to some general theory or philosophy of social life. Sorokin does not content himself, as many writers have done, with a few, often tentative and imperfectly-elaborated generalities upon so vast a theme. He makes his conclusions specific, and he uses them as a basis for a new approach to the study of sociology, or the life of mankind in groups and societies.

With this aim, he followed the publication of the first three volumes of *Social and Cultural Dynamics*, in 1937, with a fourth volume in 1941, in which he studied in detail three main groups of problems arising from his earlier findings and theories. He sought to analyse in more detail the nature of a true system of culture, of what he calls a socio-cultural system or supersystem; to distinguish it from mere chance mixtures of an unsystematic, unrelated kind that he describes as socio-cultural congeries, as well as from the miscellaneous collections of cultural systems and these congeries found in any one place which he describes as the structure of the total culture of an area. He next discussed how culture changes, and finally asked why it changes. Inasmuch as the answers to these problems will to some extent at least have emerged from the preceding chapters, there will be some risk of repetition in returning to them here. Nevertheless it should prove useful to recapitulate and round off the historical survey by directing special attention to the main deductions to be drawn from it.

An immediately striking fact about Sorokin's views on the nature of cultural systems is his insistence upon their complexity. Many, if not most, historians have, of course, been so impressed by the complexity that they refuse to believe in the possibility of detecting any order, still less any system, in the apparently haphazard, chaotic and purely casual, chance sequence of events. History on these assumptions never repeats itself. Neither does it fit any pattern or follow any plan.

Such a view, which Sorokin describes as 'socio-cultural atomism', condemns any search for uniformities as unwarranted, and thereby denies the possibility of building up any broad system of knowledge about social life or of constructing any form of sociology as a science of socio-cultural uniformities. Despite the vehemence with which this atomist view is often held, the very people who propound it may often be found introducing general ideas at some stages of their work without, however, giving any adequate definition or elaboration of their meaning.

A completely opposite doctrine is maintained by many historians and sociologists, who regard the whole mixed bag of miscellaneous aspects of social life of every kind or the total culture of any area as something which can quite properly be discussed as though it were a whole, a single thing, self-contained and complete in itself or, as Sorokin describes it, entirely integrated as a single functional system. A number of anthropologists have fallen victims to this error in discussing the total culture of areas, such as the Trobriand or Samoa Islands or of the Melanesians or other groups, primitive or not, as though they were necessarily completely integrated, static wholes. Sorokin regards the twenty-one civilizations, Hellenic, Western, Sumerian, Egyptiac, Far Eastern, Indic, etc., of A. J. Toynbee's great work *A Study of History* (1934-39), as another example of the same mistake. These integralist theories are mistaken, because they simply mix the causal, meaningful or mixed relationship, which a true cultural system must exhibit, with all sorts of purely chance occurrences, not really essential parts of that culture but consisting instead of other inessential factors derived from mere adjacency in space and time.

Between the cultural atomists and the integralists there are many other currents of sociological and anthropological thought, such as those popularized by the diffusionists, for example, who regard a culture such as that of Egypt as a completely integrated whole, but yet imagine in some obscure way that various elements of it could separate themselves from the rest of the system and diffuse, each in different directions, to take root in the various cultures to which they had emigrated.

All such theories fail to do justice to the real nature and wide range of cultural and social systems which any true culture must include and integrate. Sorokin lists language, science, religion, fine arts, ethics as the main cultural systems of mankind. Each of these systems (except language) has many sub-systems to include, for example, literature, music, theatre, architecture, sculpture and painting under fine arts and law and morals under ethics. In addition there is a large number of mixed, composite and derivative cultural systems, all of which are either composites or derivatives from the first five named, being combinations of their sub-systems. The main such derivative systems are religion-law; science-art-ethics; systems of philosophy; of economics and of politics.

Over and above these purely *cultural* systems and these sub-systems stand the *social* systems, and the men and women composing them, who act as bearers or agents through whom the cultural reality finds expression. They may be the bearers of one or two specified kinds of cultural values if they are associations for definite and limited artistic, religious, economic or other purposes, or they may be bearers of a whole collection or encyclopedia of cultural values. The family, the university or the state are examples of this omnibus social class.

Efforts to frame a general, all-inclusive view of this vast field of cultural and social systems and sub-systems have been many. The overwhelming majority try to find a reasonable theory or explanation of them by selecting some chief or prime factor, variable or principle, as a kind of central axis on which all the cultural and social systems depend and by which they are conditioned. The unity of the cultural system is thus made to result from the all-embracing power of the selected chief principle or central axis.

The many great principles which have been put forward as the clue to historical development, to serve as this 'central axis', fall into two broad groups, those which regard the axis as some compelling force existing in its own right outside the culture or society and those which select one of the factors or systems existing within the culture or society itself as the axis.

The chief *external* integrating or governing principles are the geographic theories, including cosmic theories, such as those about sunspots and the influence of the stars, and the biological theories which stress the supposed controlling influence of factors such as race, heredity, pressure of population or the evolutionary struggle for existence.

Among the factors or systems selected from within the various cultural systems and sub-systems as the key to the operation of human development as a whole have been:

Economic: Marxianism and others.
Technological: Marxianism, T. Veblen and others.
Religious: F. de Coulanges, A. Comte, Hegel (partly), Max Weber and others.
Family Forms: Le Play and his school.

Customs, Habits, Folkways, *Mores*: Sumner.

Science: De Roberty and others.

These few examples by no means exhaust the list.

Popular as the search for a single explanatory principle has been, there have also been other theories suggesting that there are but two main systems which between them can explain everything. Thus the universe has been studied under the aspects of civilization and culture, or divided according to its material and non-material aspects, or its technological and ideological aspects. All the variegated thoughts and achievements of mankind then have to be compressed into one or other of the two all-embracing factors. Whatever may be thought of Sorokin's own historical analysis outlined in the preceding chapters, it should at least have made evident the inadequacy of these and all other simpler or more arbitrarily drawn efforts to explain the nature of cultural development. He has, moreover, thrown down a very clear challenge to those who assume that no general philosophical explanations are possible. In sharp contrast with the oversimplified schemes of historical interpretation briefly alluded to above, Sorokin concludes that the total culture of an individual or of a society is neither an incoherent maze of unrelated unco-ordinated peculiarities, or 'congeries', nor is it ever likely to be one perfectly integrated system. To the extent that a considerable part of the total culture of a society or an individual is unified into one of a few great super-systems, it may be said to be rational, logical and consistent. It shows a system of meanings as its central and absolutely essential characteristic. To the extent that a people's culture consists of congeries, either parts of systems or of single cultural values, they are non-rational, non-logical, inconsistent creatures.

To contend that man and society are perfectly rational and logical as the philosophers of one main idea, or the totalitarian integrators do, or to believe as those who consider, as the atomists must, that man and society are completely non-rational and non-logical, are equally wrong. The truth is that at any given moment there are to be found in man and society rational and logical together with non-rational and non-logical opinions and behaviour; super-systems coexisting with congeries; consistency with contradiction; integration with disintegration; both synthesis and the accumulation of disunited and undigested values. Sorokin emphasizes the fact that the number of unintegrated, eclectically mixed cultures is enormous. Nevertheless, amongst the welter of confused and confusing cultural phenomena, he claims to have detected and described three great super-systems which have for long periods in the past successfully polarized for a time most of the activities and beliefs of very large numbers of people and of many societies.

After charting the existence, the growth, development and decline of these ideational, idealistic and sensate cultural super-systems, it is possible to get a new insight into the character of past civilizations and cultures.

By demonstrating the manner in which each of these super-systems successfully integrates their various component elements into a truly unified culture, so that their arts, science, social and economic philosophy are seen to have an interrelated common style peculiar to each and not shared by the other two, Sorokin makes possible a new encyclopædic grasp of the nature of past cultures to deepen and also to extend historical knowledge.

How the discovery and description of his cultural super-systems succeed in providing operational concepts for cautious use in historical interpretation becomes clearer after he has explained in the light of his facts and his theories how cultures and cultural systems change in space and time.

How changes in social and cultural life occur

Does the total culture of a given area change all together as one system, or do its various elements change atomistically and independently from one another?

Sorokin answers this question by making several important distinctions.

If a cultural system is closely integrated, it changes as a whole, in togetherness. The greater the integration and inter-dependence of the system, the greater the togetherness of the change.

If it is not closely integrated, none but considerable changes in the most important parts of it will be interconnected and able to lead to a change of all the important compartments of the culture as a whole.

If a given culture is a mere spatial congeries any part of it can change without involving any change in the rest of its elements. When, as usually happens, a given total culture is made up partly of coexisting single congeries and partly of several systems, some but not all of which are subordinated and united into larger systems and super-systems (some being coordinated with one another and some being congeries to one another), then such a culture will change differently in its different parts. All its important elements united into a super-system change together. Its congeries all change independently and at a different rate from that of the super-system.

There is the further complication which Sorokin does not fully analyse, resulting from the fact that cultural systems and sub-systems themselves evolve according to their own immanent principles, thereby influencing the super-system also. Marxist economics is perhaps one of the most striking examples of such an immanent development, for it has exercised a tremendous influence upon contemporary life and culture, although it has proved to be an influence still within the framework of a sensate super-system, as was seen on page 144.

It may seem that such an account of the matter does not explain very much and that the atomists, who think that everything is a matter of chance, are not far wrong. Certainly Sorokin does not blink the very great difficulties of going beyond the scepticism of the atomists. One immediately obvious practical difficulty is of deciding which elements are mere congeries and which are truly parts of one system. Although real, the difficulties, Sorokin holds, are not insurmountable. He is at least able to dispose quickly of a vast number of false clues. He points out that a moment's reflection upon these very numerous and complex fundamental patterns of change will soon explode all the single-factor, monistic theories of cultural change, such as Marxianism, geographical, technological or biological determinism, all of which, in so far as they purport to explain the whole history of human cultural development, Sorokin describes as hopelessly dead.

In the ideational-idealistic-sensate super-systems and their related social elements, on the other hand, it is possible to embrace satisfactorily not all but a far larger number of systems and sub-systems than any other rival theory so far propounded can hope to do. Proof of the fact becomes all the more impressive as the review proceeds of other general problems of the nature of cultural change. One of them is to discover, when systems change together, whether they do so through space? Aristotle long ago demonstrated that no motions or changes, whether of number or kind, can occur without local displacement or movement in space. Space change can happen independently of other forms of change, but these cannot occur without it.

Physical as well as social space is involved in the migrations of cultural phenomena. The steam locomotive, communism and the designs of motor cars, jazz and lipstick, Beethoven's symphonies and the theory of evolution move from one country to another, from one class to another, from city to country communities.

Movement in social space, although one of the simplest forms of cultural change involves a multitude of fascinating problems upon which all too little light has so far been shed by students of history and social life. The routes by which cultural objects and phenomena have travelled can also form an absorbing study. It involves knowledge of the direction of the streams of the cultural elements, an investigation of the importers and earliest recipients of new cultural values, an explanation of the lag in the entrance of the finished products into the culture of the rural classes, lower classes and less civilized peoples. It leads to studies of the shifting of great centres of culture, and therefore to an inquiry why certain cultural systems and values multiply and spread successfully while others do not. Of them all, it may be asked, which cultural values penetrate and are first to diffuse, the material or the non-material, and how are cultural objects and values transformed in the process of migration? It is not merely a question of migration from place to place, but from upper class to lower class, or, what usually occurs only in periods of cultural decline, from lower class to upper class. Difficult as it is to answer these questions; impossible upon the basis of single factor or monistic theories of cultural change; they become more tractable as soon as a systematic use is made of the concept of a total culture of any people or community as a conglomeration of systems, super-systems, coordinated systems and congeries of systems and single elements.

Cultural changes occur not merely from one area to another, and from one social class to another, but also from one period of time to another. The four theories of this temporal aspect of cultural change maintain:

1. That when all varieties of cultural phenomena change, they all change at the same time.

     This theory will not bear examination, particularly in the absence of any agreed time unit as the measure of change, e.g., is it a year, a generation, or a century?

2. Some classes of cultural phenomena always lead in the change, while the others lag in a certain uniform order.

     One of the best-known varieties of this theory is the Marxian notion that changes in the technique of economic production precede and determine changes in the structure of society which in turn precede and determine changes in the political, social and intellectual forms and life of society. Material culture is supposed to lead in the process of change while the non-material lags. This theory has already been illustrated by the example given on page 143. Apart from the great initial difficulties over which Marxians and non-Marxians have wrangled as to the exact meaning of the 'material factor', whether, for example, it is to include technique which, as a form of knowledge, is essentially a non-material factor; the theory of the primacy of the economic or technological factor in cultural change is simply and plainly contradicted by the historical record of the movements of discoveries and inventions in technology and natural sciences, philosophy, humanities, fine arts, and social science. Sorokin concludes that all the known varieties of a uniform cultural lag theory are fallacious, inasmuch as they elevate a partial case into a general rule.

3. All cultural phenomena change but in no uniform order and in merely haphazard sequence.

This view also is contradicted by the evident links and connections between the systems within cultural super-systems.

4. Some classes of cultural phenomena change at the same time, others at other times but uniformly in a settled order of change, while there are yet others which show no uniformity at all in their changes.

Sorokin's findings confirm that the main forms of art or science or philosophy or their categories and first principles or several aspects of law and ethics united into one system, broadly speaking, change together, causally and meaningfully, and in time, whether this time is a year, a decade or a century.

While this is true of the systems of the super-systems, there is hardly any invariable uniformity about the times of change of the minor movements of all these variables, such as painting, music and literature.

The important thing is to grasp that the system as a whole changes. It is not true that one of its components, the economic, for instance, starts the change in the first place and the other components follow.

Variations in the creative achievement in different cultural fields

Relying again, as far as possible, upon as objective a series of facts as he was able to collect, Sorokin, with the aid of a collaborator, presents an analysis of the relative importance of all the historical persons mentioned in *Encyclopaedia Britannica* (9th edition) who have contributed to each of the following fields of culture over each period of fifty years: Religion, statesmanship, literature, scholarship (humanistic, juridical and social sciences), science (including technology), philosophy, business, fine arts, and miscellaneous.

He does not place a greater value upon the results of this survey than its obvious limitations would permit. Such qualities as editorial omniscience, the perfect objectivity of contributors or the complete adequacy of their historical knowledge, for example, are not assumed. Over-emphasis upon British and English speaking people must also be allowed for, as well as the necessary absence of any personal record matching the great achievements of anonymous artists and collective enterprises in the ideational and idealistic periods, all of which must be recognized as additional shortcomings. The results shown are therefore somewhat distorted, but the distortion is not catastrophic. No better information is readily available, while that which Sorokin provides is, as he claims, the fullest, most systematic and most impartial data so far given by any theory of culture and cultural change. It at least is not the type of fact so often used by so-called scientific writers whose facts are purely and simply illustrative, descriptive shreds of pseudo-facts, quite unable to support scientifically as they are supposed to do, the generalized propositions they are brought in to sustain.

The numerical indicators produced as a result of this study give for each fifty years the geometric average of the number of persons mentioned in each field and the number of lines devoted to them in the *Encyclopaedia Britannica*. The quantitative-qualitative assessment of each eminent person's historical achievement thus results from the amount of space devoted to him. An arithmetical average of all the geometric averages in the last column gives a rough index of the total creativity of each fifty-year period in all ten fields of activity. The following table (pages 222 and 223) summarizes his general results.

Sorokin also presents the results, omitted here, from the following countries separately: Greece, Rome, France, England, Germany, Austria Hungary and Bohemia, Russian and Poland, United States.

The main deductions drawn from these findings are:

(*a*)   That in all fields of culture, both in the non-material subjects (religion, literature, art) as well as in the material subjects (science and technology), cultural achievement is accumulative.

(*b*)   The direction of the process is naturally linear, if only because of this accumulative addition of cultural achievements over time.

(*c*)   The creativeness of various periods fluctuates enormously and violently. Some periods of the ideational cultures are sterile or unanimous; some periods have no achievements of any kind. In other periods there are great explosions of creative activity.

(*d*)   Religion and statesmanship provide a more continuous stream of creative historical persons. Creativeness in economic and business achievements is most fragile, the least continuous and most apt to dry up and disappear. Again it is entirely false to claim that historically, technological, economic and scientific inventions or creativeness are more continuous or accumulative than the religious, political or humanistic activities.

(e) Religion and statesmanship provide historical persons and creative achievements earlier than any other field. Literature comes next. Business is the last to develop. Philosophy, fine arts, science and scholarship all appear at about the same period. Social, political and military organization are the earliest paramount necessities for any group.

(f) Religion and statesmanship are not merely the first to emerge, they remain the most important fields.

(g) The manner in which the ten cultural systems, summarized on pages 222-223, emerge and decline is in accord with what has been found about the succession of ideational, idealistic and sensate cultures. The record in relation to business and religion affords the best evidence of the mutual incompatibility of the ideational and sensate cultures. Reduced to the most summarized formula, it seems to show that it has indeed been found that man could not, over the centuries, serve both God and Mammon.

(h) Literature, fine arts and music for the writers of the *Encyclopaedia Britannica* meant, for the most part, the sensate forms of those arts. Partly for this reason, but above all because, in their ideational forms they are largely collective or anonymous productions, the indicators of influence and leadership in them are greater in sensate than in ideational periods.

(i) Science is predominantly a sub-system of sensate culture, and the statistical indicators show that it rises and falls with sensate culture.

(j) Scholarship and philosophy can flourish in ideational, idealistic or sensate periods as the indicators show.

On all these grounds, Sorokin bases his claim that his division of culture into super-systems with their qualitatively different dependent systems is an analytic procedure superior to that so far provided by any other classification. He also claims that it provides an historically valid, easily understood explanation of cultural changes.

His theory fits the facts and by the facts he means, if not all the facts, at any rate vastly more of them than any previous writers on the subject have thought it necessary to collect. At the same time, he recognizes that there are not by any means as many facts as could be desired, particularly relating to ideational epochs.

Rhythm and phases in cultural change

Sorokin next takes up the question whether the cultural changes show any rhythm in their movement. Rhythm, tempo, periodicity, cycle, oscillation and fluctuation are all terms that have been used

Table 9—HISTORICAL PERSONALITIES MENTIONED IN *THE ENCYCLOPAEDIA BRITANNICA* (*1875*)

Geometric Averages of the number of lines devoted to each.

Period	I Religion	II State	III Literature	IV Scholarship	V Science	VI Philosophy	VII Business	VIII Misc.	IX Fine Arts	X Music	Arithmetic Average
B.C.											
4000–3951	—	8.4	—	—	—	—	—	—	—	—	0.8
3000–2951	—	6.4	—	—	—	—	—	—	—	—	0.6
1500–1451	—	—	—	—	—	10.0	—	—	—	—	1.0
1050–1001	39.0	48.3	—	—	—	—	—	—	—	—	8.7
950–901	17.9	—	—	—	—	—	—	—	—	—	1.8
900–851	13.7	21.8	44.6	—	—	—	—	—	—	—	7.9
850–801	—	18.0	—	—	—	—	—	—	—	—	1.8
800–751	10.6	19.2	10.9	—	—	—	—	—	—	—	4.1
750–701	53.4	18.2	—	—	—	—	—	—	—	—	7.2
700–651	9.8	—	19.3	—	—	—	—	—	—	—	2.9
650–601	36.2	21.7	34.8	—	—	—	—	—	—	—	9.3
600–551	69.5	39.2	25.7	—	—	41.0	—	—	6.6	—	18.2
550–501	42.3	104.4	12.8	—	—	122.7	—	8.7	7.6	—	29.9
500–451	30.8	96.7	105.8	5.9	—	64.8	—	2.8	26.9	—	33.8
450–401	3.6	168.0	144.4	80.3	—	110.4	—	9.3	48.4	—	58.8
400–351	2.8	175.0	26.3	57.4	3.8	214.3	—	5.2	27.1	—	52.2
350–301	—	281.7	32.1	31.2	14.1	145.3	5.5	—	50.6	3.1	54.4
300–251	—	70.4	51.7	1.7	10.3	91.6	14.3	—	—	—	26.0
250–201	—	155.0	42.7	5.8	4.4	8.5	—	4.6	—	—	24.6
200–151	—	111.7	81.0	38.6	30.9	13.0	—	—	—	—	24.9
150–100	6.7	37.5	12.3	5.4	33.6	11.4	2.2	26.0	15.3	—	8.6
100–51	5.6	265.9	95.2	23.2	12.9	14.8	—	—	2.8	—	43.8
50–1	13.1	216.0	219.5	128.1	7.5	4.0	—	—	3.7	2.2	61.9
A.D.											
0–49	253.4	125.6	41.3	41.1	23.2	55.3	—	18.5	—	—	54.9
50–99	36.4	170.7	159.8	55.1	8.4	46.8	—	—	—	—	48.7
100–149	132.3	37.3	54.1	71.7	14.1	2.2	—	11.2	—	—	34.7
150–199	97.3	70.4	68.3	34.4	38.7	38.6	—	—	2.6	—	32.2
200–249	155.2	77.3	16.7	15.2	10.3	19.6	—	—	—	—	28.4
250–299	135.6	36.6	3.8	1.7	4.3	—	—	—	—	—	18.2

A.D.											
300–349	200.0	75.8	—	29.5	9.4	22.9	—	5.7	—	—	34.3
350–399	307.9	78.7	41.9	34.7	15.0	18.0	—	—	3.3	—	50.0
400–449	197.3	83.7	33.8	50.6	—	—	—	—	—	—	36.5
450–499	35.5	86.8	11.9	53.1	4.7	20.1	—	—	—	—	19.6
500–549	56.4	119.3	22.4	58.8	7.4	28.6	—	—	—	—	28.0
550–599	80.3	40.6	44.2	15.2	4.1	—	—	—	—	—	16.6
600–649	199.4	52.0	14.6	7.2	—	—	—	—	—	—	30.7
650–699	78.5	1.7	—	—	12.0	—	—	—	—	—	9.5
700–749	54.0	34.1	—	12.2	—	16.6	—	—	—	—	11.2
750–799	34.4	55.2	—	8.1	—	9.7	—	—	—	—	9.8
800–849	76.3	60.8	4.6	24.1	8.9	5.8	—	2.4	—	3.1	16.6
850–899	129.8	80.4	—	45.0	3.3	—	—	—	—	8.0	28.4
900–949	80.2	54.0	7.8	15.5	—	—	—	—	—	—	18.1
950–999	59.1	93.1	48.0	19.7	29.2	28.3	—	—	—	—	22.6
1000–1049	94.6	129.3	14.3	8.8	6.3	29.7	3.0	—	—	10.5	28.7
1050–1099	195.1	211.6	23.1	25.5	—	56.3	—	—	—	—	49.0
1100–1149	152.6	132.7	20.0	110.0	18.9	8.8	—	—	—	—	44.8
1150–1199	222.4	182.0	63.9	54.4	13.2	21.4	—	—	—	—	58.4
1200–1249	136.9	195.1	41.4	62.6	8.8	34.3	—	4.5	4.7	—	47.7
1250–1299	156.3	185.0	47.2	64.4	14.8	—	16.9	8.6	35.8	—	54.0
1300–1349	108.7	180.8	108.2	53.1	—	—	15.0	—	78.1	—	58.7
1350–1399	195.8	193.8	142.5	32.5	—	—	29.5	5.0	36.6	—	65.1
1400–1449	161.4	222.0	56.0	90.8	4.6	33.2	40.1	14.3	157.7	—	78.0
1450–1499	231.9	393.4	120.2	213.5	12.1	8.9	100.7	29.0	442.1	12.1	156.4
1500–1549	805.8	504.4	409.2	220.3	96.3	65.3	82.3	116.6	790.4	10.8	310.1
1550–1599	626.6	782.3	782.1	363.9	187.0	49.1	70.0	149.2	262.3	75.9	334.8
1600–1649	512.6	927.0	828.9	441.7	295.0	328.5	71.7	138.2	686.0	38.4	426.8
1650–1699	901.1	1063.1	942.8	389.3	420.7	303.2	68.1	57.7	560.1	78.1	478.4
1700–1749	634.2	786.4	842.6	527.7	451.0	318.8	77.9	181.2	249.0	149.1	421.8
1750–1799	452.4	2329.9	1666.5	995.2	1318.0	404.5	271.3	397.3	597.9	295.8	872.9
1800–1849	944.6	3201.0	2765.0	2022.2	2042.2	535.3	692.7	530.2	1327.7	390.4	1445.1
Totals	9287.3	14937.4	10406.2	6646.4	5199.4	3361.6	1561.2	1726.2	5423.3	1077.5	5962.9

very frequently in the social sciences, but rarely with any precision. Sorokin devotes some pains to their elucidation.

Among the many previous rhythmical theories, Sorokin calls attention to those in pairs, or dyads, such as war-peace; order-disorder; the Chinese Yin and Yang; the Hindu alternation of the materialization of the spiritual unity (Brahma) and its dematerialization; the Babylonian rhythm of the destruction and recreation of the world; the eternal struggle between strife and love of Empedocles; Campanella's alternation of religion-atheism; Saint-Simon's rhythm of 'critical and organic periods'; Fourier's anarchy-unity; A. N. Whitehead's intuition-scholarship; J. L. Lowe's convention-revolt in poetry and literature.

There are very many others. In the social sciences, writers have called attention to such dual sequences as rapid population increase followed by slow increase or stationary condition (G. Schmoller, R. Pearl, G. U. Yule); alternation of the phase of concentration of wealth and its more even distribution (G. Schmoller, V. Pareto), expansion and contraction of government regimentation (H. Spencer, P. Sorokin); rise and decline of aristocracy (Aristotle, Plato, Ibn Khaldun, Vico and others); challenge and response, withdrawal and return, rout and rally, apparentation and affiliation societies, schism and palingenesis, growth and decline of civilizations (A. J. Toynbee, O. Spengler); centralization-decentralization (Brooks Adams); technical-materialistic phase and spiritual-religious and ethical phase (L. Weber); culture-civilization (Spengler); binding and loosening (*Bindung und Lösung* of K. Joel).

This long catalogue by no means exhausts the list of various dyads or two-phase rhythms which have been proposed as clues to the processes of history. Three-phase rhythms, or triads, are yet more popular among social and philosophical thinkers, and they can undoubtedly be detected in many social and cultural phenomena. Examples are synthesis of meanings (conception)-incarnation into vehicles (objectification)-acquisition of human agents (socialization); invention-imitation-opposition (G. Tarde); appearance-growth-decline; ideological phase-organizational phase-power phase in social movements (R. Mayreder); breakdown-disintegration-dissolution of civilizations (A. J. Toynbee); architectural-plastic-pictorial phases in art (P. Ligeti); lyric-epic-dramatic in literature (V. Hugo); ancient-medieval-modern (Herder, Hegel, Ranke, Comte, Dilthey); age of gods-of heroes and-of men (G. Vico); three stages of disorderly-small tranquillity-great tranquillity (Confucius); theological-metaphysical-positive stages (A. Comte); thesis-antithesis-synthesis (Hegel).

Four-phase rhythms are also discernible. The alternations of the seasons, the biological rhythm of childhood-adolescence-maturity-old age, morning-afternoon-evening-night, all set a pattern which has been widely adopted. Florus, who flourished around A.D. 200, thought he detected such a rhythm in the history of Rome, and Spengler in our own time applied the pattern of childhood-youth-manhood-old age directly to the explanation of historical change. Four-generation rhythms were adopted by Ibn Khaldun, by Machiavelli, and by G. Ferrari.

An example of the more complicated six-phase rhythm is the well-known cycle of Polybius, monarchy-tyranny-artistocracy-oligarchy-democracy-mob-rule, which he thought was eternally repeated. Sorokin regards the division of the week into seven days as evidence of yet more complicated rhythms of which the month and the year are others. He suggests that magic numbers, such as 3, 7, 9 and 12, bear witness also to the reality of rhythms in social life. In one of his earlier works he analysed, classified and criticized the views of other writers who had studied fluctuations, rhythms, and cycles of social processes. (*Contemporary Sociological Theories*, 1928, see especially pages 728-756.)

Having established the reality of rhythmical change in social and cultural affairs, Sorokin points to the insatiable desire of the human mind to seek to establish and to explain the major rhythms of human history. The thinkers who have sought to satisfy this desire, from Confucius, Lao-Tse, Plato, Aristotle, St. Augustine, Erigena, St. Thomas Aquinas, Ibn Khaldun, Vico, Machiavelli, Hobbes, Descartes, Montesquieu, Adam Smith to Kant, Hegel, Comte, H. Spencer, Marx and others, are still eagerly studied and discussed, while hundreds of less-ambitious, fact-finding studies are neglected and forgotten.

For his own suggestion that the three-phase rhythm of ideational-idealistic-sensate cultures provides a valid and useful clue to historical change, he does not claim more than that it may unquestionably be discerned in the history of Western culture and that, in addition to disclosing one of the most all-embracing, long-term or tidal movements which has twice recurred, it also points to a number of smaller rhythms in the main fields of culture, indicating their interrelations with one another.

Sorokin does not claim for his theory, as Spengler and others did for theirs, that it is universal and applicable to all other cultures as well as to that of Western civilization, despite some evidence for it in Egyptian, Hindu and Chinese history.

The rhythms which may be discerned in the passage of Græco-

P

Roman and Western culture from a dominant ideational phase to idealistic and sensate phases have already been described. They may be summed up as follows:

1. Ideational-idealistic-visual (sensate) rhythm in painting, sculpture, architecture, *Chapter III.*
2. Ideational-idealistic-sensate rhythm in music, drama, literature and art criticism, *Chapter IV.*
3. Ideational-idealistic-sensate rhythm in the systems of truth and knowledge; in religion, philosophy, science, *Chapters V and VI.*
4. Rhythm of stationary, increasing and rapidly-growing discoveries in the natural sciences and in technological inventions, *Chapter V.*
5. Ideational-idealistic-sensate rhythm in the systems of ethics and law, *Chapter VII.*
6. Familistic-contractual-compulsory rhythm in the field of social relationship, *Chapter VIII.*
7. Theocratic-idealistic-secular rhythm in the field of political regimes, *Chapter VIII.*
8. Rhythm of the rise and decline of sensate economic well-being, *Chapter VIII.*
9. Rhythm of the rise of war and internal disturbances in the transitional periods from one phase to another; and decline of such outbreaks in the periods of crystallization and domination of ideational and sensate phases, *Chapter IX.*
10. Rhythm of leadership and domination of religion in the ideational phase, and of business and other sensate activities, in the sensate phases, *Chapter X.*
11. Rhythm of the rise of the ideational type of historical persons in the ideational phase and of the sensate type in the sensate phase, *Chapter X.*
12. Rhythm of ideational-idealistic-sensate forms of liberty, *Chapter VIII.*
13. Tidal rhythm in increase and decrease of totalitarianism and *laisser-faire, Chapter VIII.*
14. Rhythms of idealism-materialism; of eternalism-temporalism; nominalism-conceptualism-realism; of ideational-idealistic-sensate conceptions of time, space, causality and of other first principles and fundamental categories of human thought, *Chapters V and VI.*

Relationships of meaning and causality in cultural life in both their static and dynamic aspects.

The wealth of material studied and presented by Sorokin in each of these fourteen main cultural sub-rhythms has been indicated in the preceding chapters, together with brief summary indications of the way in which their true nature has been classified and rendered more comprehensible by the account given of the main embracing rhythm of the super-systems; the ideational, idealistic and sensate cultures. A firm grasp of the nature of the cultural super-system gives a firm grasp of the nature of the sub-systems in the same way as the branches and leaves of a plant may be grasped by the main stem of the plant. This is a bold claim, for it cannot be made on behalf of other theories of cultural development because, Sorokin says, they all look in the wrong places for the order of change throughout time. He summarizes the point by claiming to have discovered both a static and a dynamic meaningful-causal relationship between an enormous number of socio-cultural phenomena and socio-cultural processes with their rhythms and phases. This summarized statement contains a wealth of meaning, inviting some clarification and further thought.

'*Static* meaningful-causal relationship' may be explained as the relationships in which, where A is given, then $B\,C\,D$ are meaningfully-causally connected. Thus if the essential character A of the sensate super-system is known, it is possible to say that, if A is given, then such and such additional qualities and characteristics $B\,C\,D\,E \ldots N$ will also be given. For example, it can be predicted of such a system A that its art B will be predominantly visual, with all the essential characteristics of such an art (b, c, d, e, f, etc.) described in Chapter III (see, e.g., pages 29, 55, 65); that its system of truth C will be predominantly empirical, with concentration on the natural sciences and technological inventions; that D, supersensory religion, will play a very modest part; that its ethics and law, E, will be predominantly utilitarian, hedonistic, expedient; that its government, F, will be secular, led by military, or rich, or professional groups; that its literature, G, will be predominantly realistic, sensual, in part erotic, with a common type of people instead of gods and heroes as its main personages.

Similar schemes can be drawn up for the ideational and idealistic cultural systems. Given the nature of the super-system, there is thus a clear and tangible possibility of predicting a large number of the forms which would be assumed by its art, philosophy, religion, ethics, social organization and so on; since the A and its $B\,C\,D\,E \ldots N$ are connected causally and meaningfully.

It may be objected that this is a circular argument since A is only known as A by the character of the sub-groups $B\,C\,D\,E \ldots N$. The inadequacy of such a superficial objection may, however, be seen from the fact that the meaningful-causal relationship exists not merely between A and its $B\ C\ D\ E\ \ldots\ N$; but also between B with $C\ D\ E\ \ldots\ N$, between C and $B\ D\ E\ \ldots\ N$ and N with $B\ C\ D\ E$ and so on. The organic unity of the whole can be further shown from the fact that if A is given, $B\ C\ D\ E\ \ldots\ N$ will be there; if A is absent, $B\ C\ D\ E\ \ldots\ N$ will be absent.

'*Dynamic* meaningful-causal relationship', the second half of the claim made for Sorokin's theory on page 227, means the type of relationship which exists between A and B if, when A varies, B also varies. In the scheme just given, it means that if A varies, not only B but $C\ D\ E\ \ldots\ N$ also vary. Such a dynamic relationship exists when an ideational cultural system, A, moves to the idealistic phase, A^1. Then all the other sub-systems, $B\ C\ D\ E\ \ldots\ N$ and their related systems also move. Furthermore, if it is known what kind of fundamental transformation is being experienced by B or C or N, it is possible to foresee with considerable probability the kind of transformations which D, E and other embraced systems, with their rhythms and phases, will be undergoing. A complex net of dynamic relationships of interdependence is thereby discovered, not only between the main cultural process with its super-rhythm—the passage of the super-system from A to A^1, for example—but between the embraced processes and their rhythms.

Sorokin illustrates the theory by assuming that our culture is at present in transition from a dominant sensate phase to a more ideational phase. It would then, he holds, be probable that wars and revolutions will increase, that economic prosperity should decrease, that most sensate values should decrease, beginning with money and the prestige of wealth; that the increase in scientific inventions and discoveries would be at a slower rate; that supersensory religion should find more followers in all its varieties accompanied by increasing mysticism, religious rationalism, fideism; that utilitarian and hedonistic ethics should lose ground; that visual, sensate, sensual and erotic forms and contents of the arts should also decrease.

These changes are probable, not certain. Sorokin does not claim that the sequences he thinks he has discovered are universal and eternal. They have, however, been fairly typical and general. The fact that the sequence ideational-idealistic-sensate appears only to have occurred twice in the history of Western civilization is not, he thinks, a valid statistical reason to doubt the reality and necessary connexions he describes, for their strength lies more in their logico-meaningful interconnections than in the statistical number of their actual recurrences. This does not mean that his theories lack empirical foundation. Indeed he has good reason to claim that he has handled more relevant empirical facts, and handled them with more care than all the guardians of empiricism in sociology taken together. Despite the accusations of some of his critics, Sorokin is less concerned with securing credit for the originality of his views than with the demonstration of the way in which they carry further, amplify and correct earlier views tending in the same general direction, notably those of Vico and Hegel.

Theories of Periodical Social Change

After establishing that cultures change and that rhythmical patterns may be discerned in those changes, Sorokin next examines various theories which have sought to demonstrate the existence of periodicity in cultural change.

This review takes him far afield into a study of some strange and fantastic notions advanced not merely by mystery-mongers of various kinds, but also by profoundly original thinkers, such as Plato and Aristotle. These fanciful imaginary speculations, lumped together by Sorokin as metaempirical, are to be found especially among ancient Hindu theories, as well as in many others, including Chinese, Aztec and Arab speculations. The true nature and significance of Plato's mysterious perfect number of time which completes the perfect year, when all the eight revolutions of the seven planets and the sphere are accomplished together and they again meet at their original point of departure, have continued to baffle his commentators and interpreters. It may be taken as a more exalted sample of the many obscure outpourings of astrologers, soothsayers and numerologists whose activity by no means came to an end at the close of the Dark Ages. No less a genius than Sir Isaac Newton was much given to such speculations, some of which are to be found in his *Observations upon the Prophecies of Daniel and the Apocalypse of St. John*, published after his death in 1733. Nietzsche and Herbert Spencer in more recent times indulged in views with no better factual basis than those of the most wildly speculative theories of much earlier times.

All may be dismissed, Sorokin concludes, as curious and ingenious, perhaps; but incapable of providing any serious or tested knowledge. Many of them, for example, propose such long term periodicities that there is no means of checking their validity.

Cosmic theories of periodicity in historical change are mainly astronomical, astrological and meteorological. The idea that the course of human affairs is very closely linked with the movements of the heavenly bodies is of the greatest antiquity. One of the oldest of such varieties of cosmic theories of periodicity had its origin in the ancient Babylonian development of astronomy and astrology. The great cycle, the *annus magnus* or the world's year, was thought to be completed when all the stars assume again a position they had before, a period variously estimated at 432,000, 480,000 to 720,000 years. The idea persisted, as the reference above to Plato's views indicates. It was kept alive by the Pythagoreans and, in varying forms, is quite commonly found in Greek and Roman writers. The Gnostics and the Fathers of the Church took over similar ideas, which were also kept alive by the Arabs. The early scholastic writers, such as Abelard, William of Conches, Alexander Neckham, Adelard of Bath, were full of astrological theories and prognostications. Similar views persisted throughout the Middle Ages, as the works of Bartholomew of England, Robert Grosseteste, Albertus Magnus, St. Thomas Aquinas, Dante, Peter of Abano and Roger Bacon all testify. Sorokin also quotes many later views, down to works of similar import solemnly put forth in our own time. Considerably less fantastic and more closely tied to mundane events are theories of the geographic type. So also are those of the bio-organismic type of cosmic periodicity of which that interpreting social rhythms and periodicities by the idea of human generations is the most general. Sorokin has little difficulty in demonstrating the fallacious nature of these cosmic and biological explanations of cultural change.

That social happenings cannot be regarded as perfectly independent of the cosmic and biological conditions in which they occur is so obvious that it may readily be admitted. But it does not follow from such an admission that the dependence of social and cultural life on cosmic and biological sources is so close that any change in those sources must necessarily be tangibly reflected in social and cultural life. Any careful study of the facts is sufficient to show that the number of changes in social and cultural life which go on independently or directly contrary to cosmic and biological forces is legion.

Any reliance upon such theories must, moreover, be seen to be unjustified when it is discovered that periodicities in such matters as sunspots, the life of a generation, rainfall or climate generally, are no true periodicities at all but statistical averages, mean, mode or median, dressed up to look like periodicities. It becomes, therefore, statistically impossible to verify the periodicities in social and cultural life alleged to be based upon cosmic and biological forces. Many of the theories purporting to expound such periodicities are perfectly naïve and fantastic. Sorokin will allow no better status to the business cycles with which recent economic literature is so full. They again are purely statistical averages, not identical with a true periodicity and their description varies from author to author, from country to country and from period to period. The truth is that they are averages based upon fancifully varying intervals.

The root of the fallacy in all such cosmic and biological theories is, says Sorokin, that they look for periodicities in the wrong place, that is to say outside and not inside the world of social and cultural phenomena itself. Inside that world there are indeed periodicities, but they represent intentionally or unintentionally established social conventions. Many are of an hourly, daily, weekly, monthly or annual occurrence. There are still longer periodicities running over several years, such as the four-year term of office of an American President. All such conventional periodicities are essentially relative to the country or society in which they occur.

The application of measures of time to describe change in social and cultural life presents many difficulties which Sorokin examines, including some of the better-known efforts to deal with them, such as the so-called law of acceleration which asserts vaguely that everything in the universe tends to change faster as time goes on. For some writers this view is based upon such facts as that the Stone Age lasted longer than the Iron and Bronze Ages. But the use of stone continued with the use of iron and bronze, and both are still used to-day. For this and other reasons, Sorokin concludes that little is to be gained from such notions. He offers, instead, his own view that, when a super-system of culture passes from the ideational to the idealistic and then to the sensate phase, the rates of change in time of the quantitative, qualitative and spatial changes of the super-system, and of all its main systems and sub-systems, tend to become faster. The opposite occurs when a super-system passes from a sensate to an ideational phase, for then the rate of change tends to become slower. Within the sensate phase of the super-system the rate of change tends to become particularly fast in its later, overripe stage. Without enumerating all the arguments and considerations Sorokin advances in support of these conclusions, it will be sufficient to note that they are not merely logically consistent with the nature of the super-systems in question; they are also borne out by the facts presented in the preceding chapters. They also fit the observed sequences of events better than any other theories so far offered. They can, for example, explain retardation as well as acceleration which the so-called law of acceleration is forced to ignore. Besides being very definite, they also have the advantage of relating together the rates of change in large numbers of social and cultural processes. This study concludes Sorokin's review of the nature of change in social and cultural processes. It remains to consider how and why such change occurs.

Why Cultures Change : The Principle of Immanent Change in Social and Cultural Life and the Principle of Limits.

Relentless becoming instead of everlasting permanency was no doubt recognized by mankind as the law of life long before Heraclitus, at the dawn of Greek philosophy, proclaimed that all things are in a state of flux.

Logically, three answers are possible to the question how change is brought about in cultural systems. Change may be caused by forces or factors that lie outside the social and cultural system itself. Pressure of the environment, coupled with mechanistic and behaviouristic theories of mental and social activities, have been widely regarded as an all-inclusive and sufficient explanation of social and cultural change. The fundamental principle, according to such a view, is that of stimulus-response. Current thinking is deeply impregnated with these notions so that the explanation of many social evils, such as crime, the defectiveness of social institutions, political or economic organization, is looked for in external causes.

The opposite solution is the immanent theory of social and cultural change, which holds that social and cultural systems change by virtue of their own forces and properties. Those who hold this view do not place all their hopes for reform or for the improvement of life in some rearrangement of external conditions. Like a doctor, they view social and cultural life as an integral self-contained system, and they would not expect to change an old system into a young one, any more than a doctor would expect to transform an eighty-year-old man into a youth of twenty. Hegel is considered by Sorokin to have arrived at the most consistent and universal conception of immanent change ever created in the history of human thought. Aristotle's theory, although only derivatively immanent, is also one of the most systematic, complete and all-embracing theories of change in general and of socio-cultural change in particular. These are but two examples, analysed in greater detail by Sorokin, among at least four main types of theories of immanent change.

A third possible explanation attempts to combine both the external and immanent factors. Where a truly synthetic or integral principle arises from such a combination, it may suggest a satisfactory solution. Too often, however, real integration is not achieved. Then, although lip-service may be paid to the idea of joint influence, in practice no definite solution is achieved, but merely vague suggestions are given with some emphasis perhaps upon a single external or on an immanent factor.

Sorokin considers that the true source of change must be sought within a social and cultural system, although external factors may also play some part under certain conditions and limits. Change is from within, is immanent, because it is an inevitable consequence of the very existence of the cultural system as a going concern. The alternative to change is equilibrium, a state fatal to any organism, since it spells stagnation, atrophy and death. Change is the law of life. The environment is relatively unchanging. To look for the source of change in the environment instead of within the process of life itself is therefore demonstrably illogical. Extreme externalistic sources of change are thus ruled out unless everything is attributed, without any further attempt to find a rational explanation, to God or the Prime Mover. Mundane material external causes cannot offer a satisfactory explanation. They usually lead to a mere postponement of a solution. Sorokin gives, by way of example, the attempt to explain changes in American family life in the last fifty years (A) by some external factor (B), say a change in industrial conditions. Then the question naturally arises, 'Why have industrial conditions changed?', so that a new theory (C) is brought in to explain (B). It may be the theory (C) that there has been a change in the density of population. But then why has (C) come to be? In this way the suggested explanation is pushed back until some remote notion connected with climatic change or sunspots or other possible cause is reached. All are equally unsatisfactory, because the inevitable question must soon be asked of whatever external cause is chosen, 'Why is it capable of changing itself and of starting changes in the others?' The question is impossible to answer, especially if some material aspects of the environment, such as climate or geology or geographic factors, are proposed as the solution, because that leads to the extraordinary hypothesis that the least changing factors of all are brought in to account for the most rapidly changing of all phenomena—those of life itself.

If the search for purely external causes of change is abandoned in favour of some one of the elements of cultural life itself, such as the means and modes of production of Marxianism, the mystery is by no means solved. How is it possible to demonstrate that some elements in social and cultural life, such as the family, religion or science, cannot change themselves, while some others, such as the methods of production, density of population, art or social customs, can do that?

To believe instead that the true principle of change is engendered within the cultural process itself is not to believe that external forces have no influence in producing cultural change. The family or any other social system, for example, changes immanently, but being in interaction with the State, with business organizations, the Church and other social systems, each of which also changes immanently, the changing family is subject to influences and pressures from them as well. Sorokin likens the total situation to a constellation of immanently changing systems. Change in one member of the constellation is facilitated by changes in the others. Sorokin advances the somewhat paradoxical view that the external, biological or cosmic forces operate in a somewhat similar way. When plague germs or some natural catastrophe attack a cultural system, they provoke a reaction from a living organism which is itself in the process of change.

Among the many practical results of adopting Sorokin's view of the matter would be to introduce a much more cautious note in history text-books where, for example, they seek to expound the so-called causes of great historical events, such as the decline of feudalism, the emancipation of serfs and villeins, the Peasants' Revolt, the Crusades, the Reformation and the Renaissance. On Sorokin's view the crude inadequacy of much that has passed for historical insight into many of these great themes will at once become apparent: the notion, for example, that the Revival of Learning was largely stimulated by the expulsion of Greek scholars and their books when Constantinople was captured by the Turks, or the even more desperate efforts which have been made to find some plausible theory on the lines of the economic interpretation of history to explain the Crusades.

Instead, therefore, of historical phenomena being regarded as an amorphous lump occasionally disturbed or lifted by one or two magic levers, whether economic or bacteriological or climatic, Sorokin depicts history as a field of forces developing according to their own internal principles of evolution, and interacting not in a mechanical but in a truly dynamic fashion. Not only upon general political history does Sorokin cast fresh light. His account of various theories about economic fluctuations, particularly theories about business cycles, is also illuminating. Some of these theories look for the causes of business fluctuations in forces external not merely to the business system but also to the social system of which business is a part. There are, for example, various geographic theories of climatic changes, rainfall, sunspots or other cosmic influences used by various writers to explain the matter.

On the other hand, many business cycle theories are of the clearly immanent type, seeking their explanations of recurrent booms and depressions in the process of saving and investing, in building and construction work, in changes in tastes, and therefore in the quantity and quality of production, in banking operations or in the economic system as a whole. Others offer immanent explanations, but only after insisting that the economic sphere must be regarded as part of the larger social system. Others again collect a number of factors, some immanent and some external, social, psychological, biological and cosmic, often without apparently realizing that a mere mechanical juxtaposition of various factors mostly incommensurable with one another mixes things which cannot then be understood in their comparative roles or in their working together.

To elaborate the consequences of Sorokin's conception of the nature of the forces producing cultural change would extend the analysis beyond the realms of history and far into the field of sociology; not, of course, that there is or should be any incompatibility between the two. History, as the record and explanation of social and cultural change, must inescapably contribute to sociology and be influenced in turn by sociological theories. Sorokin's own work gives what is probably the most detailed and thoroughgoing demonstration of this historical nature of sociology and sociological nature of history, not merely in the four volumes of his *Social and Cultural Dynamics*, but in his system of general sociology best summarized in his *Society, Culture and Personality, their Structure and Dynamics* (1947). It must, therefore, suffice here to report Sorokin's own summary of his conclusions upon the 'why and the how' of social and cultural change.

1. The reason or cause of a change in any socio-cultural system is in the system itself, and need not be looked for anywhere else.

2. The external environment which is mostly composed of the immanently changing systems is an additional reason for a change of a system.

3. Any socio-cultural system changing immanently, incessantly generates a series of immanent consequences, which change not only the environment but also the system itself.

4. The destiny or life career of any socio-cultural system represents mainly an unfolding of the immanent potentialities of the system itself which are the main factor in its own destiny.

5. External forces cannot fundamentally change the immanent potentialities of the system and its normal destiny, but they may crush the system or stop the process of unfolding its imma-

nent potentialities at one of the early phases of its existence. They may also slow down or hasten, help or hinder, strengthen or weaken, the process of realizing those potentialities.

6. So far as the system, after it has emerged, bears in itself its future career, it is a determinate system and in this sense deterministic. So far as the future of the system is determined mainly by the system itself and not by external agents, such a determinism is indeterministic or free, flowing spontaneously from the system itself according to its own nature.

7. The main direction and the main phases of the unfolding are predetermined by the immanent forces within the system, but a considerable margin for variations remains free so that many of the details of development are free and become an unforeseen and unpredictable matter of chance environment and free choice.

8. The relative action of environmental factors and of self-control in shaping the destiny or life career of any system is not constant for all socio-cultural systems, but the more perfectly the system is integrated, the more powerful its self-control will be.

9. A socio-cultural system will have greater power and self-control and be more independent of the forces of environment the greater is its membership, the better the members are biologically, mentally, morally and socially, the greater the actual wisdom, knowledge and experience the system has at its disposal, the better it is organized; the greater the total sum of means of influencing human behaviour and natural forces at its disposal, the more consistently the system is integrated or the more it is able to show its solidarity.

Any attempt to look further into the nature and ground of historical change encounters very obvious and considerable difficulty. If it is asked, for example, why the observed rhythms occur or why social and cultural developments have taken the course they have done, it is not possible to advance beyond the plain and simple empirical position that such are observed facts and there is no more to be said.

Recognizing that many will want some answer to the question, 'Why is it so empirically?', Sorokin reviews several sociological attempts to provide answers and reaffirms his own Principle of Limits (see page 152) to amplify, correct and supplement them. Amongst various efforts to account for periodical movements and rhythmical changes in social and cultural developments, he examines various mechanistic theories, all of which he rejects, including all efforts made to apply the idea of equilibrium in the social sciences.

His views, summarized as the Principles of Limits, are as follows:

1. Identically recurrent socio-cultural processes are impossible.

2. Eternally linear socio-cultural processes are impossible. Any process that appears to be such is in all probability a long-time linear process which in its complete life is likely to be a non-linear process.

3. A linear trend limited in time is found in almost all socio-cultural processes. Its duration is different for different processes, but is shorter than that of the whole existence of the system.

4. It is impossible, both factually and logically, for any socio-cultural processes to have unlimited possibilities of variation of their essential traits. Therefore 'history is ever old and repeats itself'.

5. Apart from the essential traits, there is a wide, almost unbounded, possibility of variation of the accidental properties of a system. Exhausted systems may be replaced by new ones, again giving almost unlimited possibilities of variation. History is therefore ever-new, unrepeated and inexhaustible in its creativeness.

6. Since practically all the socio-cultural systems have limited possibilities of variation in their essential forms, it follows that all systems that continue to exist after all their possible forms have been exhausted are bound to have recurrent rhythms. Recurrence in the life process of such systems is therefore inevitable.

7. The recurrent rhythms will be more frequent, conspicuous and easier to detect and understand in proportion as the possibilities of variation of main forms are more limited.

8. Failure to grasp any recurrent rhythm will result from the process of the socio-cultural system having comparatively large possibilities of variation which empirically prevent the infrequent rhythm being noticed. Or the process may have too short a life span, dying early before it has had a chance to run through all its forms. Or the coexistence and mutual interference of several contemporaneous and different rhythms in the same system blur the rhythm of each, so that, to the observer or listener, they appear as unrhythmical 'noise'. Or there may be an excessively long duration between the recurrences. Or the rhythm may be exceedingly complex and many-phased.

9. In the light of the considerations in the preceding paragraphs, it is possible to assert the truth of the apparently contradictory statements that history ever repeats itself and never repeats itself.

10.   Alternative views of history excluded by these considerations include the strictly cyclical, identically recurrent conception of the socio-cultural process; the linear theory of unlimited movement in one direction; the 'unicist' view of the unique nature of historical phenomena that denies the existence of any recurrent rhythms in the socio-cultural process in favour of the idea that all happenings are brand-new and unique in the totality of their traits and properties at any moment; the static conception that there is no change and that the socio-cultural world ever remains strictly identical with itself. All such views are untenable. The valid view is that of an incessant variation of the main recurrent themes which contains in itself, as a part, all these views and, as such, is much richer than any of them.

In so far, therefore, that the broad trends of Western culture have been manifest in fully integrated cultural patterns explicable as movements of three great cultural super-systems, the ideational, idealistic, and sensate, it seems clear that none of these three can help changing, rising, growing, existing full-blooded for some time and then declining.

The possibilities of change for these fully integrated systems are strictly limited. There can hardly be more than five fundamental answers to the chief problem of all, the true nature of reality, two of which are negative. That is to say, for a fully integrated cultural system, reality must be either supersensory (ideational premise) or sensory (sensate premise) or it has both aspects inseparably (idealistic premise) or it is entirely unknown and unknowable (premise of scepticism) or it is known only in its phenomenal aspect while its transcendental aspect, if it has such, is unknowable (premise of criticism and agnosticism). Each of these several premises may, of course, show many varieties differing in detail. Similarly there cannot be more than five or six integrated systems of truth: the truth of faith, of reason, of the senses, of their idealistic synthesis or an integrated sceptical and agnostic or a critical system. Art styles also must be ideational (symbolic), visual (sensate) or idealistic (integrated symbolic-visual). More detailed patterns of art, such as classic and romantic, idealistic and naturalistic, conventional and revolutionary, linear and *malerisch*, find their development within these three fundamental forms. So also in ethics, in social, economic, political and other relationships, all, in so far as they are integrated, have limited possibilities of change.

What is said above, Sorokin is careful to emphasize, applies merely to *integrated* cultural systems. The number of unintegrated, eclectic and mixed combinations of the ideational and sensate cultural elements is enormous, but by their nature they cannot serve as a major premise of integrated systems of culture. They are characteristic particularly of transitional periods.

Such considerations arising from the Principle of Immanent Change and from the Principle of Limits, pointing to the strictly limited possibility of the main forms of change, help considerably, therefore, to throw more light on the nature of cultural change and represent a major contribution to dynamic sociology.

Sorokin pursues the analysis yet further. Given the three main super-systems of ideational, sensate and idealistic culture, it is clear that each may be either completely true, completely false or partly true and partly false.

If any of the three were entirely true, it could be expected to endure for ever, for it would give an adequate knowledge of reality, it would permit its bearers to adapt themselves successfully to their environment which they would fully understand and thereby ensure a better social and cultural life than could be attained by any system based on error.

If any of the three were entirely false, none of these satisfactory results would be possible and none of them therefore could have dominated millions of human beings for centuries as they did. Moreover after they had disappeared, it would, on such an hypothesis, be unlikely that any of them could have recurred, as they did.

The third possibility, therefore, seems inescapable, and it is necessary to conclude that the observable super-rhythm of alternating sensate-ideational-idealistic cultural super-systems is explicable only on the assumption that each is partly true and partly false, partly adequate and partly inadequate.

The vital part in each of these great cultural systems gives their bearers the possibility of adaptation and survival. Their invalid part, existing side by side with their valid part, leads their bearers away from reality. As any one of the three systems grows, emphasis is increasingly put upon its own special and partial aspects of reality; it becomes monopolistically dominant and it tends to drive out all other systems of truth and reality with the valid parts they contain. Validities are increasingly lost; falsities develop and multiply. Society and its culture, built upon such a basis, becomes more and more empty, false, ignorant, inexperienced, powerless, disorderly and base. The society of its bearers must change its major premises unless it is to perish. Change having been forced upon the society and culture in this way, the process recommences with the new system which has replaced the old and discredited system. Such is the nature of immanent change in a cultural system. It is a dialectical process rather than an organic process. That is to say, Sorokin does not rely upon biological analogies in an attempt to show that cultures die as it were of old age. He seeks to demonstrate that their failure results from the working-out of their own presuppositions or inner natures.

Despite the powerful logic of such an analysis, it seems to Sorokin to need further defence, particularly perhaps because of the evident claim it makes on behalf of the truth of faith derived from sources such as those described as intuition, inspiration, revelation, extra-sensory perception, mystic experience and so on. No honest investigator can, he thinks, deny that from some such force great contributions have been made to science, art, philosophy, religion, ethics, technology or even to economic and practical creative values. Some kind of intuition is at the very base of the validity of the systems of truth, of reason and of the senses. Intuition has been one of the most important and fruitful starters of an enormous number of scientific, mathematical and philosophical discoveries and technological inventions. The greatest artistic, religious and ethical systems of culture have been inspired by religious and mystical intuition. Sorokin has no difficulty in illustrating these contentions from the history of human thought; from the literature of artistic, musical and poetic creation; or from the lives and autobiographies of scientists and technicians.

The Theory of Truth

It is in the light of such considerations as these that Sorokin seeks to transcend his provisional assumption (see page 87) that there may not be one but six possible systems of truth. Such an assumption would indeed be difficult to substantiate upon Sorokin's own principles, for by what standards could it itself be pronounced true or valid? No ideationally-minded thinker would concede that truths of the senses enjoy an equal validity with the truths of faith. No man born and bred in a sensate culture would be likely to admit that his science based upon sense impressions has no better title to credence than the pronouncements of intuition or of religious and ideational thought. The sceptical, agnostic or critical positions are by their nature unlikely to yield positive standards of truth.

There is, therefore, one way only of avoiding the complete relativity of judgment which would inevitably result from the acceptance of five or six standards of truth, and that must be by extracting from each system of truth such elements of validity as can be combined, supported and verified by the use of the others.

Far from being a despairing eclecticism, such a conjoint standard of validity is that which has in fact been used to achieve all the major advances in knowledge. That is to say, empirically, intuition, for example, has been found to make an indispensable contribution to discovery. Of course, Sorokin does not commit the wild error of saying that because some intuitions have been fruitful, every intuition is therefore valid. On the contrary, he believes that most intuitions have probably been productive of error. However, the same verdict must be passed upon many pronouncements of the senses as well as upon many of the conclusions arrived at by the most rigorous logical reasoning or by dialectical argument.

It has not been by mere attention to the findings of the senses that modern knowledge has been secured. Mankind possessed that resource for millenia without deriving great insight from it. The sensory acuteness of many primitive tribes is notoriously much greater than that of civilized man, but it does not confer his knowledge upon them. Sense impressions without the ordering activity of the mind, its intuitive and reasoning powers, are sterile. The profound answer Leibniz made to Locke on this question, *nisi ipse intellectus*, (see page 106) is surely inescapable. Yet mere logical argument, bereft of other control, is also sterile, as the schoolmen of the Middle Ages laboured to prove to all eternity.

Intuitive insight, logical reasoning, empirical verification must therefore all play their part in establishing integral truth which may therefore be described as being three-dimensional. It is not identical with any of the three forms of truth, but it comprehends and includes them all.

It does not follow as a matter of course that integral truths attainable in this way are in fact able to comprehend the whole of reality. Almost certainly they cannot, for truth is finite, reality is infinite. All that can be said is that the resolute search for integral truth represents the best that the limited minds of finite men are able to accomplish.

Sorokin's own theories depend essentially upon such an outlook and procedure. His intuitive grasp of the real character of the great cultural systems that explain the fluctuating character of the history of civilization and his logical deductions based upon them have been carefully checked and tested against the recorded facts, that is to say by the methods of sensate science. He can, therefore, offer his results as an attempt to attain integral truth since they transcend the truth forthcoming merely from intuition, logical reasoning or accumulations of facts. At the same time he does not claim to have solved all the problems or to have removed all difficulties.

Q

If it be objected that nobody in their senses would ever try to do anything else, it is only necessary to point to the failure of each of the main great super-systems of culture to achieve such integration or to attain conscious realization of their own limitations and imperfections. For that reason they proved unable to survive. The truth, the whole truth, integral truth, was not in them. To refuse to accept such a verdict would be needlessly to impoverish the vital, cultural and spiritual heritage of mankind.

The Challenge of the Past

It would be impossible to leave the work of Sorokin, even in the bare outline sketched in these pages, without indicating in greater detail the consequences of the failure of our sensate culture to achieve integral truth or without a reference to his prophecy that crisis and disaster are about to overtake the present form of society and culture in Western Europe. It will already have become evident that, in his opinion, ours is a society and culture having all the marks of a sensate super-system in disintegration and decay. Its values are dissolving, and there is no way of halting the process which has already begun to remove the distinction between right and wrong, beautiful and ugly, true and false. It is a process which must inevitably end in anarchy. Mankind and human values will, he says, be regarded and interpreted more and more as though they could all be explained by biochemistry biology, psychoanalysis, reflexology, mechanics and materialism. The result will inevitably be a universe of atoms and electroprotons with human robots enmeshed in its huge and inert web.

Any genuine public opinion or 'world-conscience' will disappear and all that will remain will be the opinions of unscrupulous factions and the 'pseudo-consciences' of pressure groups.

Contracts and covenants will lose their binding force until democracy, capitalism and private property will be swept away, together with the free society of free men built upon the firm foundations they once provided. Freedom will become a mere myth for the majority, while the dominant minorities behave with unbridled licentiousness. Declarations of the Rights of Man will become beautiful screens for unadulterated coercion.

Might will become right. Wars, revolutions, revolts, disturbances and brutality will become rampant. Governments will become more fraudulent and tyrannical, giving peoples death instead of freedom, violence instead of law.

The family will continue to disintegrate; divorces and separations will increase progressively to diminish the difference between socially sanctioned marriage and illicit sex-relationships. Symptoms of decay and disintegration will also be increasingly evident in all other sensate values.

Instead of a cultured life and cultural values characterized by unity, coherence and by an inner harmony of style, our world will become a kind of bazaar, a cultural dumping-place into which are thrust all manner of miscellaneous cultural elements devoid of any unity or individuality.

Creative impulses will wane and wither. Galileo, Newton, Leibniz, Darwin, Kant, Hegel, Bach, Beethoven, Shakespeare, Dante, Raphael and Rembrandt will have no successors except mediocre and increasingly vulgar crowds of pseudo-thinkers, science-makers, picture-makers, music-makers, fiction-makers and show-makers.

Christianity will fall away, to be replaced by a multitude of nondescript fragments of science, shreds of philosophy, magic and superstition. Technical inventions will progressively become destructive instead of constructive.

People will take great size as a standard of excellence instead of high quality. Bestsellers, sensational hits, glittering external show will be more prized than classic renown or true worth. Thought will be replaced by 'information, please' and 'brains trusts'; wise men by Smart Alecks; great leaders by frauds.

A corresponding degradation will overtake even the greatest cultural values of the past. Reproductions of the works of Michelangelo and Rembrandt and other great artists will be used in all manner of utilitarian ways, such as in the embellishment of soap wrappers and whisky bottles; Beethoven and Bach will provide supporting programmes or signature tunes for radio advertisements for breakfast cereals, patent medicines, beer and tobacco. Yet despite all this, far from achieving sensate aims of a higher standard of living, production and real wealth will decline; economic depressions will become more severe because of increasing moral, mental and social anarchy. Security of life and property will fade and with them will go the peace of mind and happiness of mankind. Consequently mental disease, crime and suicide will spread.

The effect of these cumulative disasters will be to split societies into two main classes. There will be the great majority, the swinish multitudes in Burke's challenging phrase, who cling to the old sensate faith, 'eat, drink and be merry for to-morrow we die', who do not apparently know how to avoid the fate by which they are being engulfed or that they have any duty to resist and oppose it. But, at the same time, the ranks of the ascetics and stoics will be strengthened by the growing numbers who, revolted no doubt by the progressive degradation of life, are led to reject and despise those sensate values which will appear to have been directly responsible for the decay and ruin of civilization and culture. In this way, by tragedy, suffering and crucifixion, mankind will be purified and brought back to reason; to believe once more in eternal, lasting and absolute values. Ultimately a new era will open, owing its existence not to the decayed and bankrupt sensate society and culture, but to new ideational or idealistic values, yet to be realized.

'What an extravagant and fanciful picture of the destiny of modern man' may well be the reaction of many who read this summarized commination so reminiscent of the harsh words with which the Hebrew prophets of the Old Testament scourged and corrected their people.

Yet much of this prophecy of gloom and disaster has already been proved a deadly accurate forecast. Millions of human beings have found their fate to be far more bitter than Sorokin could have imagined when he made his predictions. For it must be remembered that the words and the opinions summarized in these pages were published in 1941 and they were therefore written much earlier. He could not have known that the arsenals of death were shortly to add atomic bombs to their weapons of annihilation becoming every year more potent. Already, within ten years of that date, the evils, the destruction, the suffering, sorrow, torture, foul degradation, massacre and butchery which men have inflicted upon other men make up a total so staggering in its horror that, if doubt is felt about the justice of Sorokin's predictions, it can surely be solely because the mind cannot grasp what their fulfilment entails. Human eyes cannot endure to look for long either at the sun or at the fires of Hell which certainly have opened under our feet, even as Sorokin said they would. 'The total of dead and injured Japanese during the Pacific War,' the New York Times estimated, on 20th April, 1949, 'was nearly ten millions.' To this staggering total must be added the appalling sufferings inflicted by the Japanese upon those whom they attacked and upon those whom they captured and enslaved with unspeakable brutality. In the West, where the struggle began, where it lasted longer and where greater numbers were involved, the catastrophe was yet more horrible.

Mercifully the human mind cannot remember sensations; it cannot feel the sensations of others. Were it otherwise, who would be able to retain his sanity after surviving through the years which followed 1940?

Those who were spared or who survived exile, robbery, imprisonment, concentration camps, assassination, mass executions, torture chambers, gas ovens, bombs, starvation and the impelling lure of suicide as the sole means of escape, can hardly refuse to acknowledge that evils on such a colossal scale have never before been inflicted upon humanity. Sorokin's conclusion that these disasters are unmistakable symptoms of profound cultural and social disease may not easily be gainsaid or queried on the ground, for instance, that there is no warrant for using biological analogies by applying the word 'disease' to describe cultural life. He is convinced that human behaviour reflects the cultural and social life of mankind at any one time; that there are no external causes, for instance, by which that behaviour is determined. We cannot find excuses for our troubles in the weather or in sunspots. There are no devils pulling the strings to make men act as they have acted. The devils are the men themselves.

It is therefore difficult to escape his conclusion that hope for Western society must be abandoned as long as it continues on its present course. He also implies that nothing can be done to halt or to divert the decline.

To question this assumption is not the task of a book devoted to the main outline of Sorokin's theories. Some readers will be struck by the contrast between this confident prophecy of doom and Sorokin's own dismissal of similar forecasts, noted for example on pages 185, 202, 228. To many others it will seem that in voicing once again, and with such convincing arguments, the most fatalistic pessimism about the course of history in the immediate future, Sorokin is in the apocalyptic tradition of that distinctive line of Russian and Slav thinkers who have always seen human destiny as tragic and doomed to suffering, possibly achieving a doubtful redemption, but only at the cost of titanic struggles against a perverse and malign fate.

The refusal in Mediterranean and Western lands to take these dire warnings very seriously may contribute to the impatience with which the East feels itself misunderstood by the West, whose sunnier optimism must seem facile and shallow when measured against the realities of life experienced within the vast cold grey depressing wastes of the marshes of the Pripet, the cradle of the Slavs.

It would, however, be singularly unfitting to refer even briefly to Sorokin's general outlook on life in a manner implying that it may be explained away by racial or geographic factors. His whole purpose has been to put the facts of history in a far wider, grander and more intelligible context. To the extent that he succeeds in imparting new knowledge and new insights it may be believed that his views give to mankind both an occasion and an encouragement to transcend the narrow determinism that appears to be their fate. The utter ruin of sensate culture may then by no means seem inevitably foreordained.

In the Victorian era, the leaders or, as Sorokin calls them, the bearers of culture succeeded at what was perhaps the high price of a very considerable increase in hypocrisy, hollow formalism and evasion, in imposing powerful restraints upon sensate man. No candid history of the nineteenth century can write-off as insignificant the achievements in Great Britain of the evangelical and the catholic revivals, of the free churches, or of the Salvation Army, to mention merely some of the religious manifestations called forth in opposition to sensate tendencies getting dangerously out of hand.

To them must be added the almost equally impressive banding together of men and women in lay and secular voluntary societies for the pursuit of worthy ends far transcending any narrow personal selfishness of a merely sensate type.

England is not the only country about which such things may be said, nor is it necessary to go back to the nineteenth century for examples. In the whole recorded annals of history, there is no precedent for the generosity which, in our own times, the American people have displayed towards other countries. It is rare for a traveller to return from the United States without having been embarrassed by the lavish hospitality he has received at American hands. That this nation-wide generosity, characteristic of all classes of American society, is no mere chance affair provoked by the unusual sight of a foreigner, is proved by the enormous gifts for charitable purposes made by Americans in America. The local community chests, hospitals, schools, colleges, museums and galleries, libraries and even complete universities, are among their more conspicuous manifestations. Then there are the great charitable Foundations many of which, such as the Rockefeller, Carnegie, and now the Ford, also operate abroad. Their activities are conceived on a vast scale and with a planned foresight, enabling them to make a positive contribution to the moral and material welfare of other countries rivalling anything hitherto achieved in the field of idealistic charitable and missionary enterprise. Since Sorokin wrote, American moral and material support has been extended to other nations on a truly gigantic scale. It is to be seen in the major contribution made by America to the creation and functioning of the United Nations and its many specialized agencies; that impressive new machinery to define, preserve and sustain the noblest human values which has been set in motion since Sorokin wrote. American aid to the rest of the free world has, in practical sensate terms, also taken the form of outright gifts of machinery and other capital and consumption goods which have prevented the most crippling shortages and have thereby averted disease, famine and premature death, not in one but in many entire and populous nations. American determination to make moral values prevail, despite a very heavy cost in American material welfare and in American lives lost in battle against the enemies of freedom in Korea, has indubitably begun a new and profoundly impressive chapter in the history of international relations.

It is true that the enemies of freedom make the most desperate propaganda efforts to depict the unselfish acts of the American people as a smoke-screen for a new form of American imperialism or Dollar Diplomacy, but the impossibility of sustaining such an argument before any audience able and willing to look at the facts before them condemns it to derision and speedy death. Generosity springing from great strength allied with high principle has the distinctive and immediately recognisable quality of true idealism. It is altogether different from that self-seeking bred by low cunning out of fear, poverty, envy and greed animating the most violent critics of the American people in recent years.

Sorokin's own conclusion that no great cultural system entirely dies away is surely vindicated by this great American example in altruism and idealism, for it can clearly be no product of a pure sensate culture. The example of Professor Sorokin's own Institute for Creative Altruism, mentioned on page 157, is as good an index as any of the seriousness with which Americans are prepared to devote themselves to the altruistic task, supposedly so unusual in a fully sensate society, of helping others. In what other country would it be possible to launch such an Institution?

The Soviet Union, for lack of resources, could understandably admit its total inability to rival American generosity so briefly and inadequately described above. When, however, it is prepared to make some such advance, even to the extent of setting up similar organizations in all the Russias to co-operate with the Institute at Cambridge, Massachusetts, the world may find it somewhat less impossible than it does at present to believe that Communism can have any genuine interest in promoting human welfare and the brotherhood of man.

It has often been said that prophecies contribute to their own fulfilment. If they are extremely distasteful, they may act in a contrary sense. Sorokin's critics clearly have the opportunity, and theirs also is the responsibility, to prove him wrong. Clearly they are able to rely upon enormous reserves of moral principle in their efforts, as the example of the people of the United States of America so conclusively demonstrates. The survival in Great Britain and in the British Commonwealth of respect for moral principle and of an analogous regard for non-material, cultural values likewise cannot be in doubt. It is manifest in many form. Without attempting any descriptive catalogue or inventory of them, it may suffice to point to the considerable share of national energy and resources now devoted under the Colonial Development and Welfare Acts to increasing the moral and material welfare of the many millions inhabiting Britain's colonial dependencies. The contribution also being made to peoples in other territories under the Colombo Plan in South-East Asia and through British participation in the Technical Assistance scheme of the United Nations is similar in purpose although it is not on the same vast scale as is the aid given to Colonial dependencies. Taking all these schemes together, it will be found that for many years Great Britain has alone done more for underdeveloped territories than have all the other members of the United Nations put together.

A more impressively spectacular illustration of British devotion to non-self-regarding and symbolic values occurred early in 1952 on the sudden death of a greatly respected King and the accession of a young Queen to the Throne upon which he had conferred additional prestige and renown.

Totally inexplicable upon any narrow sensate, nominalist and crudely utilitarian theory of social life, great manifestations of sorrow, loyalty and affection, in which huge multitudes participated throughout the British Commonwealth, gave convincing proof on that occasion of the deep latent force of idealistic values among the British peoples. The marked change in the character of monarchy over the last hundred years has been accompanied by a change in public sentiment in the United Kingdom which together illustrate some of the principles set forth in this work and throw a new light upon the occasional criticisms directed by a minority in the nineteenth century against monarchy as an outworn medieval institution which had mistakenly been allowed to survive into an age of enlightenment. It could not then have been evident that sensate obtuseness about the power of symbolism and idealism in public life which gave apparent strength to those arguments, was itself destined to have but a short and limited currency.

Against wider historical perspectives and a better balanced review of British national life and character, the belief that idealist culture should lose no more ground but on the contrary will be a dominant power among the British peoples, need be no act of despairing fideism.   Of the magnitude of the evils against which such a resurgent idealism must contend, there likewise can unfortunately be no doubt, for it is very clear that the situation is now grave. How grave it has become is the purpose of this concluding section of the summary of Sorokin's views to set forth.

Sorokin's is by no means the only warning voice to which mankind might now pay some attention. His is, however, one of the most powerful, because he speaks, or purports to speak, with an authority vastly more impressive than that based on nothing better than personal taste or even religious and moral traditions. His authority is history; the history of earlier societies; the sociology of the past.

In its light he cannot echo the glib and facile assurance that all is well with humanity and that unlimited material progress may be expected in due course to provide paradise on earth for everybody. If he rejects such shallow optimism, it is not because his own conclusion is one of despair. Consistently with his theory of immanent cultural change, he believes firmly, not merely that the creative process of building a new idealistic or ideational culture is possible, but that it is already going on. By word and example he is himself doing what he can to help forward that great cause.

One outstanding conclusion of all philosophies of history must indeed be that History can deliver no final sentence upon man's hopes and possibilities. In the first chapter of this book very brief references were made to some of the earlier views which seemed to support a contrary notion about the scope and purpose of historical study. Now at the end of this summary survey of the wide-ranging efforts Sorokin has made to find a more comprehensive, all-inclusive philosophy of history, the time has come to refer again to those mistaken earlier notions so that his own far deeper and more fully developed views may stand out all the more clearly and distinctly. Ten intervening chapters have been devoted to this theme and no attempt can here be made to summarize what is itself a summary.

Yet if it is a mistake to assume that historians ought to be prophets, it does not follow that history is studied in vain. The great gift which History bestows is none other than that sought also through Philosophy. The aim of both is to achieve that greater clarity of vision which it is the prerogative of Truth alone to confer. To strive to see more distinctly what has hitherto been the nature of man's estate is to accept a discipline enjoined upon those whose loyalty is to Truth. Their reward is an insight which all should possess who have any interest in shaping the future. Inevitably therefore, anyone like Sorokin who can throw a strong, clear and fresh light upon the past will deservedly command attention for his views upon the problems of to-day and to-morrow. But (to work out, even in the most sketchy detail, the main lines of guidance for the sociology of the present and of the future suggested by his work is no part of the purpose of this book. There could, however, be no more fitting sequel to Sorokin's vast and encyclopaedic survey of the past, so summarily indicated in these pages, than the claim that it should serve also to prompt sincere, earnest and fruitful reflection upon the future hopes and upon the destiny of mankind.

INDEX OF SUBJECTS

INDEX OF NAMES

The names of the thinkers and philosophers contained in the lists on pages 91-3, 116-18 and 125-6 are not included in this index.

Smollett, T., 79
Socrates, 101, 108, 136
Sophocles, 55, 65, 67
Sorokin, P. A.
  early career, 6
  works, *passim* espec. 6, 127, 150, 163, 235
  cyclical theory of history, 130-1, 212-48
  Harvard Research Center in Altruistic Integration, 157, 247
Spencer, Herbert, 5, 19, 95, 123, 127, 224, 225, 229
Spengler, O., 5, 7, 9, 17, 19, 107, 127, 130, 224
Spenser, Edmund, 78
Spinoza, 107
Stael, Mme. de, 76
Stalin, 143
Stendhal, 76
Sterne, L., 79
Stirner, 114, 115
Strachey, Lytton, 81
Stravinsky, 62, 63
Strauss, Richard, 63
Sumner, W. G., 215
Swift, J., 75

Tacitus, 69
Taine, 37
Tarde, G., 224
Tasso, 78
Tawney, R. H., 77, 142
Taylor, Jeremy, 78
Terence, 68
Terpander, 54
Thales, 97
Theocritus, 66
Thrognis, 65, 67
Theophrastus, 67
Thierry de Chartres, 134
Thrasymacus, 115, 158
Thucydides, 2, 108
Tolstoi, 80, 115
Toynbee, A. J., 5, 9, 19, 213, 224

Trajan, 47
Trevelyan, Sir G. O., 160
Troeltsch, 77, 142
Tschaikovsky, 63
Tutankhamen, 26

Unwin, Sir Stanley, 82

Vaihinger, 107
Vanburgh, Sir J., 78
Van Dyck, 36
Van Eyck, 37
Veblen, J., 214
Velasquez, 36
Verlaine, 76
Vico, 5, 108, 129, 224, 225, 229
Virgil, 68, 70
Vittoria, 53
Voltaire, 75, 82, 130

Wagner, Richard, 56, 61, 63
Walton, Izaak, 78
Warner, Richard, 165, 168
Webb, S., 115
Weber, L., 224
Weber, K. M. von, 63
Weber, Max, 77, 142, 180, 214
Whitehead, A. N., 136, 224
Wilde, O., 166
William of Conches, 136, 230
Winckelmann, 28
Wölfflin, 36
Wordsworth, Wm., 13, 94
Wu-Tao-Tzi, 27
Wyatt, Sir Thos., 76
Wycherley, Wm., 78
Wyclif, 73

Xenocrates, 101

Yule, G. U., 224

Zeno, 106, 108
Zeuxis, 35
Zola, 75, 76, 80